THE BOYS' CLUB

ALSO AVAILABLE IN ENGLISH BY

MARTINE DELVAUX

Bitter Rose
(translated by David Homel)

The Last Bullet Is for You
(translated by David Homel)

Nan Goldin: The Warrior Medusa
(translated by David Homel)

Serial Girls: From Barbie to Pussy Riot
(translated by Susanne de Lotbinière-Harwood)

White Out
(translated by Katia Grubisic)

THE BOYS' CLUB

The Many Worlds of Male Power

MARTINE DELVAUX

Translated from the French by Katia Grubisic

Talonbooks

Talonbooks
9259 Shaughnessy Street, Vancouver, British Columbia, Canada V6P 6R4
talonbooks.com

Talonbooks is located on xʷməθkʷəẏəm, Sḵwx̱wú7mesh, and səlilwətaɬ Lands.

First printing: 2024

Typeset in Minion
Printed and bound in Canada on 100% post-consumer recycled paper

Talonbooks acknowledges the financial support of the Canada Council for the Arts, the Government of Canada through the Canada Book Fund, and the Province of British Columbia through the British Columbia Arts Council and the Book Publishing Tax Credit.

This work was originally published in French as *Le boys club* by Éditions du Remue-ménage, Montréal, Québec, in 2019. We acknowledge the financial support of the Government of Canada through the National Translation Program for Book Publishing, an initiative of the *Roadmap for Canada's Official Languages 2013–2018: Education, Immigration, Communities*, for our translation activities.

LIBRARY AND ARCHIVES CANADA CATALOGUING IN PUBLICATION

Title: The boys' club : the many worlds of male power / Martine Delvaux ; translated from the French by Katia Grubisic.
Other titles: Boys club. English
Names: Delvaux, Martine, 1968- author.
Description: Translation of: Le boys club. | Includes bibliographical references and index.
Identifiers: Canadiana 20240364724 | ISBN 9781772016024 (softcover)
Subjects: LCSH: Mass media and women. | LCSH: Sexism in mass media. | LCSH: Men in motion pictures. | LCSH: Men on television. | LCSH: Male domination (Social structure) | LCSH: Feminism and mass media.
Classification: LCC P96.F46 D4513 2024 | DDC 302.23082—dc23

I am the chosen one.

—Donald Trump

We are legends.

—*The Riot Club*

Warning:

This text includes discussion of sexual
assault and sexual abuse.

INTRODUCTION

Liberty, Equality ... Boys' Club?

I'm writing this introduction a few years after the original French version of *Le boys club*[1] was published in Québec and then in France. Since then I've had countless interviews, discussions, public presentations, and radio and television appearances, all of which have led me to conclude that I have become a target. A pack has been unleashed against me, with online masses of mostly men storming my social media, and columnists letting loose their fury before they've even read the book. Insults, mockery, sexism, and threats of rape and even murder, all because of a woman taking the liberty of denouncing the ways men organize themselves to control the world.

All around the world, for as long as sex discrimination has existed, feminists have been interested in how men are positioned in the world – a world that doesn't truly belong to everyone. It's still a man's world, the world of men, and only some men at that. The chosen ones tend to be white, heterosexual, educated, wealthy, well-born. Despite what we are led to believe, the world we live in isn't some egalitarian playground where all of us gambol about freely. It's a world dominated by groups of men, groups made up of certain men who get to decide how the world should be run.

•   •   •

In 2018, the American sociologist Suzanna Danuta Walters published an op-ed in the *Washington Post* asking, "Why Can't We Hate Men?"[2] She was writing after Donald Trump was elected, and after Harvey Weinstein's fall from grace, among countless others in film and television; after #MeToo and #TimesUp. Why can't we women hate men, Walters asks; why is hating men forbidden? She was asking in light of the demonstrable fact that men have hated women for thousands of years; surely there are plenty of reasons for women to hate them back. Since the dawn of misogyny, we've been armed with encyclopedic knowledge of the violence men inflict on us, the power they appropriate, and the control they exert over our bodies, our minds, our money ...

Yet despite everything we know, we refrain from talking about men as a single category, we not-all-men piously, loathe to stoop to such an outrageous generalization. We continue to defend them: no, they're not all like that! Basically, Walters suggests, it's women's anger that's banned, our feminist anger, anger that demands that things change once and for all. Anger that would tell men that if, in fact, they're not all misogynists, as they keep trying to convince us, then they must be able to understand and accept that they're part of a system that doesn't give women their rightful place, and once they've understood and accepted that truth they must commit to fighting with us to change it. If you're really on our side, if you're not one of those men, then give us space! Trust us! Stop demeaning us, stop bulldozing us with your words. Listen to us. Let us work. Stop undermining our physical integrity. Agree to learn from us. Stand back. Chose to stay quiet instead of speaking over us. In other words, be feminists alongside us.

Walters received a barrage of hate mail in response to her short opinion piece, just as I did. And yet ... where exactly is the hate here? How is it hateful to analyze a system using extensive scientific research and statistical study and to denounce that system, in this instance sexism, which is based on the supremacy of a segment of the population, and only a happy few among them at that? Why is it hateful to point to male dominance, to masculinity as the standard, and to the power that men wield together, from sea to sea to sea? How can it be hateful to shine a light on the male inner circle that organizes our world in a thousand ways that are as obvious as they are covert, those boys' clubs that orchestrate the exclusion, invisibility, and disappearance of the female[3] half of the population, and ultimately impede diversity?

Like so many feminists, my weapons are words – words that analyze, reflect, dissect, and document. Words are weapons that harm no one, unlike fists or bullets, unlike blades like the one used to attack the University of Waterloo gender-studies professor Katy Fulfer and two students recently. Words are a weapon to fight against indifference, silence, and disregard, against all the things that have been used to muzzle women since the beginning of time, to make us weep.

Writing about the boys' club is a way of resisting a structure I refuse to accept. I refuse to bow, to give in, to give up, to stay silent in the face of what is so obvious: the boys' club is everywhere. The slightest glimpse of its undoing, of loosening the ranks and letting in new faces, is only ever a fake-out before it rebuilds, regroups, and slams the door, forever reborn out of its own ashes. In the school-yard of life, the boys' club keeps all the goodies: power, money, recognition, freedom.

When I set about carving up the boys' club in 2019, I'd hoped an autopsy might allow me to find a series of characteristics to identify it, diagnose it. I wanted to strip off some of that veneer, that shine. What I especially wanted to do was throw a wrench in, to make life a little harder for the boys' club and prevent it from slipping quite so far under the radar. I wanted us to be clear-eyed, to know everything about that covert, charismatic, commanding Everyman: his habits, his gestures, his words, his clothes, the way he talks, walks, sits, what he eats and drinks. How he operates in the world to make it his own, against our will and at the cost of our lives.

The boys' club is toxic, and it contaminates everything, like a virus spreading arrogance and condescension, contempt and violence. The boys' club thinks it can do anything, because it usually gets away with everything. Those men are convinced they are entitled to whatever they want, so they take advantage of the weaker and more vulnerable as their own stock goes up and up.

I take up my pen again now at the end of 2023, having heard hundreds of women and men who aren't part of it ask how we can put an end to the boys' club. I'm more certain than ever that the answer is to keep talking about it, analyzing it, and calling it out. The Hockey Canada scandal[4] and other cases of abuse in athletics; the rise to power of right-wing statesmen around the world; the repression of feminism, anti-racism, anti-capitalism, decolonialism, and other liberation movements, including Woman, Life, Freedom in Iran; the shadow of Donald Trump looming once more at the door of the White House ... All of it is evidence that the sociopolitical figure of the boys' club remains all too timely.

In the meantime, the climate crisis is getting worse, with women and children bearing the brunt, while the fate of humanity rests in the hands of a group of men in positions of power.

But silence shall not win out, dear boys' club. For years we've been screaming, shouting; we're done being quiet. When one of us goes to the front, she goes for all of us, and all of us keep up the fight. We'll wear masks to protect ourselves from you. We'll stand two metres away. We will wash our hands of you. We'll wait until most of us are inoculated and ready to take a stand, to reject your monopoly, your excesses, your obsession with hoarding everything. Your way of taking bodies, of taking our bodies – to hurt us, make us sick, make us waste our time and our money. To push us off course. All the things you do to try to make sure there aren't enough of us or we're not strong enough to break away from how you've hemmed us in and kept us at bay to keep your game secret, mysterious, invisible, and beyond our reach. So that we don't know whom or what to attack.

But don't be fooled. We're very patient. We are multitudes. We are here, and we are not going anywhere.

—**MARTINE DELVAUX**

Montréal, December 2023

CHAPTER ONE

Men Ask Me Questions⁵

After a public interview one day, I got a question. From the end of the last row, at the very back of the room, a voice called out, a man's voice. He didn't raise his hand, didn't wait for his turn to speak; he just started talking. He spoke loudly and clearly. He did not look at me, though I was standing at the front of the room, and it was ostensibly to me that his question was addressed. Rather, he looked towards me as he spoke, gazing off to the side, where no one was sitting, looking at nothing.

He was the very picture of nonchalance, slouching in his chair, almost holding himself apart from the audience, yet at the same time his tone, the words rushing out, suggested great hurry. Leaning back in his chair, his head tilted slightly, he spoke like someone who understood everything and who'd come that day to put me on the spot: "Who's behind this domination of women? Whose fault is it?"

A noticeable shudder went through the audience. Sitting at the table, microphone in hand, I stayed quiet. I looked at him and waited. In my head, I was turning his question over every which way, trying to work out whether it was sincere or if he was just baiting me: was this a naive, humble lack of knowledge or a show of contempt, an attack? It felt like he was really asking, *who's behind the so-called domination of women?*

I spoke up, answering his question with another question: "Monsieur, are you asking me to explain to you what patriarchy is?" I gave a little laugh. Now he was looking at me straight in the face, pleased with the confrontation. "Would you like me to summarize the thousands of studies that have been carried out, all the research, the essays and manifestos? There's really nothing to explain, and I have nothing to prove that hasn't already been proven over and over again. I cannot and I will not answer your question. The best thing to do would probably be to go find out for yourself."

In answering without answering, I answered anyway. That's what made a fool of me – it wasn't so much that man himself, it was the culture that taught me my place. In spite of everything, I didn't tell him off, I didn't raise my voice, I didn't get mad, I didn't humiliate him, I didn't pretend not to hear him, as if he didn't exist. At most, I gave a hint of mockery and maybe winced a bit, my reply tinged with exasperation. I shouldn't have replied at all. I should have dropped my gaze to the side, just like him. I shouldn't have dwelled on his question. I shouldn't even have considered it. I should have done to him what is always done to women: I should have erased him, made him invisible, so that he didn't count.

There aren't just mansplainers[6] in this world – men who explain life to us, who interrupt us before we're done talking, who finish our sentences, who pretend to listen or to read our books but who instead of being interested in our words just wait with a full set of prejudices, knowing in advance what we're going to say. It's not just mansplainers; there are also questioners, who ask impossible things, interrogations that are detours, the smack of a cue bouncing billiard balls off in every direction, to get us off track. There are those who demand evidence, like television-show detectives, following a series of tiny pebbles on the road to a guilty verdict. What was I guilty of, in his eyes, as a feminist? Wanting to disturb the harmony of the world as he knew it and as he wished to preserve it? I was guilty of demanding equality, of demanding justice. I was guilty of constantly bringing up the image of the bodies of women who have been raped, beaten, and murdered.

What he was really asking was, *Whose fault is that big, bad (or maybe not-so-bad) male dominance? To whom can we attribute that?*

"The desire for attribution is a desire for appropriation," Jacques Derrida writes in *The Truth in Painting*, in matters of art as it is everywhere else. To say: this (this painting or these shoes) is due ... to X, comes down to ... saying: it is due to me, via the detour of the "it is due to (a) me." Not only: it is properly due to such-and-such ... to a subject who says me, to an identification.[7]

In asking his question, the man at the back of the room aligned himself with the perpetrators of male dominance, these anonymous, faceless perpetrators whose existence he questioned, implicitly passing the buck to women and implying that women themselves submit to that domination. By asking, he identified with them, lending them his face.

His question was a kind of confession – of his control over how the world works, the role he played and wanted to keep playing, along with his peers, his brothers, all anonymous like him. He didn't look at me because his question wasn't meant for me; he wasn't looking for an answer because it wasn't a question, it was a statement. Alone at the back of the room, he didn't need to speak to me; he was addressing his own kind. It didn't matter whether they were there or not; he was speaking on his own behalf but with the strength of a community that outweighs all else: the company of men. I think back to Marguerite Duras's words to Jérôme Beaujour during the interviews that became *Practicalities*:

> If you're a man your favourite company ... is the company of men. And it's in this context that you approach women. It's the other man, man number two inside you, who lives with your wife ... But the chief man inside you, man number one, has real relationships with men, his brothers.[8]

As Simone de Beauvoir writes at the beginning of *The Second Sex*, "A man never begins by presenting himself as an individual of a certain sex; it goes without saying that he is a man."[9] And Virginia Woolf, in *A Room of One's Own* a few decades earlier, asks, "Have you any notion how many books are written about women in the course of one year? Have you any notion how many are written by men? Are you aware that you are, perhaps, the most discussed animal in the universe?"[10] Woolf, in asking why so many books about women have been written by men while the reverse is not true, is asking, why are women so much more interesting to men than men are to women?

> Professors, schoolmasters, sociologists, clergymen, novelists, essayists, journalists, men who had no qualification save that they were not women, chased my simple and single question – Why are some women poor? – until it became fifty questions.[11]

We note the absence of women, we think of their erasure or domination, their humiliation, their sacrifice, so why can't we consider the omnipresence of men? That is what Virginia Woolf calls, in *Three Guineas*, the "hypnotic power of dominance,"[12] and which could be described as the de facto state of the cloistered networks of chosen men, a homogeneity so vast, so widespread, and so ordinary that it goes unnoticed.

CHAPTER TWO

From Serial Girls to Boys' Clubs

The Italian American artist Vanessa Beecroft made a piece in 2000 in which she posed Navy SEALs. Using as her subject a specialized United States army corps trained to fight on land, on water, and in the air, a strategic, highly trained team, often first in, capable of hand-to-hand combat and ready to kill, was a departure for Beecroft, whose photographs and performances at the time tended to feature half- or completely naked women teetering in high heels. Instead, her *VB39* (1999) and *VB42 Intrepid: The Silent Service* (2000) featured sailors in uniform. The first performance, *VB39*, showed sixteen Navy SEALs from the Naval Special Warfare Command, in San Diego, dressed in their summer whites, standing in the centre of a completely white room. The second, *VB42*, took place at night on the deck of the SS *Intrepid*, an aircraft carrier anchored in New York Harbour: thirty troops from the Undersea Warfare community, dressed in blue, blend into the darkness as the audience mills about. According to the art critic Gilda Williams, the men looked like chess pieces.[13]

Unlike the so-called female performances created by Beecroft, in which models, perched on spike heels, gradually fall to the ground from pain, fatigue, cold, and boredom, the men hold the pose. They hardly blink; their self-control is impeccable, suggesting that they can do even more, much more. Williams notes the Hollywood aura of the SEALs, and indeed there is an action-movie feel to the scene.[14] Bit by bit, an imperial aesthetic surfaces: the soldiers are glorious, they are superhuman. The public is no match for them: they will not be intimidated, they can barely even be looked at. If there's any tension in the visual field, the SEALs win. As one of the platoon members put it, "Once we walked in we're into the military mode. We're focused, and what was going on out in the audience didn't distract us. You're in a mode where you're not supposed to move or fidget, so it can give you the feeling of being a statue." [15]

Beecroft's performances say something about the meeting of art and war: like Leni Riefenstahl, Beecroft positions herself in the service of fascism. As a good dictator does, she reveals the slippage between the aesthetic and the political. That is my starting point.

•　•　•

VB42, Vanessa Beecroft Performance, 2000
Intrepid Sea Air Space Museum, New York, USA
© Vanessa Beecroft, 2024

VB39, Vanessa Beecroft Performance, 1999
Museum of Contemporary Art, San Diego, USA
© Vanessa Beecroft, 2024

VB35, Vanessa Beecroft Performance, 1998
Solomon R. Guggenheim Museum, New York, USA
© Vanessa Beecroft, 2024

From Serial Girls to Boys' Clubs

Gilda Williams describes *VB39* and *VB42* as a new version of Duchamp's 1917 *Fountain*,[16] which placed a urinal in the centre of an art gallery. But Beecroft does the opposite: in *VB42*, she forces the public to leave the gallery to attend a performance on a warship. It's as if Duchamp, instead of bringing the urinal into the gallery, had dragged the public into a washroom to watch a man take a piss. My book is meant to unfold along those lines, an invitation to follow me and see what men do together, what kind of club they come up with.

Right off the bat, then, there are two images. Two ways of occupying space. Two parallel but opposing figures: on one side, models strutting along a runway, stopping for us to look at them; on the other, military troops, training. Sometimes the models fall over, their feet caught in the hem of a dress or their ankles twisting in their stilettos, or they have no energy because they eat almost nothing. In the second group, no one falls, they stay in line, posing blankly. On one side, a corps de ballet, ballerinas dressed in white tutus, lined up and synchronized, performing *Swan Lake;* on the other, football players in a huddle, pressing their heads together so the other team can't hear them. Standing side by side or one behind the other, the girls don't talk to each other, they don't look at each other. They are offered up to the gaze, made to be seen, staged in order to be observed. What are the men – the boys – doing? Are they there just to be looked at too, to be appreciated for their beauty? They do look the same. They're wearing what we accept as a masculine outfit – a military uniform, perhaps, or a sports jersey, a suit, coveralls, a morning coat. Whereas the girls are immediately reduced to their appearance, to the aesthetic they create together, for purely ornamental purposes – staged to look pretty – the boys' uniformity has to do with defending something – a fundamental value, a nation, a country, a religion, a language, some form of power to which they want access, as do others like them.

On the one side, beauty. On the other, power. For the girls, a figure that relies on a form of anesthesia, the waking dream of sleeping beauties. For the boys, it's about networking and exchange.

The girls are young, slim, white; they move as a single unit. The boys are young or old, rich, white, sitting in a circle around a table or standing in a circle [17] around a ball. The table is the board of directors, a political party, a jury, a university body, an editorial board, a newsroom, a bunch of guys running a social network, coders working on a video game, scriptwriters in a brainstorming session, just some friends hanging out. The ball is the constitution, the sacred text, the game plan, the book or movie being reviewed, the orchestral score, the animal about to be eaten, the woman about to be fucked. What matters is that they're together. They are turned towards each other. They look at each other, watch each other, listen to each other. They exchange words, figures, ideas, beliefs, documents, money, weapons, women. In every case, they trade something that has to do with power in one way or another, power they have or power they want. Power they want to keep for themselves.

When I think of that image, when I see the table they're sitting around, with nothing but emptiness in the middle, I wonder if there's actually something they need or if, on the contrary, they come together around nothing at all – there's no centrepiece, no feast, no scapegoat, no trophy. Perhaps all they need is the gaze of someone who looks like them, the gaze they meet and in which they see themselves. Women, as Virginia Woolf writes, "have served all these centuries as looking glasses possessing the magic and delicious power of reflecting the figure of man at twice its natural size," [18] but maybe the ultimate mirror is in the eyes of another man, maybe a glance between two look-alikes either shrinks or swells. As James B. Twitchell writes in *Where Men Hide*, "women become feminine against the backdrop of men, while men become masculine in the company of men. Might that partly explain why men in groups are such a perplexing cultural force to both sexes?" [19]

Sitting in a circle, they look at each other, becoming larger than their individual selves as they see themselves reflected. Seeing themselves in each other's eyes is enough for them. People don't really need a common object around which to form a community, I think; the common object is the self. What connects men is the very figure of man, writ large, in the centre. One for all and all for one, in defence of the group: the boys' club.

CHAPTER THREE

Lights, Camera, Action

The repetition of a figure or image is the admission of a system. It is a symptom of the state of the body social, what we know about it and what we ignore, or prefer to ignore. Ergo this montage: I won't try to explain the images as much as show them, expose them, develop the syntax to allow meaning to unfurl from the examples all lined up. I want more showing than knowing, in the hope that seeing will lead to doing.

It's all about shock. Between ambling around in the nineteenth century and sitting in a movie house in the 1920s, a war happened, and trauma. In the words of art historian Jean-Philippe Uzel, "that was precisely the shock, which was at once cultural, social, psychological, and physical, that a film montage manages to replicate."[20] To put it in film theorist and director Sergei Eisenstein's words, the aim of what he called a "montage of attractions" refers to "influencing [the] audience in the desired direction through a series of calculated pressures on its psyche."[21] The idea is to "grab the stunned spectator by the hair and, imperiously, bring them face to face with today's problems,"[22] to trade contemplation for amazement, and to impel a reaction on a social level. It's a matter of facing and being faced with what's in front of you. A montage forces us to "not stay silent in the face of murder recorded in real time."[23] For me, that means writing one image at a time, unpacking them piece by piece, and trying to move forward so that in the end, we can understand (and condemn).

> We know full well, before a particular montage, that the same material in a different montage would without a doubt reveal new resources for thought. In that way, a montage is a work

that is able to reflect on and critique its own results. In that way, a montage corresponds exactly to the essay form. It operates by gathering and reading a range of things. [24]

I want to borrow Theodor Adorno's words on the essay form as a tool of the dominated, enacting a gaze that enables them to "perhaps become masters of their own suffering" and a way of thinking that "in fact is a vision rather than a thought." [25] I am film-haunted, and this book will be like that, a movie we've been acting in since forever and where we see first, foremost, and always in the foreground, the figure of men, together. I am betting on montage to replicate the shock of life under male domination. I will be the flâneuse wandering traumatized through this ordinary war, the everyday war men wage on women, on all those who don't fit into the category *man*. Like the narrator of *Three Guineas*, who wonders what women can do to prevent war, we must never stop thinking about it; we must never stop questioning our "civilization." [26]

• • •

But how can I talk about men when I'm not a man? How do I capture a figure that's not about me, that's none of my business, and therefore about which I shouldn't say anything?

Men have always written about women, imposing their point of view, their analysis, their sociological, psychoanalytical, anthropological, philosophical, misogynistic, or romantic interpretations of who we are, in order to invent the definitive woman, the one they desire, the one they fantasize about, the one we should all embody.

I'm not one of those authors. I have no desire to define what men are, and even less to dictate what they should be. I have no desire to understand everything and impose my own knowledge on the world. What interests me is looking at the way people are portrayed, particularly when there are several of them in groups. I'm interested in the representation of men together – that movie, in this instance a made-in-America Hollywood blockbuster that saturates our perception, largely defines our imagination, and thus lays the foundation of our society.[27]

This book is a hunt for images. I want to look head-on at what all too often eludes us, even today – an invisible, transparent image that we look right through because it's so ubiquitous. I want to trace the contours of that shape, which is invisible because it's everywhere and therefore nowhere. I want to flush it out, to bring it out of hiding, make it less elusive, to bring it out into the light so that it loses some of its majesty, its sheen, and so that our affection for it is undermined – the comfort we take in a familiar image, the ordinary laziness that encourages us to let images wash over us, without fear, without thinking about what they're saying about the world, without taking into account the actual, concrete harm they do.

I want to expose the boys' club, to parade its various versions in the street in order to dissociate it from tradition or habit, from the cult devoted to it; I want to reveal it as a mechanism of power. I want to show the boys' club for what it is: an organization of bodies, a choreographed cog in the wheel of patriarchy, the mechanism that allows male domination to be fulfilled every minute of every day of our lives.

• • •

This is not just about masculinity as such.[28] Masculinity, like femininity, is a set of stereotypes, clichés, and scripts that humans adopt and through which they construct an identity.[29] The idea is to consider masculinity as collective.

This book therefore looks at boys' clubs as both figure and device and examines the way certain individuals associate with power in order to keep it in place and preserve the organization of the world as it is.

In an interview published in 1977, Michel Foucault defined a "dispositive," or an "apparatus," as "a thoroughly heterogenous ensemble consisting of discourses, institutions, architectural forms, regulatory decisions, laws, administrative measures, scientific

statements, philosophical, moral, and philanthropic propositions –
in short, the said as much as the unsaid."[30]

Following Foucault, Giorgio Agamben adopts the term, and
locates it always in a power relation. Extending Foucault's category
still further, he defines an apparatus as

> anything that has in some way the capacity to capture, orient,
> determine, intercept, model, control, or secure the gestures,
> behaviours, opinions, or discourses of living beings. Not only
> therefore, prisons, madhouses, the panopticon, schools, con-
> fession, factories, disciplines, juridical measures, and so forth
> (whose connection with power is in a certain sense evident),
> but also the pen, writing, literature, philosophy, agriculture,
> cigarettes, navigation, computers, cellular phones and – why
> not – language itself.[31]

The boys' club borrows from both the machine and the discipline;
it is a grammatical object in the language of gender relations.

As for the women I'm talking about, and among whom I include
myself, they are, here, cisgender, trans, and non-binary, in other
words, women insofar as, one way or another, they are not men;
women who exclude themselves or are excluded from the category
of men and who find themselves on the margins, outside the club,
or who are sometimes invited to join temporarily or for a particular
purpose, but who are more often than not completely excluded. I am
taking the "risk of essence,"[32] to use Diana Fuss's phrase. I will take
the gamble of sticking to the terms "women" and "men," thereby
building on the binary logic on which the West is founded, but with
the aim of dismantling it. And, in the end, I hope, to offer a glimpse
of a different horizon.

● ● ●

To echo Walter Benjamin, I want to organize my pessimism by dis-
covering a space made up of images that are "the world of universal

and integral actualities."[33] I want to look at this world because it is mine, it is ours, and because it needs to be interpreted and analyzed in an attempt to identify what is repeated here, what is said and said again, shown and shown again, so often that the image ends up disappearing. Like deer in the headlights, we see nothing.

I want to expose the boys' club to take away its magic, its surreal, immortal quality: "a unique manifestation of a remoteness," as Benjamin puts it, "however close it may be."[34]

I want to separate boys' clubs "from the realm of tradition," substituting "for its unique incidence a multiplicity of incidences,"[35] so that our understanding of the boys' club is no longer based on ritual, but on politics.

I want to make the existence of the boys' club self-evident no more: bring it out into the open, expose it, and make sure that from now it's going to be under surveillance.

CHAPTER FOUR

Origin Story

A boys' club is an organization that traditionally excludes women and is controlled by men.

It is a group of wealthy older men who wield political power.

It is a group of people in a position of power who use that power for their own benefit, usually indirectly. In England, the old boys' networks refer to men who attend private boys' schools and who, after graduating, become the old boys.

It is an expression that implies the desire to preserve an elite. It's who you know, not what you know, as the saying goes. The boys' club is a tight-knit group of male friends who protect each other.

The boys' club is a very specific type of group. It's not a crowd of indistinct faces, it's a network, a clan, a family, a regiment, a team, a council, a fraternity, a government. It is a group the members of which are connected, dependent on each other, relating to each other, and united by common interests and beliefs, an ideal all of them share. In some cases, the structure is clear and transparent – the Catholic Church, for instance, and the Vatican in particular, or the army. There are some women in religious and military organizations, but not at every level (and indeed very few, in the case of the army) or in the same capacity as men (at least in monotheistic religions). Men make up almost the entire membership, and certainly the main leadership. The Catholic church and the army are the hypostasis of the boys' club, its absolute incarnation. What interests me here, however, are the more subterranean version, the invisible, incognito boys' clubs, which everything conspires to not let us see.[36]

• • •

At the turn of the twentieth century, there were over two hundred private clubs in Britain. The waiting lists for admission were lengthy, with people waiting up to twenty years. From nineteenth-century coffee houses, which were based on commercial interests and political affiliation, we've shifted to non-profit schemes, clubs whose income derives from membership fees and which are built around professions, hobbies, and political positions. As counterparts to the Woolfian dream of a room of one's own (other than the matrimonial chamber), over the years, we've had the club, the bachelor pad, the garage, locker rooms, hunting cabin, saunas ... so many spaces for men. Private clubs are part of the practice of separating the sexes socially and spatially; the word "club" even comes from "cleave," to split or sever. [37] In Britain at the end of the nineteenth century, gender relations were not all smooth sailing: there was a modern push to advance the rights of some women against the supremacy of others, but Queen Victoria was not in favour:

> The Queen is most anxious to enlist every one who can speak or write to join in checking this mad, wicked folly of "Woman's Rights," with all its attendant horrors, on which her poor feeble sex is bent, forgetting every sense of womanly feeling and propriety ... It is a subject which makes the Queen so furious that she cannot contain herself. God created men and women different – then let them remain each in their own position. [38]

The Victorian era, Jan Marsh writes, was almost synonymous with the ideology of so-called great men – the individuals celebrated in the National Portrait Gallery (founded in 1856) and in the 1885 *Dictionary of National Biography*. Their exploits were extolled in texts like Thomas Carlyle's *Heroes and Hero Worship* (1841) and Samuel Smiles's *Self-Help* (1859). Manly values of courage and enterprise were linked to military campaigns and economic expansion, while women's role was to be patient and sacrificial. Motherhood was idealized, as was virginal innocence, but in general women were denigrated, inferior. To quote John Ruskin, a woman was to be "the centre of order, the balm of distress, and the mirror of beauty," [39] while a man was "the doer, the creator, the discoverer, the defender." [40] The inequality between men and women held the day, a state of affairs denounced by John Stuart Mill in 1867:

> Think what it is to a boy, to grow up to manhood in the belief that without any merit or any exertion of his own, though he may be the most frivolous and empty or the most ignorant and stolid of mankind, by the mere fact of being born a male he is by right the superior of all and every one of an entire half of the human race ... Such people are little aware, when a boy is differently brought up, how early the notion of his inherent superiority to a girl arises in his mind; how it grows with his growth and strengthens with his strength; how it is inoculated by one schoolboy upon another; how early the youth thinks himself superior to his mother, owing her perhaps forbearance, but no real respect; and how sublime and sultan-like a sense of superiority he feels, above all, over the woman whom he honours by admitting her to a partnership of his life. Is it imagined that all this does not pervert the whole manner of existence of the man, both as an individual and as a social being? [41]

Although women began to have access to university education in England from the 1860s onwards, only certain fields were considered suitable, all others being open to men, who thus attained more advanced levels of higher education. While many women gradually entered the workplace, middle-class and bourgeois women did not work outside the home, devoting themselves to the domestic sphere and the care of children, the elderly, or the ailing.

The domestic realm of women was closely linked to the invention of private gentlemen's clubs:

The deep desire for male affiliation implies a need to be separate from women that persisted until the early twentieth
century with the resurgence of mixed-sex society. Instead
of a flight from domesticity, the gentlemen's clubs may well
be considered a flight from women and their social events.
Nineteenth-century clubmen embraced the concept of domesticity in such a way as to provide for their own comforts
while undermining the influence of the home.[42]

The club was convivial, a place of rest and comfort where men
could network without the distracting presence of women. It was
a locus of homosocial and heterosexual desires, the latter serving
as a screen for the former, and both founded on a misogyny and
replicating the camouflage of homophobia. Gentlemen's clubs were
defensive: they calmed the anxiety caused by women, those angels
in the house,[43] and also thereafter by the suffragette movement.
What was disturbing was perhaps precisely the aim of gatherings
of women to be other than merely ornamental – a threat to the
social, conjugal, and sexual equilibrium. As one London clubman
put it, a club was "a place where women ceased from troubling and
the weary were at rest."[44]

•   •   •

Even while gentlemen's clubs were flourishing, there was an increase
in the number of women in the workforce, laws were passed giving
women power over property and access to divorce, and the British
empire was withering with the increased presence of America and
Germany in the geopolitical arena. The average age of marriage was
going up, and the birth rate among the middle class and the bour-
geoisie was going down: "Victorian men faced 'the double threat of
extinction and degeneracy.'"[45] In the face of the pressures placed
on men to provide for their families, the club was a liminal space,
offering passage between the house they had grown up in and the
marital home.

The clubs helped create a public persona for men. As extensions of private schools, they were "gentlemen factories"[46] that allowed men to explore the city in a different way, from the centre of urban life.[47] The club was the domain of dandies, of elegant men, torn between masculinity as ephemeral and muscular. At the club, men could be powerful and delicate, evolving in a demanding man's world in which gender performance was complex, and where it was impossible to assert virilization or feminization and to affirm heterosexuality or explore homosexual desire, because it was all of those things at the same time. In *A Room of His Own: A Literary-Cultural Study of Victorian Clubland*, a book about private club culture in Victorian England, Barbara Black cites Laura Morowitz and William Vaughan, defining "clubland" as a "rehearsal for patriarchy"[48] – for the performance of patriarchy. Clubs had everything to do with the empowerment of men; as a second home, clubs also represented a threat to the institution of marriage by providing a surrogate home for both single and married men.

Clubs were a refuge, a home base; the club was the first stop for men when they got to London. It was where they went to escape domesticity and its attendant femininity. Black argues that men from the single-sex world of private schools felt uncomfortable in the domestic sphere and sought to replace conjugal domesticity with domesticity between men. Gentlemen's clubs included all the rooms of a home – a dining room, a library, a dormitory, a sauna, an office – and were intended to be a sanctuary from the stress and worries of everyday life. It was a place where friends felt like family. With their palatial decor, clubs were prestigious, distinguished homes; the luxury, the finery, and the feasts (with food choices that were said to be more varied than they were at home) made clubs a home away from home, and better. The home was the domain of the angel, and men instead sought that power at the club. Quoting Roy Porter, Black highlights how

their popularity among the married, as foreigners observed, called into question the truth of "home sweet home." By their superb comforts, critics jibed, clubs encouraged "the cult of egoism, the abandonment of family virtues, the exclusive taste for material pleasures, and a deplorable laxity of moral of which the whole nation will someday feel the baneful consequences." [49]

As Black explains in her preface, she chose to look at the structure of gentlemen's clubs because of the vestiges that persist, from the clubs, most of them single-sex, she recalls from childhood, to the fraternities and secret societies at university and the Freemason ring on her father's finger, the secret handshakes and the hazing. Club culture remains relevant today; just look at social networks like Facebook, Instagram, and others. The culture is still alive and well, as is the segregation that goes along with it. The private clubs of the Victorian era turned London into a male city, a "monster," in the words of the writer Flora Tristan, who disguised herself as a man in order to gain access to clubs and who lambasted their cultivation of "immobility of the soul" and the fetishization of "social materialism" that produced the British elite; [50] what remains of that culture today? How do our lives now still mimic the exclusively male clubland of yesteryear? We are living in a grandiose mansion with multiple glass ceilings.

As an interface between the private and the public, the windows of the clubs looked out onto the street, but their walls (that is, the door fees, membership cards, and membership fees) had been from the beginning a means of demographic division – a "flight from difference," the art critic Abigail Solomon-Godeau [51] calls it – a withdrawal, in other words, a refusal of and an escape from those who did not look like their members. As George Augustus Sala put it in his 1857 caricature of clubs, they were a weapon used by savages to keep white women at bay. [52] In her analysis of the club phenomenon, Black mentions the anthropologist Clifford Geertz, who studied "the definition, creation, and consolidation of a viable collective identity." [53] It is the English private clubs' creation of a collective masculine identity, and the construction of that identity as contained within the walls of the club, that interests me here. As Black defines them, clubs are made up of

> groups of "brothers" who are not blood kin but nevertheless
> form a vital community, an associational culture heavily reliant
> on sameness sharpened on the whetstone of difference and on
> the maneuverings of exclusion and inclusion, on a keen sense
> of social distinction that keeps the socially ineligible at bay.[54]

The clubs made London an "imagined community," to borrow Benedict Anderson's phrase, that spoke volumes about what it was like to be a man,[55] specifically in this case a bourgeois man:

> As an institutional culture that operated upon fraternal ideolo-
> gies to construct a public, professionalized masculinity reliant
> on a set of shared cultural practices and male bourgeois social-
> ity, Victorian clubland provided a way of structuring class
> relations and encouraging – indeed, regulating – identification
> with one's own class.[56]

The Man in the Club Window, as the frontispiece illustration in the 1859 *The Habits of Good Society: A Hand-book of Etiquette for Ladies and Gentlemen* was captioned,[57] was clubland's most famous metonym. Like the flâneur, the man in the club window gives the impression of observing things calmly from a privileged, protected vantage point inside a posh club. But also, like Sherlock Holmes after him, from his position he can read the signs of social class, because he knows that social identity has to do with performance and self-exposure, and he knows that gentlemen's clubs allow for cultural production and consumption.[58] The door of the club is the threshold between propriety and impropriety, and the man in the club window is the arbiter of human behaviour.

CHAPTER FIVE

Men, Together

I write from the perspective of the woman outside the club window. Unlike the man who's watching what's going on outside from inside the luxurious private club, I'm standing here on the sidewalk outside, trying to see what's going on inside – more like voyeurism than anything from a flâneur scene. I'm trying to gain access to what inherently excludes me: the secret factory of power and masculinity.

• • •

In his preface to the reissue of Eve Kosofsky Sedgwick's influential LGBTQ+ literary essay *Between Men: English Literature and Male Homosocial Desire*, Wayne Koestenbaum highlights the fact that the 1985 essay, which was the first to deal with homosociality, was published in a feminist collection. "Sedgwick was a woman," Koestenbaum writes, "wedging herself boldly into the male-male buddy huddle, [and] she incarnates her argument by making clear that the fraternizing of men is a traffic that passes through and over her body, and that she, as woman, is uniquely qualified to comment on the traffic jam."[59]

Sedgwick refers to Heidi Hartmann's definition of patriarchy: "a set of social relations between men which have a material basis, and which, though hierarchical, establish or create independence and solidarity among men that enable them to dominate women."[60] She adds,

> in any male-dominated society, there is a special relationship
> between male homosocial (*including* homosexual) desire and

the structures for maintaining and transmitting patriarchal power: a relationship founded on an inherent and potentially active structural congruence. For historical reasons, this special relationship may take the form of ideological homophobia, ideological homosexuality, or some highly conflicted but intensively structured combination of the two. [61]

Unlike the simple continuum of relations between women, which presupposes that there is no marked difference between women who love women and women who defend women's interests (a continuum that makes for some fluidity between the erotic, social, familial, economic, and political), relations between men seem to be not only be more rigid, but their associative life, the fact that they meet among themselves, is based on both misogyny (opposing women and differentiating from them at all costs) and homophobia (differentiating from homosexuals who are considered effeminate, and hiding any homoerotic desire). Men with other men would seem to constitute a defence of heterosexuality and of the trade value of women bartered between groups of men.

Sedgwick refers to René Girard's notion of mimetic desire, but she points out that Girard does not sexualize the players in his triangle (the vertices of which can be occupied by humans or by heroes, gods, works of art, and so forth), though they are almost always two men vying, in one way or another, for a woman. As Claude Lévi-Strauss outlines, with regard to marriage, the trade relationship does not take place between a man and a woman, but between two groups of men for whom the woman is an object of exchange, and not one of the subjects involved. The triangle, writes Sedgwick, makes "graphically intelligible the play of desire and identification by which individuals negotiate with their societies for empowerment." [62] The boys' club reflects that triangle, as men's organizations that exclude women in order to preserve their trade value.

The decor of the French Travellers Club in the Champs-Élysées is fairly blatant: "paintings of naked women adorn each of the heavy carved wooden doors. Above the bar, a large painting depicts a beautiful, scantily clad woman from behind."[63] According to club lore, the painting represents La Païva, a famous nineteenth-century courtesan, one of whose lovers had the mansion that now houses the club built for her: "In a place frequented by businessmen who work in finance, it is amusing to see amid the mouldings and wood-work so many female representations even though membership is restricted to men only."[64] Women are only allowed in as images, reminiscent of pornographic photos in military barracks.

What is the rationale for the exclusion of women by current members of French, British, and American gentlemen's clubs? One gentleman, requesting anonymity, mused, "the rooms are small; we wouldn't know where to put the women."[65] Graham Snell, secretary of Brooks's, a gentlemen's club in London, said, "the question has never arisen. In fact, it's not a topic of conversation." Anthony Lejeune, seventy-seven, a member of White's in London, argues that clubs are "the only place where you can really be relaxed. When a woman enters a room, the decibels go up. It becomes difficult to take a nap after a good meal."[66] When asked about the exclusion of women, Mel Keenan, vice-chairman of the venerable Royal Northern & University Club, replied, "men change in the company of women and vice versa. Men talk to each other differently, they confide in each other."[67] The club owner suggests that the men can engage in camaraderie and banter with no women around, which is not the case when they're there, while one member complains that women talk too much.

In 2014, Anthony Layden, chairman of The Travellers Club in London, consulted the club's two hundred members about the inclusion of women. The responses, as noted in his report, fell more on the side of members who displayed antipathy towards women and felt discomfort in their presence.[68] One member commented that he would find it "distinctly inconvenient to have to sit up and look civilized because a lady might appear," [69] while others feared that the presence of women would jeopardize the club's status as a place to enjoy "the company of male banter and without having to bother with the etiquette that one inevitably must adhere to in female company." [70] The lawyer Ardavan Amir-Askani, who was interviewed about the French Travellers Club, in Paris, opined that, "in this all-male world, we avoid the source of trouble that women represent. We're not going to play the rooster and try to shine." [71] What does shine, however, are the shoes, notes journalist Brice Perrier, polished by a woman working at the bottom of the carved onyx staircase. [72] As recently as 2018, the Automobile Club de France refused admission to women: "We've brought the members back to the centre of the circle," the Auto's president explains ... [73] so to speak, perhaps, since members are so important that men sometimes swim in the club's Gustave Eiffel–designed pool, which no woman has ever entered, completely naked.

Private clubs still exist in Paris. As well as the Travellers and the Auto, there's the Jockey, the Tir aux pigeons, the Polo de Paris, the Cercle interallié, the Club de la Chasse, the Cercle MBC, and the Saint James – all gathering places for powerful people in politics, the media, law, business, and academia. Ninety percent of the Jockey Club's membership are French aristocrats, though all clubs are founded on some form of kinship: a club should include people like us with whom we can pleasantly eat and drink and share various kinds of power. People like us, of course, are predominantly white and male.

•　•　•

The boys' club has everything to do with contempt and even hatred of women – misogyny in the truest sense of the word. However homosocial a space the boys' club may be, it is nonetheless steeped in a homophobia that is the flip side of rejecting the feminine. While male homosocial groups may indeed blossom into homosexuality, the club structure itself functions as a beard or an alibi: the hierarchy between men and women is reflected in the inequality between heterosexuals and homosexuals, which serves to conceal the true desire behind the closed doors of the boys' club. The boys' club is doubly masculine, at once genuinely homophobic and genuinely homoerotic, made up of men who want to be with men, and who even want (albeit covertly) to sleep with men, and who are deeply attached to and invested in their identity and the power that goes with it.

CHAPTER SIX

The Faithful

The television drama *Patrick Melrose*, adapted from a series of five novels by Edward St Aubyn, explores and condemns the cruelty behind the boys' club's power. My intention is not to associate boys' club with cruelty or pedophilia, which are central to the miniseries, but to note how the television series reveals how power can be perverted by those who reign from the sort of peak status conferred by a hefty bank account and high-culture membership. As we meet and follow the protagonist, Patrick, a drug addict and the son of a wealthy heir who repeatedly raped and tortured him as a child, we discover the dark side of men of power, their capacity to do evil with impunity.

In the first episode,[74] Patrick leaves London and crosses the ocean to retrieve his father's body in New York. In the United States, he joins some of his father's friends in one of New York's many private clubs. The men all look alike – they're wearing the same uniform and they have the same haircut, and they're drinking the same drink, a bull shot, a mixture of beef stock and vodka. "Something of an acquired taste," one man says, a taste you develop when you belong to that club, and to a certain social class. The meeting is short, but long enough to reactivate Patrick's trauma as he recalls his father's cruelty. The father's friends, who are in one way or another complicit in his sadism, seem like an extension of evil, and the club, with the men sitting around in red-leather armchairs, is a satellite of the father's house where the child was raped. "The gang's all here," one of the friends says as he sits at the table, implying that those who matter are there.

The men describe Patrick's late father as a great man, a gentle-man who refused to compromise, who demanded nothing but the best. "Never apologize, never explain," Patrick adds sarcastically to the chorus of praise; "that was another one ... Never try, effort is vulgar, things were better in the eighteenth century. Oh, and despise all women, but your mother most of all." The room goes quiet. The waiter arrives with the glasses. "What a lot of faithful gun dogs," Patrick says, ostensibly describing a hunting scene in a painting in front of him, referring both to the animals and to the men seated around the table. One man begins to obliviously recount a hunting anecdote, to the dismay of the others, who clearly have heard it before. Patrick interrupts him, offering instead another hunting story he heard from his father when he was eight. One of the friends, Nicholas, who was there when Patrick's father told the story, is shocked and angry, and tries to stop Patrick from saying anything, but Patrick goes on. In the 1920s, his father went hunting in India with a bunch of judges and generals. One of the men was bitten by a wild dog and started showing symptoms of rabies. They were three days from the nearest hospital, and the men hoisted him into a hunting net over their heads for the rest of the meal. The man wouldn't stop screaming, so Patrick's father shot him in the head.

A flashback follows, with the father telling Nicholas the story, and the men laughing as little Patrick sits nearby. The father clearly takes pleasure in recounting the cruel scene to scare his son. In the club, music is playing; someone is at the piano. Patrick is triggered, traumatized, nauseated. The scene ends with him vomiting into the bathroom sink. A club member chides him: "You might have used the stall." "Good idea," Patrick replies, and locks himself in to shoot up.

The episode establishes a connection between clubs in the United States and England and highlights the sadism that underpins them all, in one way or another. It illustrates the web of privilege, power, and cruelty that shapes gatherings of men, and leads not only to violence against women, but also against boys, as another feminine, fragile figure, in opposition to stereotypical (and toxic) masculinity. Patrick is faced with an impossible choice – becoming like his father, or breaking the mould by getting high. He is the son of a rich man, but he's also the son of a boys' club complicit in the evil he experienced as a child. It's almost as if he was raped, humiliated, and tortured not just by his father, but by the entire community. The sexual violence inflicted by the father on his son (and, as we learn over the course of the series, on the mother too – Patrick is a child of rape) is part of the wider wielding of privilege. The father is a wealthy white man who socializes with the upper crust, advances into foreign lands like a colonizer, and towers above the fray: he is often portrayed looking through his bedroom window on the top floor of the mansion where they live, shouting orders to members of the household. He is part of the group he represents, a group in which his son automatically becomes a member through his inheritance, but from which he wants to get as far away as possible, rejecting the spell cast on him at birth by the evil fairy of the boys' club.

• • •

There are still currently a number of private clubs in London that do not admit women as members: the Beefsteak Club (founded in 1876), Boodle's (1762), Brooks's (1764), Buck's Club (1919), the Garrick Club (1831),[75] the London Sketch Club (1898), and the Travellers Club (1819). At the East India Club (1849), women can be guests. The Flyfishers' Club (1884) used to allow women to access the club at particular moments as members' guests but has recently implemented an "all-male guest policy at all times."[76] The Savile Club (1868) allowed a trans woman who had originally joined as a man and who had been part of the club for years to remain a member, even after she began identifying as a woman.[77]

Among the existing clubs, there are some notable hold-outs. Pratt's (1857), a club for aristocrats, only recently began admitting women. When the journalist Amelia Gentleman contacted Pratt's Club for a 2015 article to ask whether women were admitted, the friendly steward (a woman) explained that they were not, with a logic that wasn't entirely easy to follow: "They still don't allow women in because it is a supper club; we only open at seven at night. Only at private lunches – women are allowed then – as we do the lunches on a different floor." She did not explain why seven is too late for women to venture out, or if there is a reason why women must have lunch on a different floor. At the Turf Club, the person who answered the phone would not confirm whether or not women are admitted (they aren't), and promptly hung up.[78]

Then there's the Savage Club, which still maintains an all-male membership:

> The Savage Club was founded in 1857 and remains one of the leading bohemian gentleman's clubs in London. Clubs elsewhere have borrowed both the name and the style, which continues to be the "pursuit of happiness" – a quest made infinitely more agreeable by the fellowship of members who are known to each other by the sobriquet "Brother Savage."[79]

Women are not admitted, except on specific evenings: "Several times a year members invite ladies to share both the dinner and the entertainment – sometimes as performers. On these occasion guests always include widows of former Savages."[80]

Finally, White's (founded in 1693), the oldest still-active gentlemen's club, is considered the most exclusive, and therefore the most prestigious. It is the only club that expressly states that women are not welcome, either as members or even as occasional guests.

Ultimately, the prestige of a group or establishment is determined by its ability to exclude other categories of people. Whether or not gentlemen's clubs accept women, they remain created for men by men and in a traditionally masculine spirit, from the decor (wood panelling, dark colours, portraits of great men, sculptures of naked women) to the activities offered (sports, card games, gambling, themed steak evenings, Scotch, cigars, and so on). [81]

•   •   •

In January 2018, Robert Verkaik published a sweeping excoriation of London's men-only clubs in the *Guardian*. [82] The secretive, sexist culture of these institutions, Verkaik says, has shaped the notion that it's okay to host an event that results in a veritable festival of sexual harassment. London's clubs, Verkaik explains, were born out of a need among the wealthy to get together in a dining room full of cigarette smoke but empty of women in order to enjoy masculine pleasures, namely alcohol, gambling, and women-as-entertainment. Then as now, club members come from private schools and university societies. That is the case for the famous Brooks's, and for White's Club, where then Prince Charles celebrated the end of his bachelorhood the night before his wedding to Diana, and the lesser-known but fiercely male-only Beefsteak Club, whose members must promise to keep everything that happens there a secret.

Verkaik's aim in exposing current boys' clubs is a warning against the role they play: these places where politicians, bankers, and investors meet to strike deals and form alliances are a threat to democracy. The membership lists are kept secret, and it's impossible to know which ministers belong to which clubs and what the impacts are on public policy; the same is true of the judiciary.

England still allows clubs to be set up on associational principles: clubs can admit only women, or only people from a specific cultural community. However, since the majority of clubs are formed by privileged white men, the law is de facto elitist along the same lines, unlike political parties, for instance, which aren't allowed to restrict membership on the basis of race or gender. Verkaik calls for club membership lists to be made public to ensure that governance and justice are not being meted out in the smoky halls of men's clubs.

• • •

In Paris, the club Le Siècle has been attracting a fair bit of attention. The high-end club, which was described by Marie-Béatrice Baudet as "the eternal France,"[83] organizes monthly social dinners that bring together a clever mix of politicians, CEOs, bankers, lawyers, judges, ambassadors, military personnel, scientists, big bosses, and star journalists. Le Siècle is the inner circle of those in power ("not elected power, the other").[84] The mission of the club, 85 percent of whose seven hundred members are men, is to "produce consensus."[85] Membership is by invitation or sponsorship and includes a probation period of one to two years before members are officially included "within the ruling class."[86] Most members are graduates of a political studies institute, of the École nationale d'administration, or of engineering or business schools. Very few women are members: after being admitted at the club's foundation, they were excluded from the club in 1949 on the grounds that they "disrupted the debates," especially when they were members' wives or mistresses, and things became "unmanageable."[87] Membership was once again open to women in 1983, when the left came to power. Whether in gender, age, ethnocultural origins, qualifications, or social class, what is striking is the homogeneity and the secrecy: "Nothing that is spoken inside must be shared outside."[88]

In early 2021, the Duhamel scandal shone a light on Le Siècle. Olivier Duhamel, who had been president of the club since 2020, was accused of sexual assault by his daughter-in-law Camille Kouchner. Kouchner's memoir *La familia grande* details Duhamel's abuse of Kouchner's twin brother, whom she dubs Victor in the book. Duhamel was an eminent political scientist who was inducted into Le Siècle at the age of thirty-three, the age at which he met Évelyne Pisier, "Victor" and Camille's mother. Duhamel confessed and stepped down as Le Siècle president and as president of the Fondation nationale des sciences politiques. A number of other club members left as well, including Marc Guillaume and Jean Veil, Duhamel's friends, who, it was said, knew of the abuse.[89] *La familia grande* hinges on the matter of silence – the silence kept by the extended family, by what Kouchner calls the "mafia" that included the family and friends who hung out at the summer house in Sanary. Beyond Olivier Duhamel's resignations from his leadership positions, however, students and other members of the Paris Institute of Political Studies (familiarly known as the Sciences Po) called for Frédéric Mion, then Sciences Po director, to leave over his handling of the sexual assault and incest allegations against Duhamel. The scandal, the signatories wrote, was "symptomatic of an absolute boys' club made up of French elites, who are ready to protect themselves at the expense of the victims of sexism and sexual violence."[90]

• • •

In the third episode of the British television series *London Spy*,[91] Scottie, a former secret agent, takes the young Danny to a London private club, Whitehall, of which he is a member. Out on the street, before they come into the club, Scottie gives Danny some advice:

> Affect an air of mild boredom ... It needs to feel effortless.
> Making an effort is the surest giveaway.

A man at reception discreetly hands Danny a list of the club rules. The two men walk into the room and sit down in red leather armchairs around a low table in the centre by the fireplace, under a huge chandelier. White men sit in the armchairs around them, reading the paper or chatting quietly over a drink. Huge exposed beams support a very high ceiling. Pedestals on either side of a stage display two busts of famous men. Danny looks at the menu, surprised. Scottie explains that it's just assumed that members can afford to pay their way; there is never any mention of actual money.

At one point, Danny bends over to pull up his reindeer socks. Scottie smiles, amused. "There are more women in a gay club," Danny says. The club doesn't allow women, Scottie answers. "Is that legal?" Danny wonders, to which Scottie points out that not very many are likely to apply.

Scottie has made an appointment with James, a fellow Whitehall member and former colleague, to ask him for information about the murder of Danny's lover. "Have you lost your mind?" James replies. Looking at Danny, he adds, "Your acquaintances are beginning to rub off on you." "Oh no," Scottie answers. "I learned these tricks from the top."

"I'll tell you a joke, how about that?" James offers. "An Englishman, a Chinaman, a Frenchman, an American, a Russian, an Israeli, and a Saudi walk into a bar. And they all agree."

Scottie sinks down in his seat, dejected. Danny doesn't get the joke. "You better explain it to your boy at a later stage," James says, getting to his feet. Scottie is stunned and gets up immediately after James leaves. He and Danny cross the room, followed by the men who were sitting around them. By the exit, the butler asks Scottie to settle his bill; he is being seen out of Whitehall for good. Once the men are outside, Danny asks Scottie what the joke meant.

"Substitute the nationality for the security agency: British MI6, the Chinese Ministry for State Security, American CIA, Israeli Mossad, Russian FSB, the Saudi GIP ... The punch line was that they all agree."

They all agree despite their differences: the boys' spy club gathers around a common cause (in *London Spy*, this is research into how to recognize when someone is lying, which all the national surveillance agencies want to prevent being broadcast, which is why Danny's lover Alistair was murdered). During this bit of dialogue, the camera starts to spin around the characters, faster and faster, as if to isolate them from the rest of the world, and especially from the members of the private club and its politicians, businessmen, and secret agents. Who are Scottie and Danny once they are excluded from the male community?[92]

It's noteworthy that the two characters are gay, one old and one young – the old boy or old friend, and the "boy," the word James uses to disparage Danny, implying that he's a one-night stand, a sex worker, or a criminal of some sort, and who in any case belongs to a lower class and deserves to be despised.

Danny is a boy who doesn't deserve access to the boys' club.

CHAPTER SEVEN

Good Old Boys

Boy: a young male, usually a child or adolescent. As in, *It's a boy!*, shouted upon first seeing the genitals of a child assigned male at birth.

Boy. From Middle English "boi" or "boye," meaning both boy and servant, domestic servant, slave, sometimes even demon, but also referring to a young man who grooms racehorses (1872), an Indigenous servant in certain African or Asian countries (1890), or a music hall dancer (1947). From the Dutch "boef," which means a criminal, scoundrel, rascal, boy. [93]

The Germanic, Proto-Indo-European, and Norwegian roots all refer to the word "brother," and boys are indeed brothers. It is the name given to groups of adult men engaged in an activity that binds them together (in English, we speak of male bonding, a word also used to describe the close relationship between, for example, a parent and child). Boys are therefore members of the same sports team, a group of friends, brothers in a fraternity, coworkers in a particular field (the police, for instance), or army troops: "our boys." Boy is used to name a superhero or a fantastic creature (Aquaboy) and the word is used in many expressions, such as bad boy, boy-crazy, boys will be boys. [94]

• • •

Today, we tend to use "boy" instead of "man" in hierarchical social contexts. Bear in mind also the racism that underlies the use of the word by a white person to designate a Black person, the notion of fraternity, and the evocation, including etymologically, of criminality.

The eternal youth of boys is at the heart of the concept of the boys' club or, to put it in Michael Kimmel's terms, of "Guyland."[95]

Stuck in eternal youth, boys never age. Their grey hair and wrinkles are valued socially, unlike the fate of aging women. For women, we deplore the passage of time, favouring the "magnificent" bodies of young women (as the writer Yann Moix said in an interview given when his book *Rompre* was published [96]), while the old boys are allowed to live out their years and hold history aloft while retaining their youthful status. It's a status they confer upon each other and which they enforce. Not only are men ubiquitous, they're also eternal, at least those in positions of power. The good old boys are not marked by time; together they dominate it, and the world, too, through the network of relationships they build, maintain, and defend. According to Michel Foucault,

> power in the substantive sense, "le" pouvoir, doesn't exist. What I mean is this. The idea that there is either located at – or emanating from – a given point something which is a "power" seems to me to be based on a misguided analysis, one which at all events fails to account for considerable number of phenomena. In reality power means relations, a more-or-less organized, hierarchical, co-ordinated cluster of relation. [97]

Foucault's words resonate with what Pierre Bourdieu writes in *Masculine Domination*: "Manliness, it can be seen, is an eminently *relational* notion, constructed in front of and for other men and against femininity, in a kind of *fear* of the female, firstly in one-self."[98] Or to quote David Mamet, specifically with regard to the United States, "Women have, in men's minds, such a low place on the social ladder of this country that it's useless to define yourself in terms of a woman. What men need is men's approval."[99] Men's clubs are structured specifically in opposition to the feminine, against it, as a barricade, but also close by, pressed up against it. Men's fear of women, or of anything remotely associated with the feminine, is just another manifestation of rejection, of the disgust that comes with desiring the very thing that is despised. It is symptomatic of the feeling of shame described by Emmanuel Levinas, the effect of which is experienced in the body as the expression of the impossibility we suffer from, of not being able to break with ourselves, to escape from ourselves. Beneath their suit-and-tie armour, the boys of the boys' club are naked, they're on their own, no matter how well surrounded; they are bound to themselves, that is, they are bound to the human condition, which instead of setting them apart from women links them. "What shame discovers," Levinas writes, "is the Being that *discovers* itself,"[100] who discovers their own humanity; it is, to come back to Agamben, "overcome by its own passivity."[101] That passivity, which is closely linked to femininity, is reviled and rejected by the boys' club (as the men go to the club to do business, both economic and political, together) and at the same time it's sanctioned: well dressed and settled into their leather armchairs, the boys drink, smoke, eat, read, and chat, thus lending themselves to what would be designated as feminine expressions, sharing gossip[102] and trading secrets. With regard to the clubs' gender representations, there is at once a chasm and a tiny step between the masculine and the feminine. Despite their best efforts, the misogynists in the boys' club are constantly on the cusp of what they scornfully, arrogantly associate with the realm of femininity. In that sense, they are old boys: eternally childish.

• • •

Lili Loofbourow describes 2018 as the year of the old boys[103] – the old boy-in-chief being, of course, Donald Trump. If the masculine ideal that has always been glorified in American culture is rough and unrefined, a Marlboro Man who shoots faster than his shadow and for whom chivalry is effeminate, the Trump model is an illbred, capricious, spoiled brat who has no manners and doesn't give a shit, who takes pride in his boorish ways and ignorance. He spews insults unscrupulously, disregards protocol, refuses social graces.

He's a boy who is old and for whom everything is permitted.

Boys' clubs are everywhere in the United States and elsewhere, and no one ever believed that the White House stood apart, but Trump's uniqueness is the uncompromising, unabashed way he embodies what the boys' club stands for. Trump doesn't fit the image we have of a man of power, not only wealthy, but educated, well bred, well dressed, who crosses his legs when he sits down and knows how to soften his voice; but he is utterly the boy in the club insofar as he stands for its basic principle: he exudes those characteristics, unfiltered – how they know how to be cruel, how they humiliate and intimidate; how they resort to shouting, jeers, and mockery; how they place themselves above the law and act with impunity. These are all childish traits that are unacceptable in power situations.

But the boys don't change. Quite the opposite, in fact. They insist and defend and protect that identity at all costs: that's what motivates them. From Donald Trump to Brett Kavanaugh, and with a nod to Roger Ailes, Les Moonves, and Roger Stone, the old boys, whatever costume they wear to etch their masculinity, remain "puffy," as Loofbourow puts it.[104] They're puffy and greedy, always wanting more – more power, more money, and more women, too. They can never have too much. And they can't stand being questioned about it. If they are, they puff themselves up like pigeons, go red in the face, and shout and bang their fists on the table or cross their arms, sulking. Sometimes they even start to cry, great big crocodile tears like Harvey Weinstein[105] when one of his victims told him off or when a journalist threatened to leak the charges against him. They lie without even hiding it, and when their lies are pointed out to them, they get mad – not because they've been caught, because truth doesn't matter to them; they're annoyed that they're being pestered again. They'd rather turn to their allies, the men who are like them and who play the same game – everything is a game to them, and whoever scores the most points wins – those who abide by the system of falsehoods because it allows them all to acquire power. The old boy also has a strange relationship with his father: he is his heir, he simultaneously depends on him and repels him, a disturbing rival he keeps at a distance because the only people to whom he can be loyal are other boys like himself.

The same could be said of his relationship with the institutions he represents or within which he works. "It's tough to react" to Trump, Loofbourow says,

> because you don't even know at what point to start explaining why that's a problem. Communication requires a shared frame of reference, but it's not clear whether *any* premises of governance are held in common. Trump is a public servant, but there is no public interest in his framework; there's only Trump.[106]

There's only Trump; Trump and his ilk, Trump and all those who can gain something by standing close to him one way or another. This is where the notion of the club itself becomes central: the boys exist only through the network they're part of and which enables them to evade the law. One will be the lawyer of another who is the financial partner of a third who invested in the business of the fourth who was accused of sexual assault, for which the first will defend him. It's all about the network, held tight by financial interests between boys who tap each other on the shoulder during a game of golf, and strengthened by a loyalty that allows them to feed their addiction – not to power or money, strictly speaking, but to having and wanting more, always more. As for the child screaming in the store aisle at a parent's refusal, more will never be enough.

• • •

The television series *The Good Fight*,[107] about a Chicago law firm, is based on current events. The plot is a commentary on the Trump era, reflecting bluntly on how to resist in a world where real life is so unbelievable that it merges with fiction. In season 3, episode 1, the main character, Diane, a lawyer in her sixties, is lying against the back of her sleeping husband. As she speaks, she is staring at a yellowing bruise on his shoulder, which suddenly comes to life and becomes the face of Donald Trump. Diane's husband, who is a ballistics expert, was shot with buckshot by Eric Trump or Don Trump Jr. while on a safari in Tanzania. They waited to bag their prey before taking him to the hospital. From its very first episode, which aired on CBS a year after the Trump election, *The Good Fight* lambasted the American right, white and male supremacy, racism, sexism, and misogyny. At the heart of the series is a law firm in the Midwest at which most employees are Black, and where women play a predominant role. At the heart of the series, too, is the constant, persistent denunciation of Trump and the Republican Party, of which Diane's husband is a member. Diane, a Democrat through and through, loves her husband in spite of his political allegiances because, she says, he is a profoundly good man. But, curled up behind him as he sleeps, she rebukes him for having turned into a "footman to the king." "What has happened to men?" she wonders out loud.

> What happened to Paul Newman and Burt Lancaster? What
> happened to men who were slow to anger, and responsible,
> and wouldn't cry like whiny little bitches? When did Trump
> and Kavanaugh become our idea of an aggrieved man?
> Quivering lips, blaming everyone but themselves. [108]

She imagines Trump blathering back arrogantly, and herself biting back, "God, I hate you! I don't believe in hell but sometimes I wish people like you ended up there. Or I tell myself you're really unhappy in all your gilded happiness." [109]

•   •   •

Diane's monologue is reminiscent of Trump's famous open letter, published in newspapers on May 1, 1989, after the brutal rape of a white New York City jogger in Central Park. While the victim was still in a coma, and before the trial of the five teenaged perpetrators (who were Black and Latino, aged fourteen, fifteen, and sixteen), Trump paid $85,000 for advertising space in four New York papers, calling for the return of capital punishment: "Bring Back the Death Penalty. Bring Back Our Police!" Although he never names the five boys outright, the implication is clear.

The lawyer's words in *The Good Fight* echo Trump's in his letter: "What has happened to our City over the past ten years? What has happened to law and order? ... What has happened to the respect for authority?"[110] Trump condemns the "roving bands of wild criminals"[111] and takes the opportunity to once again oppose the mayor of New York and express his hatred, hatred Diane returns thirty years later:

> Mayor Koch has stated that hate and rancour should be removed from our hearts. I do not think so. I want to hate these muggers and murderers ... I recently watched a newscast trying to explain the "anger in these young men." I no longer want to understand their anger. I want them to understand our anger. I want them to be afraid.[112]

The case of the Central Park Five fed Trump's thirst for fame and served his desire to be the centre of attention, everywhere and all the time. Trump poured more fuel on the fire and stoked the collective hysteria surrounding a horrible, unacceptable crime, which was one among the more than three thousand rapes committed in the same year,[113] the majority of the victims of which were Black or brown, and none of which attracted as much attention. Yusef Sallam, Raymond Santana, Kevin Richardson, Anton McCray, and Korey Wise, all minors, were violently interrogated without lawyers or their parents present, they were starved and kept awake, and they were terrorized into making false confessions. None of them actually admitted to committing the crime, but they all admitted they had witnessed it, implicating the whole group.[114]

The boys were found guilty in a trial by jury and sentenced to prison. While awaiting trial, and following publication of the letter signed by Trump, they and their families received death threats. In 2002, the real culprit, Matias Reyes, who was serving a life sentence for other crimes, confessed to the rape of Trisha Meili. DNA testing confirmed his guilt and the innocence of the five boys.[115] After a lengthy civil suit, the five reached a settlement with the City of New York and were awarded $41 million in compensation. Trump, meanwhile, never apologized; on the contrary, he doubled down in anger, describing the settlement as the "heist of the century."[116] Speaking at the White House on June 18, 2019, he said of the Central Park Five and his comments thirty years earlier, "you have people on both sides of that. They admitted their guilt."[117] Trump expressed himself in similar terms after the 2017 events in Charlottesville – the two opposing and simultaneous anti-racist and white supremacist protests and the subsequent murder of an anti-racist activist by a white supremacist. Trump clings to a Manichean understanding of events – from his point of view, there are two sides, two groups of individuals who do not see things in the same way – and in doing so, he defends the police and the justice system responsible for convicting the boys. Even after the opposite has been proven, he maintains the guilt of the five: they confessed, he says.

The "sentimental journeys" Joan Didion[118] talked about at the time of the trial of the Central Park Five are still relevant today. Didion was decrying the media polarization between the jogger, who stood for all that was good about New York, and the Five, embodying all that was bad about the city. It was easier to look at New York through that Manichean lens than to try to think about the corruption that affected the city at every level, whether inflected by gender, socio-economic status, or skin colour. Any analytical complexity gave way to a romantic, sentimental reading, a narrative to which Donald Trump still clings today with his never-ending refrain, "Make America great again."[119]

CHAPTER EIGHT

The Donald

Donald Trump is a boys' club unto himself: he surrounds himself with white men, as power hungry as he is and for whom the law is a fairly fluid concept (like Roger Ailes, Roger Stone, Roy Cohn, Steve Bannon, and Michael Cohen, among others), and he lives his gilded happiness in a gold-plated life[120] – the privilege of those who, on the strength of their economic heft, which is itself spurious, the sum of a string of debts, do not need to be competent in order to succeed. Trump is the personification of cynicism. He single-handedly represents everything that is harmful to women: sexual aggression, discriminatory policies, the kind of sexism that reduces women to objects and encourages violence. His happiness is gilded unscrupulously on the backs of others.

Since Trump was elected president of the United States on November 8, 2016, feature films and television series about him have proliferated, most of them a tarnish job, scraping off a fairly flimsy veneer. Trump is a plaster president.

In his documentary *Fahrenheit 11/9*,[121] Michael Moore tells the story of Trump's rise to power, from his youth to his election. One of the milestones in the billionaire's life takes place in Flint, Michigan, the town where Moore grew up, and to which he always returns.[122] In 2014, Flint's water was contaminated, a tragedy caused by the state's governor, Rick Snyder, who made the decision to draw drinking water from the Flint River, rather than from the previously used Lake Huron and Detroit River. The Flint River's lead levels were too high and poisoned the town's population, particularly children. The residents were abandoned by the Democrats: in one shot in the documentary, Barack Obama is shown at a town hall gathering feigning thirst and asking for a glass of water, which he then pretends to drink to confirm the official finding that lead levels were perfectly acceptable – a betrayal of a predominantly Black population by the first Black president of the United States, and a significant electoral distraction. It might seem relatively trivial, but what happened in Flint happens every day in a million ways: collusion between powerful men of power who protect their own economic and partisan interests. As Moore suggests at the beginning of *Fahrenheit 11/9*, the United States is not predominantly Republican, nor are Americans predominantly right-wing; what is right-wing is the boys' club that holds the reins of power.

The 1980s were the golden age of Trump, who prided himself on having a "killer instinct."[123] Trump's name is mentioned about thirty times in Bret Easton Ellis's novel *American Psycho*, whose protagonist, Patrick Bateman, is a psychopath and a serial killer in a long line of the same, including Tony Soprano, Hannibal Lecter, and Walter White, a boys' club of beloved criminal antiheroes. Ellis's character keeps a copy of Trump's *Art of the Deal* on his work desk, and he dreams of being invited on the millionaire's yacht. When the *New Statesman* magazine featured a caricature of the president on its cover with the headline "American Psycho,"[124] the link was clear.

While Ellis's novel caused controversy when it was published in 1991, not least among some feminists, the 2000 film adaptation,[125] which was directed by Mary Harron, who is not only one of few female directors, but whose first film was *I Shot Andy Warhol*, feels oracular. There is an immediate telescoping from the Reagan years to the Wolf of Wall Street era and what we are living through today. As Ellis pointed out in 2016, if he'd written *American Psycho* in the last few years, Bateman would be dining at the French Laundry with Mark Zuckerberg or at Manresa with Netflix's Reed Hastings. He'd be wearing a Kanye West Yeezy hoodie and teasing girls on Tinder. The contemporary Bateman, the book critic Dwight Garner suggests, would probably attend a Trump rally wearing some designer version of the Make America Great Again baseball cap.[126]

• • •

Trump is said to be all about publicity, preferably good, but he'll take either.[127] He wants to see his name printed in big letters on helicopters, planes, buildings, a multitude of objects. As the pioneering talk show host Phil Donahue said in 1987, "This guy can't get up in the morning without being surrounded with himself." Trump, when asked which actor could play him in a film of his life, suggested he should play himself.[128]

Trump is a hollow shell, an empty suit, a character in search of an author: he is void of text – the poverty of his language and rhetoric bear witness to this.[129] He inherited millions from his father and proceeded to reinvent himself as a self-made man. Driven by his desire to surpass his father, who had amassed his own fortune thanks in part to Trump Village in Brooklyn, the son improvised himself into a New York property tycoon in prestigious Manhattan, where he established himself among the "big boys," as the journalist George Arzt put it.[130] Manhattan was the stage on which Trump put on his show. Many have compared his life to a movie, evoking Trump's one-time teetering between Hollywood and real estate; perhaps he ended up confusing the two.

In the 1970s, Trump turned the Commodore Hotel into the Grand Hyatt. Then he built Trump Tower, the first of a series of high-rises sprinkled around the world like so many monumental phalluses bearing his name, a real-estate colonization that helped make Trump into a brand name he described as "luxury, successful, gets things done, does well."[131] Trump styled himself as Midas, the embodiment of the American dream. He wanted people to believe that everything he touched turns to gold, when the opposite was closer to the truth: in the 1990s, he lost a lot of money and rose from the ashes largely thanks to various shenanigans, and to *The Apprentice* television show.[132]

There was a direct link between the reality show (which rivalled the popular sitcom *Friends* in terms of ratings) and the televised reality of US elections. Initially, Trump's office in Trump Tower wasn't that chic and had nothing to do with the empire that *The Apprentice* aimed to market. So the show's producers rebuilt everything: a cardboard conference room, a chair that looked like a throne, a set created from scratch to create an intimidating atmosphere. Then there was that shot of Trump coming down the escalator – the very same on which he announced his candidacy for the presidency, on the advice of Roger Ailes, then CEO of Fox News. It was a scene much mocked in the media: "Only losers walk. Presidents take Stair Force One," Jon Stewart quipped on *The Daily Show*, mimicking Trump's voice.[133] Even *The Simpsons* re-enacted the scene: Homer comes down the escalator behind the future president, whose tentacular hair wraps around him like a lasso before swallowing him.[134] The escalator has become famous, the setting for the billionaire's television interviews and now a tourist attraction.

Trump Tower can be considered the creation of Donald Trump's pièce de résistance : the building landed him on the cover of magazines and in the media. We might even see the White House as just a larger version, as if Trump were not merely its tenant, as the sitting American president is usually referred to, but the owner. For Trump, buildings are trophies, just as women are objects to be possessed. When Trump's first wife Ivana started to get on his nerves (she'd borne his children, and, in Trump's words, "I don't want to sleep with a woman who's had children"[135]), and when he was already in a relationship with Marla Maples, who would become his second wife, he saw the Plaza Hotel from his office in the tower, decided to buy it, and asked Ivana to manage it. Trump just had to own the building;[136] he couldn't bear not being the owner of the New York City landmark. But he also couldn't handle seeing Ivana running the Plaza, and shortly afterwards the couple went through the divorce of the decade.

•　　•　　•

The person in charge of the Trump Tower construction site was, unexpectedly, a woman: the then thirty-one-year-old engineer

Barbara Res. Since the election of the real estate magnate, Res has given interviews, written opinion pieces, and published two books.[137] She is one of few former Trump employees willing to talk openly about him, without fear of reprisal.

Res refers to Trump Tower as her creation. She was the only woman in a sea of men when the building was going up. She stood up to Trump; she knew how to stand up to him, although that was before he became the man he is today. According to Res, between the man she knew and the man Trump became, there seems to be a kind of fall: his features have hardened, as have his arrogance and contempt, his desire for revenge, his need to humiliate others. Res isn't shy: she says of her former boss that he is a bad president, and that she is now working against him. He's "out of control,"[138] she says, he can't tell right from wrong, he's less and less human. Res describes him as a megalomaniac and a predator who scrutinized women constantly, commenting on their appearance, boasting about his sexual prowess, and treating his female companions as trophies.[139] While Trump at the time allowed Res to voice her opinion, today she finds that he exudes a toxic masculinity that refuses to be challenged: "Now, I don't think he respects anybody. I don't think there's a person alive that he respects, because he thinks he's God."[140]

A part of Res remains loyal to the man with whom she claims to have had a real relationship. He liked strong women. He called Res a "killer"[141] and believed that "men are better than women, but a good woman is better than ten men."[142] He would later describe his business dealings with women as follows:

> "I have really given a lot of women great opportunity. Unfortunately, after they are a star, the fun is over for me. It's like a creation process. It's almost like creating a building; it's pretty sad."[143]

During construction on the tower, a gigantic figure of a woman was painted on one wall. She was dubbed Sarah, and the seven-metre-high pinup was meant to encourage the workers.[144]

● ● ●

For Trump, there's only one step (or escalator ride) between a woman, a building, and a country.

Trump flirted with the presidency three times. As far back as 1980, when Rona Barrett asked him in a television interview what he would do if he lost all his money, he replied, "maybe I'd run for president."[145] In the late 1980s, presidential rallies were organized as a publicity stunt to promote *Trump: The Art of the Deal.* In the early 2000s, Trump again announced that he was running for the presidency. He used the media to amplify the announcement: he made them wait, forcing them to turn the cameras on the crowds waiting to hear him speak.

The fourth time was the charm, as it turned out, not least because Trump had Roger Stone in his corner. Trump seemed to fancy himself a Pygmalion for the women he meets; Roger Stone was Pygmalion to powerful men, a kind of head boy of the boys' club. It was Stone who made Trump: "I suggested Trump should explore a bid for the presidency," Stone said; "I was like a jockey looking for a horse. You can't win the race if you don't have a horse. And he was a prime piece of political horseflesh, in my view."[146]

Trump as stallion. Trump as caricature of the man's man[147] (that is, a man who likes men) who reassures his electorate – male, white, and not university-educated – who fear the loss of male power, however slight: "The fact that Trump's impetuousness and thoughtlessness are rewarded rather than punished only further evidences the boys-will-be-boys system."[148]

● ● ●

The Trump ghostwriter Tony Schwartz describes him as a man with a binary view of the world: there are victims and there are predators. He has no conscience; he doesn't know the difference between right and wrong; in the end, Schwartz says, he's a sociopath.[149]

We know all too well by now that Trump is a liar. The *New York*

Times helpfully listed all the lies he has told since he took office.[150] His reality is fake just as his television show was fake, and nothing can stop him. The rather discreet kid who followed in his father's footsteps has become a ruthless old man, a power machine that runs amok and stops at nothing.

Trump surrounds himself with men – men like him. He speaks to them, he inspires, he incites. Whether they're businessmen or journalists, lobbyists or politicians, they share his tendency towards harassment and aggression. From surprise visits backstage at the Miss Universe pageant while half-dressed contestants are getting ready, to numerous accusations of sexual misconduct (twenty-six women had come forward as of 2023[151]), to the famous "Grab 'em by the pussy"[152] video leaked on the eve of the election, which Trump explained away by saying he had been discussing clothes,[153] Trump's behaviour reveals the true face of a man for whom the presidency is just a game in the vast schoolyard of power. Trump likes strong men, Michael Moore says, and he has "always committed his crimes in plain sight."[154] Americans elected a boy-in-chief who is also a criminal-in-chief, in the image of a mafia don, à la *The Godfather* trilogy, for whom family matters more than anything else – a family made up of other men like him, men who, if they don't want to be kicked out of the club, have to accept everything.

Trump swears by those he considers good men, like the white alt-right supremacists, nationalists, neo-nazis, and militiamen[155] who protested in Charlottesville in August 2017 (in the Unite the Right rally, led by Richard Spencer, among others[156]) to protest the planned removal of a statue of a Confederacy general. One protester drove his truck into anti-racist counter-demonstrators, killing the civil rights activist Heather D. Heyer. "There's blame on both sides," Trump said after Heyer's death, of what he saw as the defenders of the dream of making America great again: "You had some very bad people in that group, but you also had people that were very fine people on both sides."[157]

Although Trump did have to retract to some extent, the mask (if there ever was one) had nevertheless been torn off, and with it the realization that the United States was run by a racist, a man who not only defends white supremacist violence, but provokes it, fuels it, and leads it, a man who was building a wall between Mexico and the United States and deporting or locking up refugees in camps, separating parents and children and leaving them to die. As Ta-Nehisi Coates put it, "certainly not every Trump voter is a white supremacist, just as not every white person in the Jim Crow South was a white supremacist. But every Trump voter felt it acceptable to hand the fate of the country over to one."[158]

With his trademark yellow hair, a reflection of the gold he surrounds himself with, Trump is the paragon of the whiteness he defends. And not just any whiteness: it is masculine, wealthy, heterosexual, hale. In the wake of the election, Toni Morrison, with angry irony, coined the Trump project as "making America white again," with white people standing at the ready for sacrifice.[159] Their fear is so great and their bitterness so powerful that they're prepared to do anything to defend the perceived superiority of white people. The people who chose to vote for Trump aren't so much angry as terrified, Morrison writes; they're so afraid that they're choosing to vote for the man whose real estate firm was sued because it refused to rent to Black people. The man who asked to see the birth certificate of his predecessor in the White House. Who refused to employ Black people in his casinos. Who is friends with David Duke and backed by the Ku Klux Klan. The man who eggs on the Proud Boys, the extremist right-wing, misogynist, and racist group whose exclusively white, male members describe themselves as "Western chauvinists," and who call for among other things the closure of American borders, the absolute right to bear arms, and the return of women to the home; the man who encouraged those Proud Boys to descend on Capitol Hill on January 6, 2021, telling them during a presidential debate in fall 2020, to "stand back and stand by."[160]

As in William Faulkner's *Absalom, Absalom!*, writes Toni Morrison, "rather than lose its 'whiteness' (once again), the family chooses murder."[161]

CHAPTER NINE

Crown Jewel of Palm Beach

I didn't boycott the United States after Donald Trump was elected. I still regularly fly to Florida; Mar-a-Lago, Trump's private club and second home, is never far from where I go. Walking through the streets of Miami, I can see how close extreme wealth and extreme poverty are. Trump is never far away, and neither are the watchdogs of his power. He is omnipresent, in our world today and in our thoughts, and the reason he takes up so much space in this book is that he is everywhere, all the time. His influence is viral, and every appearance he makes, every mention of his name, confirms the existence of the boys' club. Trump is the personification of a phenomenon that is most often diffuse and even invisible because, although it may be embodied by a particular man, it never has a single face. Trump is the figure of a uniformity of bodies that undermines all political diversity[162]; he represents the ultimate whiteness of the boys' club as an all-powerful, omnipresent vehicle for power exercised over bodies that look different than his own.[163]

• • •

Donald Trump is the influential owner of the private Mar-a-Lago club, which has a $200,000 membership fee and hefty annual dues (up to reportedly nearly $20,000).[164] Members are required to spend a minimum of $2,000 a year on meals. Between June 2015 and May 2016, the club raked in $29.7 million in gross revenue.[165] During Trump's term as president, Mar-a-Lago became an extension of the White House. Laurence Leamer, author of *Mar-a-Lago: Inside the Gates of Power at Donald Trump's Presidential Palace*, sees the club and Palm Beach, where it was established around a hundred years ago by its first owner, Marjorie Merriweather Post, the daughter of the Post cereal mogul, as a testing ground: when it came to transforming the stately home into a private club, Trump managed to divide the island between those who were for and against, as he went on to do with the whole of the United States. The way he fights to get what he wants – the right to turn a mansion into a private club and get a tax break in the process, for instance – is one of the things his electoral base likes about him. Trump describes himself as the King of Palm Beach, beloved and boot-licked by billionaires before they turn around to say he's awful: "They all come over, they all eat, they all love me, they all kiss my ass. And then they all leave and say: 'Isn't he horrible?' But I'm the king."[166]

Mocked by Palm Beach old money, and hated by many of that coterie, Trump nevertheless settled in to stay, folding the White House and the private club into each other, condensing the presidency and his claim to Palm Beach royalty. Royalty indeed: Trump's tastes run to Louis XIV. The ballroom at Mar-a-Lago, a 2,000-square-metre extension, is a copy of the Hall of Mirrors at Versailles. Even the toilets are tiny palaces, Leamer writes: "Everywhere the gilded palace screamed out its affluence. Gold. Gold, and more gold."[167]

While American presidents have always liked to have a second home where they can spend their holidays, Trump is different: Mar-a-Lago is not his home, but a club where hundreds of people are constantly on the move. Just two weeks after taking office, Trump flew to Mar-a-Lago on Air Force One, accompanied by his acolytes Steve Bannon and Reince Priebus – an unprecedented act. Over time, Trump's weekends spent in Palm Beach cost American taxpayers nearly $130 million. The club's membership list includes dozens of real estate developers, Wall Street financiers, energy executives, and other businessmen. When Leamer published his book, at least three club members were up for ambassadorial positions. Mar-a-Lago is a select boys' club, most of the members of which got in before Trump was elected; there are few spots available today.[168]

• • •

Mar-a-Lago was business as usual for Trump while he was president, whether he was discussing a foreign policy crisis on the patio or entertaining the prime minister of Japan. Getting into Mar-a-Lago could be decisive in getting something out of the president: all it took, according to Robert Weissman of the non-partisan group Public Citizen, was the opportunity to whisper a few words in Trump's ear. That was the problem: we've witnessed a commodification of the presidency seldom if ever seen in American history.[169] While there had always been a circle of elected representatives from the wealthiest classes, being part of a club and paying to spend time in the company of the president was new.

In the wake of Trump's comments in response to the Charlottesville riot, many Mar-a-Lago members left the club, taking their money with them. Foundations that organized fundraising events there cancelled their planned events, all as discreetly as possible. Where all sorts of people, from film stars to tennis players, had once hung out at Mar-a-Lago, the club dwindled to businessmen and politicians, and unsavoury types like boxing promoter Don King, who murdered two men years ago, was paroled after four years in prison, and was finally granted a pardon from the governor of Ohio.

King was the court jester.[170] In March 2018, at the end of an evening when King had been talking his ear off, Trump retired to the family's apartment with his wife Melania. As they walked down the empty hallway, King's cries rang out after them: "The president!!! The great president!!!"[171]

CHAPTER TEN

Xanadu

Donald Trump's favourite films include *Bloodsport*; *Goodfellas*; *The Godfather*; *The Good, the Bad and the Ugly*; and *Citizen Kane*.[172]

In a 2002 interview in which the director Errol Morris asked a series of celebrities about their favourite movies, Trump commented on the Orson Welles film: "*Citizen Kane* is really about accumulation, and at the end of the accumulation, you see what happens, and it's not necessarily all positive ... I think you learn in *Kane* that maybe wealth isn't everything, because he had the wealth, but he didn't have the happiness."[173] When asked by Errol Morris what advice he would give Kane, Trump replies, "Get yourself a different woman."[174]

But the story of *Citizen Kane* is very different from Trump's interpretation. Rather than the story of a man who fails, what Orson Welles shows us (and denounces through fiction) is the fate of a greedy man who sells his soul to the devil. It's the story of the sort of man Welles loathed: an ambitious heir who, after investing his fortune in newspapers, makes up news in order to sell papers. When that's not enough, he goes into politics, but is derailed by a sex scandal that his newspaper editors deflect by crying electoral fraud. With politics proving to be the wrong path, Kane decided to promote his wife's singing career; she has little talent, but he manufactures her fame, and she is mocked so extensively that she tries to commit suicide. Kane retires to Xanadu, a palace that looks like a fusion of Trump Tower and Mar-a-Lago, and dies alone with his servants.[175]

Orson Welles made *Citizen Kane* in 1941, shortly before Pearl Harbor, at a moment during World War II when the United States was debating whether or not to jump into the fray. Welles was interested in the idea of fascism and had just secured the film rights to adapt Joseph Conrad's *Heart of Darkness*. When that project fell through, he teamed up with Herman J. Mankiewicz, a screenwriter who had tried for several years to make an anti-Hitler film called *The Mad Dog of Europe*, which Hollywood had refused to finance for fear of damaging trade with Germany. Together, in *Citizen Kane*, Welles and Mankiewicz paint a picture of what fascism might look like in the United States. But behind *Citizen Kane* is the story of Welles himself: Franklin Roosevelt had asked him to run for senator in Wisconsin in an attempt to shift the state from dairy farmers to the liberal left. Welles refused, convinced that he had no chance of being elected because he was left-wing and, worse still, divorced. In the end, the win went to Joseph McCarthy, who famously hunted socialists and communists in the 1950s. Around the same time, Trump's future mentor Roy Cohn came to power; he was feted at Mar-a-Lago a few months before his death in 1986.

●　●　●

Orson Welles played Charles Foster Kane, based on William Randolph Hearst, the newspaper magnate acknowledged as Welles's inspiration, who was basically Donald Trump. In the last image of the film, Kane, multiplied in a row of mirrors, is in and of himself a boys' club, representing all the powerful, money-hungry white men, driven by boundless ambition, who make up the United States of America and the world in general. The house at the centre of the film is not insignificant: Xanadu.

Xanadu is a castle and a kingdom, a mishmash of baroque and medieval architecture, both Romanesque and Gothic. It is Kane's "literally incredible domain,"[176] as Welles and Mankiewicz describe it in the script. Set in the Casa del Prado in San Diego's Balboa Park, Xanadu stands in for Hearst Castle in San Luis Obispo County, California. The story goes that William Randolph Hearst saw so much of himself in the character of Kane that he did everything he could to sabotage the film: he lobbied the Oscar Academy not to award it a prize (which worked!), he refused to advertise the film in his newspapers, he tried to get his hands on the soundtrack so that it could be destroyed, and he managed to persuade J. Edgar Hoover to look into Orson Welles, an investigation that lasted a decade. Hearst invited himself into *Citizen Kane* with his former companion, the actress Marion Davies, in the character of Susan Alexander, Kane's singer wife, whom Kane wants to make a star.

But Xanadu is more than Hearst Castle: it's the estates of Michael Jackson (Neverland Ranch, where we now know what went on behind the gates), George Lucas (Skywalker Ranch), Tom Cruise (Telluride), Bill Gates (which has been dubbed Xanadu 2.0) and, of course, Donald Trump (Mar-a-Lago). The age-old desire to own the biggest house is featured in the television series *Billions,* where the hero, who has bought a mansion in the East Hamptons, sits in his private cinema to watch *Citizen Kane.* He became a billionaire by investing in travel and aviation on the European stock exchange right when the World Trade Center towers fell; he had recently been laid off and was negotiating his severance package in a law office as his ex-colleagues were dying. He gets interrupted constantly by various business he must attend to and documents he has to sign, and never manages to get past the beginning of the film. That opening scene is precisely what caught my attention, that establishing shot of Xanadu.[177] Xanadu is a super-castle, just as Kane is a superman. The script describes precisely how the mythical home must appear on screen – enormous, imposing, monolithic:

> Camera travels up what is now shown to be a gateway of gigantic proportions and holds on the top of it – a huge initial *K* showing darker and darker against the dawn sky. Through this and beyond, we see the fairy-tale mountaintop of Xanadu, the great castle a silhouette as its summit, the little window a distant accent in the darkness ... Its right flank resting for nearly forty miles on the Gulf Coast, it truly extends in all directions farther than the eye can see ... The castle

dominates itself, an enormous pile, compounded of several genuine castles, of European origin, of varying architecture – dominates the scene, from the very peak of the mountain.[178]

A series of shots show different aspects of the estate, from the entrance gate to a lit-up palace window – a light which, as soon as the camera focuses on the window, suddenly goes out. When the light comes back on, the image is blurred by "big, impossible flakes of snow"[179] falling on a country scene, a cottage, a snowman. Close-up on Kane's mouth: "Rosebud ..."[180] The camera pulls back to reveal that the country scene is contained within a snow globe that falls from Kane's inert, dying hand. A nurse enters the room, pulls his arms back over his stomach, and lifts the sheet to cover his face. A description of Xanadu later follows: it contains "the loot of the world." Its resident has just died, the Kubla Khan of the United States: Charles Foster Kane.

• • •

Orson Welles's film follows the investigation of a journalist who wants to find the significance of Kane's last word. He interviews his widow and two of his closest collaborators, he reads Kane's guardian's memoirs, he steps into the enigmatic life of a man who was larger than life. The film's central question is one of proportion: how does a man become too big for himself?

A sort of Alice in Wonderland, Kane drinks a magic potion – ambition – and grows like a giant in a world smaller than he is. From the huge room with its oversized table where the journalist reads the guardian's manuscript beneath an oversized portrait of Kane, to the final scenes, everything is a game of magnitude: near the end of the film, Kane's wife, who is dwarfed by the gigantic setting, is doing a jigsaw puzzle. After she leaves, Kane, furious, destroys the flimsy decor of his wife's too-small rooms, making them seem like a dollhouse. It's almost as if the world begins to shrink until it ends up in a snow globe. The architectural scale is a comment, too, on the human scale: Charles Foster Kane is taller than all the other men around him, the boys' club of his employees, whom we see sitting around a table during a banquet while a group of chorus girls entertain them. The boys' club is also centre stage during Kane's run for state governor: standing before a crowd, under a poster of himself whose size is reminiscent of fascist propaganda, Kane is surrounded by dozens of men who look alike and who reflect his own image.

Like Trump, who, when he turns on the television or flips through the newspapers, can only see himself wherever he looks, Kane is a figure multiplied – a proliferation of the self, Welles and Mankiewicz tell us, that is the cause of his downfall. Kane wanted everything and lost everything; he wanted to be the best and he disappeared. Rosebud turns out to be the name of the sled he was playing with when his parents entrusted him to his guardian. In the last sequence of the film, the sled burns along with a bunch of other objects of little or no use or value, without anyone ever understanding what it actually means.

● ● ●

Is part of the commentary of *Citizen Kane*, through the representation of Xanadu, about men and architecture, power-hungry men who build the world in their own image, architects who hold the world in the palms of their hands?

Welles's use of scale is reminiscent of the work of design star Philippe Starck. With the Delano South Beach Hotel in Miami, Starck played with irony, inventing a universe from the other side of the mirror. Like Welles's Xanadu, Starck combined different eras and genres to create a surreal effect, a dream or nightmare world where a luminous beach leads to a dark, mysterious Scottish castle; what an odd place to come home to, in a bikini, from the seaside. But when architecture is logical, Starck said, it's not erotic, hence the need to do the opposite of what is expected:

I shall make it a dark castle in Scotland. When we shall go on the beach in the sun, in our small bikinis, we shall come back in this castle and it will be incredibly sexy. It will be a little disruptive to be almost naked in the middle of an Irish or Scottish castle with a fireplace and fur covers. That was the idea and it works. Before, there was something saying that on holidays you don't need culture. It's not true. On holidays you have time to appreciate culture. That's why I put the Salvador Dali chair and all the art. It was very, very chic and it was ambitious for Miami at this time. [181]

Starck's very chic work, like Welles's fictional world, is linked to the practice of accumulation and collage, borrowing from different eras and styles – a way of evoking, in Welles's case, European imperialism, which looted everything to fill its museums. As Welles and Mankiewicz wrote in the *Citizen Kane* script:

One hundred thousand trees, twenty thousand tons of marble, are the ingredients of Xanadu's mountain. Xanadu's livestock: the fowl of the air, the fish of the sea, the beast of the field and jungle – two of each; the biggest private zoo since Noah. Contents of Kane's palace: paintings, pictures, statues, the very stones of many another palace, shipped to Florida from every corner of the earth, from other Kane houses, warehouses, where they mouldered for years. Enough for ten museums – the loot of the world. [182]

Charles Foster Kane personifies the kind of colonialism-by-theft which can never have enough loot, and the architect-designer Starck was making a similar gesture, albeit tinged with irony or even cynicism. The Delano, too, is about not only accumulation, but also over-dimensionality: an individual who moves through that space and rubs shoulders with that kind of furniture is dwarfed by it, losing their bearings as if they had crossed through the looking glass. Is it an acknowledgment of the architectural ego?

Or cynicism from someone who claims to be changing things, making design accessible, making ethical choices, looking after the less privileged, like Charles Foster Kane at the start of his career, when in fact his work is in and for the world of the wealthy?

While Starck prided himself on taking everyone's desires into account, he actually worked according to an incredibly binary structure, where women and men exist separately and consume from that divided standpoint. Starck invented and sold luxury goods that secured his spot on the chessboard of architecture and design, but under the guise of humour, irony, and lightness, as if he had nothing to gain, as if his relationship to his work and to the world he operated in were utterly nonchalant. That indifference, or distraction, recalls Walter Benjamin's words on architecture:

> The distracted mass ... absorbs the work of art into itself. Buildings, most obviously. Architecture has always provided the prototype of a work of art that is received in a state of distraction and by the collective. The laws governing its reception have most to tell us ... Buildings are received twofold: through how they are used and how they are perceived.[183]

Tonya Neely in the film *The Architect* (2006) wants the architect who designed a public housing complex in Chicago to sign a petition calling for its demolition: "Funny to think that someone thought them up, you know, a man or his son. It always feels as though they just happened."[184] As if buildings just magically appeared. As if the architect were some kind of god.

CHAPTER ELEVEN

A World of their Own

What Philippe Starck, Orson Welles, Donald Trump, and private clubs can lead us to question is the boys' club not just as a configuration of male individuals gathering in the confines of a specific place, but as a place in and of itself. The boys' club is like the buildings, most of which are designed and built by men, that house our institutions, our governments, and our states. The boys' club is a building that we enter collectively at any given moment, but distractedly – in other words, forgetting or not quite realizing or understanding where we are.

The boys' club is a building in a city where, in theory, everyone has the freedom to move around. But as we know, all too often, to varying degrees throughout the world, cities belong to men, especially after sunset. In her book on gender and violence in public spaces,[185] the sociologist Marylène Lieber shows how women are subjected to a series of reminders or reinings-in that are not necessarily serious when taken in isolation, except that they constantly point out that women are potential prey in the public space: salacious comments, sexual innuendoes, smiles, drawn-out looks, wolf whistles ... So many gestures or interactions out in the street can be interpreted as microaggressions. Intimidation, harassment, exhibitionism, threats, attacks, sexual violence – these are the risks women run when they dare to venture outside what been entrusted to them since the Victorian era, that is, the family home. The notion that a woman's place is in the home has become one of the founding principles of American architectural design and town planning since the nineteenth century, a practice denounced by Dolores Hayden in 1980.[186] Relegating women to the domestic sphere, to suburban houses far from the city centre, isolated from each other by yards, swimming pools, and fences, also separates housewives from the boys' club. As the French feminist group La Barbe's[187] Pascale Lapalud put it:

> Women find it much harder to adapt to urban life. Cities aren't made for women because they bear such a mental and social load throughout the day ... There's a lack of legitimacy that women experience in public spaces ... Cities of the future will also mean changes in society, notably in accepting all identities. We're going to free ourselves ... from all these stereotypes and gender norms.[188]

• • •

When women are out in public, they're usually doing something or going somewhere. Unlike men, women don't quite have the right to just hang around in the public space, or at the very least, it's fraught for them to do so: if they walk the streets, they risk becoming – well, streetwalkers. As the sociologist Irene Zeilinger explains, a woman who's not moving is a woman who is available. Pascale Lapalud and other members of La Barbe undermine these prejudices by gathering in public to speak out against male domination at the National Assembly and elsewhere. Along with Chris Blache and others, they founded the research and activism organization Genre et ville to challenge and understand "the largely insidious and imperceptible role of gender stereotypes in the city."[189] Little data exists, so the collective walks the city to raise awareness, noting the different appropriation of public space, based on samples.

> We noticed that, around Belleville, 95 percent of the people who were sitting on benches were men. The use of benches varies by gender. Women take up activities in public spaces; while men take up public spaces. On a bench, women will read, smoke a cigarette, eat a sandwich, or chat with a friend. Men, on the other hand, are more likely to be idle and simply

watch passers-by. They might be called gladlings ["ravis"].
Out on the street, women push, pull, carry, and go from point
A to point B. Men, meanwhile, might be said to be propping
up the walls.[190]

These ways of being in public space are perhaps more specific to
certain European cities than to North America, but the analysis
of streets as the territory of men, a territory occupied by men,
transcends national borders: peeing in public against bushes or
walls; talking and laughing loudly, shouting; clustering to take
up the sidewalk without sharing, slowing down, or standing to
one side ... There are myriad ways men occupy space, putting up
what Guy Di Méo calls "invisible walls": "mental barriers that keep
certain parts of the city out of the imaginative world of woman."[191]
Manspreading on public transit has been criticized in recent years,
with some women imitating the way men tend to sit, with their
legs spread apart, which not only calls attention to the genitals, but
doubles the surface area that is occupied, forcing the person next to
them to squeeze in.[192] As Lauren Bastide writes, echoing the words
of the urban anthropologist Chris Blache, "faced with a man, it's
always the woman who steps aside. Or the person of colour."[193]

What would a gender-neutral city look like, Dolores Hayden
asked.[194] Shared cooperative spaces with apartment buildings built
around inner courtyards, or neighbourhoods where car sharing
is possible; safe streets and parks (that is, accessible and well lit);
public transport networks, including subways, buses, and bicycles
with schedules adapted to the lives of women, who are more likely
to travel several times a day, who still bear the brunt of domestic
chores and care work in addition to paid work, and who are more
often freelancers than their male peers. In Vienna in 1993, town
planners developed the Frauen-Werk-Stadt (Women-Work-City)
project, designing apartment complex blocks with green spaces and
inner courtyards, and including daycares, drugstores, and medical clinics. The city of Vienna itself took up the torch, widening

sidewalks, lighting footpaths and alleyways, and redesigning parks to make them safer to walk in.

Virginia Woolf called for women to be given a room of their own, which for a long time was interpreted quite literally.[195] What we now need to understand in the word "room" is the ubiquity of space, and to see not just a room in a house, but a building, the street, a city, our institutions: in short, the whole world.

• • •

Men are the surveyors of the world; it is designed for them, and named by and after them. Toponymy is predominantly male, with cities highlighting the achievements of men, usually white men, by naming streets, highways, boulevards, bridges, subway stations, and airports in their honour – yet another way of putting the male stamp on territory and etching a single, one-sided commemoration and an act of "mentrification," the gendered version of gentrification coined by @thelilithnoir.

If gentrification describes the process by which one "improves" a place so it "conforms to middle-class taste," mentrification achieves an equal status transformation by taking the history of female participation and achievement and festooning its narrative with phalluses.[196]

The names of women in urban spaces are almost non-existent by comparison.[197] The French geographer Yves Raibaud notes that, in Bordeaux, "men take up 92 percent of street names, and the biggest thoroughfares,"[198] while in Paris, 123 out of 130 avenues are named after men – presidents, ministers, marshals, generals, colonels, commanders, professors, poets, philosophers; each one has his own street, and women share the dregs. In Montréal, in 2014, only 6 percent of six thousand place names were women's.[199] Chris Blache and Pascale Lapalud, who were tasked with redeveloping the Place du Panthéon, worked to make it a mixed space, not only by widening the sidewalks (which reduces the risk of street harassment), but by placing granite blocks and platforms bearing the names of 160 women, including artists, activists, and scientists, as well as anonymous markers to represent victims of femicide, women migrants who died along the journey, and women facing homelessness, who died in the street.[200] And so the "Panthéon des femmes" was born.

A space like that, reserved for women, is an exception in the French urban landscape; places only rarely pay homage to women by bearing their names. Perhaps women's work isn't considered honourable enough, or maybe their achievements are simply less known; there just isn't much of a need or a desire to find out. The same can be said of ethnocultural and Indigenous communities, which are grossly under-represented. In France 4 percent of streets are named after women; only thirty-seven of 350 statues in Paris represent famous women. Montréal, meanwhile, claims that its heritage division has already been practising affirmative action for over twenty years. The city's action plan, cited in 2014, stated that, when choosing a place name, "if there is a choice between a man's name and a woman's name, the latter will be given preference."[201] It's not just a matter of choosing one over the other, however; it's about getting out of the boys' club, of not making the moral, ethical, and therefore somewhat false choice – that is, choosing a woman because she's a woman and thus implying that the man's name was best but had to be set aside for political reasons.

● ● ●

Men name cities. First they name it as a woman "to be penetrated like a female body," as Pierre Sansot[202] writes; writers and artists have long represented cities as places of sexual conquest and love. Those men "of good breeding and good whiteness"[203] extol erotic cities around the world – the red-light districts, exotic destinations full of charming and very young women. That eminent literature needs to be reread through the prism of sexual harassment and violence to take note of male representations of cities that women pay for, and which exalt and trivialize unfettered aggressive seduction.[204] Then they name it after themselves. They put their stamp on it. Raibaud speaks of the city as androcentric, referring (in the case of France, though the phenomenon can be extended to the whole of the West) to athletic facilities for sports practised mainly by boys. "Show me a specific facility in the city," Raibaud writes, "where sixty thousand women can indulge in their favourite pastime!" [205]

We're led to believe that male activities are more important than activities girls tend to favour (as a result of socialization); the cultural objects preferred by adolescent girls and their status as fans have been shown to be devalued in comparison with those adolescent boys choose. Raibaud states,

> girls want to go out, have fun, play outside, with each other or with boys. But they are prevented from doing so either implicitly, by a lack of amenities, services, and dedicated spaces, or explicitly, because of the boys' aggressiveness and cautionary advice from parents and friends. [206]

Single-sex spaces exclude girls and all too often become places for the expression of not only exaggerated masculinity but also sexism and homophobia. Boys thus become men, but the club they form is built on violence against women and in opposition to traits somehow considered feminine. In the words of the French philosopher Françoise Collin, the street is a holding ground for the main enemy. [207] Ultimately, the city has a masculine name and face, which is not unrelated to the fact that commonplace harassment happens every day on every street. How do you get around in the city, how do you live there, who occupies it and how, and how much? These are questions that can be asked about the place of bodies – all bodies – on the sidewalk, in cars, on bicycles, on foot, in daylight and in the dark. Street harassment has been increasingly studied and condemned – in Sofie Peeters's documentary on Brussels, *Femme de la rue*, [208] the creation of the Hollaback! site, [209] poster campaigns against street harassment, graphic novel projects featuring experiences of street harassment such as *Projet crocodiles*, the #BeenRapedNeverReported[210] movement, various slutwalks and Take Back the Night protests, and so on. Testimonies abound, as do efforts to mobilize: for example, the Between Stops service offered by the Société de transport de Montréal public transit corporation, the Take Back the Métro campaign by the French group Osez le féminisme! (which also led an initiative to rename Paris landmarks for one night in August 2015, with the Quai de la Tournelle becoming the Quai de Nina Simone, for instance).

• • •

Have things really changed since Virginia Woolf's description in *Three Guineas* of the world as seen by women "from the threshold of the private house; through the shadow of the veil that St Paul still lays upon our eyes; from the bridge which connects the private house with the world of public life?"[211] What a strange world, Woolf writes, which, at first sight, "is enormously impressive. Within quite a same small space are crowded together St Paul's, the Bank of England, the Mansion House, the massive if funereal battlements of the Law Courts; and on the other side, Westminster Abbey and the Houses of Parliament."[212] Fathers and brothers spent their whole lives in those spaces, and "it is from this world that the private house ... has derived its creeds, its laws, its clothes and carpets."[213]

Those places caught Woolf's eye first by their "colossal size":[214] buildings are like clothes, hairstyles, jewellery, and accessories, a decorative arsenal, like the ceremonies performed "always together, always in step, always in the uniform proper to the man and the occasion."[215] While men had places of their own (private clubs were an integral part of the social landscape in Woolf's day, on the eve of World War II), women did not; they lacked spaces where they could write, create, or reflect. The places that did exist, instead of including them, excluded them, such as the colleges Woolf mentions, which remains true of many institutions today – hence the importance, in thinking about the boys' club, of considering its spaces, and therefore its architecture.

CHAPTER TWELVE

Architects of the Universe

It might be said that architects have been erecting the edifice of male domination and housing boys' clubs since the beginning of time. There are no buildings without money, there is no architecture without banks, and there are no architects without businessmen or members of government. There's no government without parliament buildings, no major corporation without a head office, no university without lecture halls: institutions exist through the real estate they take up, but do we really see the buildings around us? Do we know who designed them? Or do we walk past them without quite realizing what we're looking at, except maybe when the building is a monument, if it's recognized as work of art and the person who designed it is a bona fide artist, someone important in the history of creation? In a way, we have to decide to take an interest in architecture in order to see it and to see the face behind the facade.

• • •

It's no secret that the world of architecture is predominantly male. While architecture schools have seen an increase in the number of female students, who now make up around half of the student body,[216] professorial ranks remain predominantly male: in 2021, in the United States, only 25 percent of architecture professors were women. In France in 2018, in project-based teaching, the architecture professor and researcher Stéphanie Dadour points out, only three women had professor status, compared to forty-one men; among senior lecturers, the ratio was two hundred and thirty-five to seventy-eight.[217] "It's not uncommon," Dadour points out, "to see professors giving students advice on what to wear, suggesting that they match their outfits to the models they're presenting," to say nothing of comments on cleavage and smiles.[218] Assessments of students' project presentations are an important part of their training but often seem like more of a hazing process to test and harden them for later client presentations.[219] (Reports of moral and sexual harassment and sexist violence, such as those that surfaced at the École nationale supérieure d'architecture de Montpellier in 2020,[220] further up the ante.)

In the United States, the percentage of women interns in architecture firms is 10 percent lower than the number of female graduates. Only around 20 percent of architecture graduates are women, and only 17 percent of architecture firm partners.[221] In France, 32 percent of architects registered with the Ordre des architectes are women (but 50 percent of architects under the age of thirty-five).[222] Inequalities persist. Women architects earn far less than their male colleagues – €54,757 (approximately $93,000) annually on average for men in 2020, compared to €33,495 (approximately $57,000) for women.[223] Systemic sexism persists even beyond salary discrepancies. As Anne Labroille and Christine Leconte point out, men tend to go into traditional project management, while a large number of women go into more varied practice, including project management, consultancy, and teaching.[224] They engage in care-related architectural practices, which are discredited and invisible. Working hours are incompatible with the roles that women still play in society and with the mental and physical loads they carry in their private lives. As Stéphanie Dadour points out, the age at which women become project managers is also the age at which most women who want to become project managers become mothers. All-too-common all-nighters play a part in the silent discrimination to which women are subjected as well. Moreover, in France as elsewhere, not only is the world of construction still male-dominated (as Leconte quips of construction sites, "You don't always find size 38 boots there!"[225]) but access to professional associations often takes place through male networks, sports clubs, outings, and so on.

Over the last few years, a number of publications have reported on the discrepancy between men and women in architecture, a gap that widens even further when other factors, such as skin colour, ethnocultural origins, and gender identity are taken into account. Architecture is the intersection of privilege. The majority of architects, and most of those who are remembered by history or who currently have an international reputation, are white men. Several recent books and articles denounce the inequality, sexism, and even misogyny that still dominate the world of architecture, a kind of boys' club par excellence insofar as, unlike elected governments who represent the population (albeit often inadequately, but nonetheless), architecture remains male turf. Architects, whose practice combines art, science, engineering, and business, are Renaissance men.

In 2018, the American Institute of Architects (AIA) in San Francisco surveyed nearly 15,000 respondents in every American state and on six continents. [226] White men, whose presence is tentacular at all levels of architectural practice, and after them Black, Latino, and Asian men are still hogging the top of the ladder. Female architects and designers and those from traditionally underrepresented backgrounds earn less than their male and white colleagues and are less likely to rise to leadership positions. (In Québec, the Ordre des architectes reported an increase in the number of women, but there are still twice as many men in the profession. [227]) Mothers in particular pay a professional price, and architecture firms are slow to adopt best practice in terms of equity. Generally speaking, the architects interviewed in the AIA survey suggested that architectural culture is toxic and that women are not only victims but actual targets (which was confirmed by a *New York Times* reader study conducted after the sudden death in 2016 of Zaha Hadid, the only female recipient of the prestigious Pritzker Architecture Prize). [228] Women architects describe being mistaken for assistants or secretaries; they get comments about premenstrual syndrome or pregnancy; and they find that some colleagues refuse to be managed by a woman. In the *New York Times*, the American architect Yen Ha says,

Every single day I have to remind someone that I am, in fact, an architect. And sometimes not just an architect, but *the* architect. I'm not white, wearing black, funky glasses, tall, or male. I'm none of the preconceptions of what an architect might be, and that means that every time I introduce myself as an architect, I have to push through the initial assumptions. Every new job site means a contractor who will assume I am the assistant, decorator, or intern. It usually isn't until the third meeting that the project team looks to me for the answers to the architectural problems. [229]

• • •

The typical portrait of the architect as a tall white man wearing black-rimmed (preferably round) glasses on his nose is a persistent stereotype: for example, the very successful Danish firm BIG owns the domain big.dk. [230] That dick joke alone sums up what's wrong with architecture, as Allison Arieff points out. [231] Mentors and women who have made their mark in architecture are rare: "Apart from Zaha Hadid, how many female architects can you name?" she asks.

The story of Denise Scott Brown and her collaboration with her husband, which was underestimated and devalued because their work was systematically attributed to her spouse, is typical of women's place in a macho world. "The heroically original modern architectural revolutionary with his avant-garde technology, out to save the masses through mass production, is a macho image if ever there was one." [232] Even today, women tend to be omitted from syllabi; they are invited less often as critics or lecturers and those who run construction techniques courses in university programs are almost exclusively men: female students, both because of socialization and because of the attitude of male colleagues, are still reluctant to use many tools and machines. After graduation, women architects' choices about the buildings they want to design tend to be devalued; we still swear by male genius and the skyscrapers of Frank Gehry, Norman Foster, Daniel Libeskind, among others. As a result, the sociopolitical aspects of architecture are sidelined – issues that presumably most often concern architects from marginalized and underrepresented backgrounds. As the American architect Liz Ogbu explains, "In many ways, architecture is a profession that has been the epitome of the dominant white patriarchy, from most of the celebrated starchitects to the all-too-frequent obsession with buildings that are better known for the beauty of the object than the quality of life that they enable." [233]

The question of use over beauty, of quality of life over aesthetics, is central not only to contemporary architectural creation but also to understanding the history of architecture. Since Vitruvius and antiquity, [234] the language of architecture has been rooted in the sexualization of forms and materials. Architecture was inspired by the human body – that is, the male body, harmonious, orderly, powerful, muscular, and unadorned. [235] Women were considered uncertain, as Cennino Cennini wrote in the fifteenth century, because they did not adequately represent the proportions of the human body (woman, that irrational animal, he said, has no fixed proportions), [236] and were associated early on with mere ornamentation, with frivolity. Soft, supple, submissive in the service of the whole, powerless, fragile ... Manly lines support the drawing, while feminine lines decorate it. As Leonardo da Vinci's *Vitruvian Man* shows (applying the recommendations of Vitruvius himself in his books on architecture), men dominate the way we represent the human figure. That domination continues to this day in contemporary architecture, with Le Corbusier, for example, creating the Modulor (1945), the standardized human silhouette that informs the design of his housing units. Le Corbusier wanted to establish a link of maximum comfort between Man and the space in which he lives – capital-*M* Man, rather than men or women. Everything is about proportions: the French neologism "Modulor" is portmanteaued from "module" and "or" (gold), referring to the golden mean, which determined the proportions of the Modulor. [237]

The Boys' Club: The Many Worlds of Male Power

• • •

The world of architecture, following broad, gendered categories, relegates the feminine to the decorative and makes the masculine the vector of formal essence: masculine space is created by stripping architecture down to its bare essentials. As Mark Wigley points out, according to classical architectural theory, buildings should correspond to the male body, although that architectural body is in fact closer to the traditional feminine, as an object to be observed, admired, dressed, or undressed; hence the importance attached to ornamentation. Together, male architects design buildings in the image of the male body, creating objects they treat as they do women. What is interesting, then, in the reading proposed by someone like Mark Wigley is understanding architecture itself as a feminine object domesticated by male architects – architecture as the place from which the gaze originates, as a thing to be seen and which is inhabited by the gaze, by the man who looks, whether he is the owner, a neighbour, the public, or a critic. As Wigley points out, feminist thought has clearly shown how representation, in the act of looking or of being seen, is sociopolitically significant: "What is so attractive in the feminine is the advertised presence of the masculine. What the man is attracted to is the myth of himself." [238] It is a thin white line, [239] Wigley suggests, that separates structure and decoration, domesticating the (feminine) building in order to make room for the (masculine) discipline of architecture:

> The task of architectural theory becomes that of controlling ornament, restricting its mobility, domesticating it by defining its "proper place" ... The practices of ornamentation are regulated so that ornament represents and consolidates the order of the building it clothes, which is that of man. It is used to make that order visible. The domesticated woman is the mark of the man, the material sign of an immaterial presence.

In fact, classical architectural theory dictates that the building should have the proportions of the body of a man, but the actual body that is being composed, the material being shaped, is a woman. Clothes maketh the man, but they are woman. Man is a cultural construction which emerges from the control of the feminine. [240]

A thin coat of whitewash on the walls of the modern building is associated with masculine traits such as logic, hygiene, and truth. Despite its apparent invisibility, that veneer speaks for itself: it is an added layer, a form of clothing applied to the surface of building – a white skin, as Alberti described in the fifteenth century, which acts as a screen, decorating the building by covering it, but in a way that drives home the point about masculinity. While Alberti describes the building as being built "naked" and then dressed, that white skin is not really an ornament; it is the male costume, an affirmation of masculinity as neutrality. [241] The ideology of white, as Wigley writes, has been at the heart of architecture since Alberti (and before him Brunelleschi): the construction of the gaze on a white surface is inherent in the institutions that have framed architecture over the centuries, whether with regard to classical white marble statues, art gallery walls, the white lab coats of Beaux-Arts students, or the white walls of modern design. [242]

Today, white still evokes Le Corbusier and his "Law of Ripolin":

Every citizen is required to replace his hangings, his damasks, his wallpapers, his stencils, with a plain coat of white ripolin. *His home* is made clean. There are no more dirty, dark corners. Everything is shown as it is ... Once you have put ripolin on your walls you will be *master of yourself.* And you will want to be precise, to be accurate, to think clearly. [243]

It's the law of an "extraordinarily beautiful white":

If the house is all white, the outline of things stands out from it without any possibility of mistake; their volume shows clearly; the colour is distinct. The white of whitewash is absolute, everything stands out from it and is recorded absolutely, black on white; it is honest and dependable ... It is rather like an X-ray of beauty. It is a court of assize in permanent session. It is the eye of truth. Whitewash is extremely moral ... Whitewash is the wealth of the poor and the rich – of everybody, just as bread, milk, and water are the wealth of the slave and of the king.[244]

Purity and perfection: according to Le Corbusier, we need to come to terms with our own "cowardice in not facing a separation," to do away with "ugly accumulation," and acknowledge that "we set up the cult of the souvenir."[245] We need to be rid of a certain materiality, which is a blemish and contributes to clutter; we ought to stick to pure thought. To be rid of ornamentation and stick to the walls, to the structure and its efficacy, to the purity and accuracy of white, a way of freeing the mind and creating a symbiosis between the house and the conscience: "When you are surrounded with shadows and dark corners, you are at home only as far as the hazy edges of the darkness your eyes cannot penetrate; you are not master in your own house."[246] But that whiteness isn't innocent; white has become the favourite colour of the boys' club in general, and the architectural boys' club in particular.

• • •

The whiteness of the architectural community is being called out by more and more people. Julian Rose, in 2017, noted the significance of then first lady Michelle Obama's comment a year earlier that she lived in a house built by slaves.[247] Obama's statement had its skeptics, with some right-wingers refusing to acknowledge that enslaved people had made the seat of government possible. What the controversy highlights, however, is the transparency of architecture – how

Architects of the Universe

we tend to forget that it depends on human hands (craftspeople, labourers, carpenters, plumbers, and so on) who, depending on the time and the place, and on the architects and contractors involved, are treated more or less poorly. A building's whiteness is no guarantee of purity. Consciously or not, we hold the Renaissance architect, a thinker and creator who most often does not build, apart from the workers and craftspeople who do the physical work. The figure of the modern man, who is portrayed as universal when he is in fact European and colonial, is contrasted with the bodies of the workers responsible for the actual construction of the building.

What Julian Rose and Mabel O. Wilson emphasize is the way in which colonial architecture is "literally constructing whiteness," as Wilson puts it, and attempts to universalize a cultural history of that is above all European. America, Wilson says, was born of that colonial process, the genocidal conquest of Indigenous communities and the dehumanization of sub-Saharan peoples by enslavement. She is wary, she says, of the tendency to see architecture as an "agent of progress":

> Whether we're talking about the Vitruvian Man in classical antiquity or Le Corbusier's Modulor Man in the twentieth century, and architecture has always excluded other ways of being human … Architecture has always been an agent of power, perhaps not unwittingly, but unselfconsciously; it has been the means through which the powerful literally constructed their world. [248]

The whiteness Le Corbusier dictated erases memory, history, and crimes. Buildings pop up out of nowhere, neutral, with no connection to politics or ideology, as if they were uninflected places "facilitating the free interaction of sovereign subjects in space." [249] Structures appear like Venus rising from the seafoam, like Athena emerging fully armed from Zeus's head. First and foremost, they are embodiments of beauty.

CHAPTER THIRTEEN

An Eye for Beauty

Sometimes unwittingly, Hollywood has shown us the political dimension of architecture, to which the field of architecture itself all too often turns a blind eye. Architects as movie heroes are revealing of the way architects build the world: it was true of Juror Number Eight, Henry Fonda's character in *12 Angry Men*, [250] who is the very personification of justice, and who manages to sway the positions of the other members of the jury. The same applies to the character of Leo Waters in *The Architect*, [251] whose social housing complex has become a hotbed of crime because of its design; he eventually agrees to sign a petition calling for its demolition. Finally, Flipper Purify, played by Wesley Snipes in *Jungle Fever*, is also an architect. [252] While the Spike Lee film tackles racism in love and sexual relationships, the fact that the hero is an architect is no accident: architecture is still a white world, which was even more the case when the film was made. The most common representation of the architect is a white man like Howard Roark, the hero of Ayn Rand's cult novel *The Fountainhead*, which was adapted for the screen by King Vidor. [253] In the seventy-five years since its release, the film has been watched countless times by architecture students, who simultaneously venerate, mock, and fear its hero.

Howard Roark is an ideal of both architects and men (in Rand's words, he is "the presentation of an ideal man" [254]). In *Stud: Architectures of Masculinity*, Joel Sanders describes Roark as a man who embodies the relationship between masculinity and architecture:

> Rand's hard-edged prose lodges both masculinity and architecture in a transcendental natural world: "His face was like a law of nature – a thing one could not question, alter, or

implore" ... Roark's robust physique, composed of "long straight lines and angles, each curve broken into planes," seen silhouetted against the sky, reads like a description of Frank Lloyd Wright's famous house *Fallingwater*.[255]

Roark's power stems from a popular belief that building designers, like the structures they create, represent the essence of masculinity.

> Rand's architecture of masculinity offers one of the most dramatic, although certainly not the earliest, renditions of the notion that buildings derive from the human form itself – specifically from the unity, scale, and proportions of the male body.[256]

Vidor's 1949 film adaptation of *The Fountainhead* stars Gary Cooper as Howard Roark, an architect of integrity and a pure artist, a model of humanity and genius, an archetype of masculinity. Sixty-five years later, director Denys Arcand's *An Eye for Beauty* (*Le règne de la beauté*)[257] takes up the clichés surrounding architecture and masculinity.

Although Arcand's film wasn't screened in French theatres,[258] Arcand, a Québec director who is a regular at Cannes, where he screened *Jesus of Montreal, Stardom, The Barbarian Invasions*, and *Days of Darkness*, is a household name in France. Arcand is a fan of the Québec architect Pierre Thibault, several of whose works he shows in *An Eye for Beauty* and throughout the closing credits, and he depicts the architect of the material world in the image of the great, divine creator. The first sequence of his film picks up where *The Fountainhead* left off: in the sky. At the end of Vidor's film, Roark stands at the top of the skyscraper he is building, waiting for the love of his life, Dominique Francon (the only female character in the film), to join him. *An Eye for Beauty*, meanwhile, begins soaring above the Trocadéro. The hero, Luc Sauvageau, is in Paris to accept the fictional Levinson Award for Architecture. In his speech, he declares, a civilization is always judged by its architecture. Building is an activity of hope. The hope that what we create will be useful and beautiful. The hope of telling future generations who we were. And the hope they will be moved, as we were by the architecture of those who came before us. [259]

Throughout the film, Arcand explores the idea of a civilization fabricated by its architects.

• • •

In *An Eye for Beauty,* we recognize that same cynicism and sarcasm of the professors in *The Decline of the American Empire,* the falseness of some of the characters in *Jesus of Montreal,* and the criticism of a world where appearances take precedence over existence. Thibault's chiselled houses, their openness to nature, and their transparency are soothing in their beauty and exhausting in the silence that underpins them – a silence that could be heavy with secrets, with words unspoken, but which can also be seen as a sign of emptiness, of a hollow inner life, a beauty that signals the reign of superficiality. The characters on screen really have nothing to say, as if the world itself had nothing to say, or everything had already been said, or there was nothing left to say in the face of so much beauty so devoid of meaning. [260]

Arcand succeeds perfectly in making beauty reign supreme. In fact, he achieves two things at once: he promotes beauty, and he shows its dangerous side. The film's visual grandeur is reminiscent of the majesty of Greek or Roman architecture, with Thibault's houses as monuments, where the characters (who are all white and good-looking) might be said to be hollow shells, in the image of these magnificent architecture products. Arcand gives voice to the lament of an architect in need of recognition, convinced that what he designs is fundamental. Throughout the film, that pretentiousness is coupled with a masculine arrogance: Luc Sauvageau, the architect, shows a condensed version of humanity, its ultimate representative as a man who marks its past and establishes its future, the man who traces the contours of a house where history, art, knowledge, thought, and beauty are housed. The businessman, the creative, the engineer, is also a man of houses, and the emphasis on aesthetics might suggest that he is the man of the house, too, but nothing could be further from the truth, since the man/architect/hero holds every position. Like an omnipresent god, he stands before women who are nothing and who say almost nothing; most of them only appear in relation to cooking and food, sports, and sex – in short, in relation to the body – including the lesbian doctor played by Marie-Josée Croze. She is probably the only woman who holds her own at all in the dialogue, and she is belittled in a scene at the medical clinic where Sauvageau, who is worried he might have a sexually transmitted disease, stands in front of the doctor, who crouches down to examine him as if she were fellating him.

Women are reduced to the world of appearances constructed by men. The most perfect expression of that reification is Stéphanie, the protagonist's passive blond partner, a kind of sleeping beauty, depressive and lapsed, magnificent in her evanescence, languor, and anorexia. When the women are lively, like Lindsay Walker, Luc Sauvageau's brunette lover, we associate them with prostitutes. On two occasions, when Sauvageau confesses his infidelity to friends, they ask, "a prostitute?" "An escort?" In Arcand's film, women are either pure or impure, on the side of the church or the brothel. In every case, they are the warrior's rest. The character of the architect from the beginning of the film brings it also to a close. He has grown old, with a beautiful young woman on his arm, her face and accent reminiscent of Frida Kahlo, wearing a dress in the same red as the ribbon on the medal he has just received. Woman as ornament; woman as trophy.

The movie's key scene, the mise en abyme, is a hunting scene: dressed in camo gear, like warriors, the men try to lure geese to a beach so they can shoot them. Sauvageau and his friend Nicolas, who's also an architect, plant a number of plastic geese in the shoals (like birthday flamingos in the suburbs), and as the real geese land among their presumed friends, the two men shoot the birds; later, back at the house, they behead and skin them. Sauvageau, as his name – "sauvage," savage – suggests, is a wild man, a man of history, a primal man. He brings out a traditional side of Québec that the radio host Serge Bouchard describes as the heyday of Québec gentlemen's clubs:

> Traditional Québec was built on [private] boys' clubs, where prime ministers, ministers, and deputy ministers would go up to their luxurious chalets to visit the rich Americans and English to whom they had handed over the country's most beautiful wilderness on a silver platter ... There were two thousand private clubs in Québec in 1966 [during] the reign of feudal lords: forestry companies, politicians, big businessmen, whose scandalous privileges nobody questioned ... The Cercle de la Garnison in Québec City, or the Club Saint-Denis in Montréal ... Secrets and closed doors, all for the benefit of the American and English gentlemen and the French-speaking bourgeoisie, who drank and laughed, in impenetrable circles that protected them from commoners ... Those gentlemen understood each other so well. [261]

Hunting is a traditionally masculine activity. While the practice Bouchard talks about hearkens back to a European social hierarchy, the practice and representation of hunting in North America makes it a privileged place of male alliance: camaraderie born out of respect for nature, and the forest in particular, as well as for the animal world, with which men have been associated in the popular imagination since the dawn of time. Deer hunting is part of masculine mythology and of a foundational American notion of brotherhood. (It was notably important enough for William Faulkner to announce he would miss his Nobel ceremony because he was going hunting; his publisher convinced him to change his mind. [262]) Hunting is linked to boys' initiation into masculinity, to male bonding and the exclusion of women (especially girlfriends and wives) and their rules. As hunter James B. Twitchell says, "Deer camp is what men have for a slumber party."[263] Hunting hangs between fraternity and barbarism, bringing together firearms, animal calls, blood, slaughter, cooking with meat and fat, alcohol, smoking, joking ... "Manners are held in abeyance," Twitchell writes, "jokes turn blue, there's no shaving, bourbon appears before 5 p.m., cigar smoke turns the air to haze, endless fun is poked, and pissing is elevated to a sacred ritual."[264]

The hunting scene in Arcand's film, which combines reality and make-believe, being and seeming, takes on certain characteristics of a typical hunting trip as a staging of masculinity; it's also a reflection of the forces that run through the whole film. Luc and Nicholas's hunt is almost like the trial of artifice or ornament, a criticism of what is commercial or soulless because it is reproduced technically (like the motel Sauvageau stops at in a Québec City suburb and which he leaves immediately to return to his mistress's room at the Château Frontenac); this is a core conflict in architecture, and it caricatures the gender divisions in the field. The juxtaposition of real and fake geese is echoed by the relationship established between the trees and the marijuana plants the architect grows in the forest so that they blend in with the landscape. Nature and artifice fold in on each other, like geese made of flesh and plastic. The hunting trip is evoked again in another scene in which Stéphanie, Luc's depressed wife, points her rifle at the window of their sublime house, a window that becomes the camera lens behind which we, as viewers, now stand, as if Stéphanie is threatening to make us disappear just when we think she's about to turn the gun on herself. She's aiming at the camera and at the audience, both of which are threats because they consume beauty. In that instant, the film seems to be saying what it never really articulates: between what is true and what is fake, between reality and its representation, there is a two-way mirror. Artifice looks upon reality without reality being able to look back.

By making an architect his hero, Arcand makes architecture appear to be a representative of a system coded in the same way as cinema or television. As Beatriz Colomina points out in the introduction to *Sexuality and Space*, [265] if we take up the challenge and question the connection between gender and space, we displace architecture, and by displacing architecture we displace the boys' club of architects who create places in which other boys' clubs set up their own reigns – conference rooms, locker rooms (Arcand has a shot of a series of men showering naked side by side), hunting grounds, studies, museums, churches ... The characters in *An Eye for Beauty* move within and through each of these places, which are variations on the concept of the private club.

On the surface, Arcand's film reveals something of a totalitarian ideal reminiscent of fascism (the World War II version, to be sure, but also that other fascism known as neo-liberalism). The fascist ideal is encapsulated both in the cult of nature, sport, and the body (particularly the male body, whose smooth skin and taut muscles the camera caresses), and in the modernism of the aesthetic. If the images of Thibault's houses purport to show man in his own universe, in harmony with rural or urban space, what remains are angles and unadorned, stripped-down lines, and a certain material harshness or dryness: an environment that gives the impression of being perfectly controlled. The houses reflect the discursive forms that run through the script – sentences, aphorisms, and commandments; a discourse that presents itself as truth. As both a critic and an apologist of that way of looking at the world, Arcand, through a lens that's at once mocking and friendly, has his hero say, "Ugliness is a crime against humanity." Arcand urges us both to admire and to assess the risks of beauty, to ask ourselves what crimes it is actually being used as an alibi for, and which crimes are being committed against what segment of humanity.

CHAPTER FOURTEEN

Terrorists

In the aftermath of 9/11, Steven Spielberg directed *Munich*[266] as if in response to the attacks. It's a film about men, Olympic athletes who are taken hostage by terrorists. The terrorists are hunted down by Mossad secret agents obsessed with the manhunt. The film follows the group of agents coming together, their deployment, and them killing the presumed perpetrators of the hostage situation, but it also shows their lives: how the team leader, Avner, prepares sumptuous meals for his accomplices, how they all sit around the table like a makeshift family-cum-powerful boys' club financed by the Israeli government, which provides them with weapons, bombs, planes, and apartments in order to carry out the assassinations. The film explores the relationships between the Mossad agents, their collaborators, and the people they're looking for.

• • •

There are few women in Spielberg's *Munich*, and most of them are mothers: the mother of Israel, Golda Meir; the hero's mother, the wife of an Israeli soldier for whom only homeland matters; the hero's wife, whom we see first pregnant, then in labour, and finally in her role as a young mother welcoming back the warrior-father, traumatized and weakened, whom she must now also look after. The last scene of the film speaks volumes: Avner, who we can guess is suffering from overwhelming flashbacks, is shown making love with his wife, haunted by images of what he has just been through. The low angle shows us her gaze, and we understand she is watching her husband, as if she were trying to accompany him in his suffering, without herself enjoying the sexual act.

There is a fourth female character, who is important particularly given the maternal dimension of the other women in the film: a hired assassin and femme fatale who plies her charm to ensnare the men she is hired to kill. She appears briefly, twice: we see her first in a hotel bar, cigarette and drink in hand, as she tries to seduce Avner, who resists the woman he describes to his colleague as the "local honey trap."[267] Avner is close to that colleague, who confides in him one evening about how hard their work is, and who is later found naked in his hotel room, murdered. The scent of the hitwoman's perfume betrays her as the killer, and she is later found by the terrorist hunters (this is her second appearance) on a canal cruise in Amsterdam, reclining seductively on her bed wearing only a silk bathrobe.

When the men arrive, she asks to be allowed to get dressed and suggests that they hire her now that they know how good she is. In a final attempt at seduction, she lets the sleeve of her robe slip, revealing her breasts. The men draw their weapons and fire silent bullets that slice through the young woman's throat and sternum. She staggers out of the room and over to the kitchen counter to stroke her cat; the animal continues to groom itself as the woman slumps into an armchair. A low shot shows her point of view as she watches the men shoot her one last time, in the head, and she dies before their eyes, her robe open over her naked body. The hero, in a gesture of modesty, folds back the robe, but his older colleague angrily rips it back open: "Leave it!" he snaps, referring to the robe, or perhaps to the woman, who has become a thing, an object. Stripping a woman, leaving her naked even if she is dead – a humiliation even beyond the grave. Assassination is not enough, there has to be one more gesture, a desecration of the body, to reduce the hitwoman to her weapon of choice: her sexuality.

The next scene shows Avner cooking up a veritable feast, his hands busy chopping vegetables at breakneck speed as his companions look on with some concern: he seems to be trying to forget something. At the end of the film, the agent who undressed the killer expresses his regret at refusing to let the body be covered, as if that act of desecration reflects the manhunt itself, which the hero will also question at the end of the film: will these murders really be able to foil future attacks, or was it just about revenge?

The femme fatale is an outlet for the protagonists, a pretext for them to unload together, in a film in which the dramatic tension rises constantly, not only because it is a thriller – from murder to murder, from escape to escape – but because it is about family conflicts, between the motherland (symbolized by Golda Meir and Mossad), the family of origin (represented by the hero's mother), and the hero's two families, the one he creates with his wife in Brooklyn, far from Israel, and the other he belongs to far from her, in the secret group of terrorist hunters. The murder of the young Dutch woman, riddled with holes, almost like stigmata, is an act of revenge against a threat to American family values: a professional murderer is put to death, but the trap of female sexuality is also curbed. Only the naked female body could release that tension; the murder had to be fully enjoyed rather than called into question. Above all, that naked woman had to lie there in the middle of a group of men, her body had to be the focal point of their attention and, as they looked at it together, they had to see each other hating and desiring at the same time. The splayed-open female body is the genesis of a world of their own.

●   ●   ●

In 2005, in the aftermath of the 9/11 the attack that gave the Bush-Cheney government permission to embark on a so-called war against terrorism, the lawyer Catharine A. MacKinnon tried to think about a "Women's September 11." MacKinnon described how asexual the victims were, those Wall Street men in suits and ties, compared to the highly gendered terrorists' bodies. She also pointed out that the number of victims of 9/11, between 2,800 and three thousand, is equivalent to the number of women murdered by men in one year in the United States alone, a third by someone close to them. MacKinnon also suggests that, when we look at the faces of the women who died on 9/11, we should ask ourselves who hurt them before that day: if, on that day, a spouse had killed them instead of the terrorists, would the media, public opinion, the government, and the entire nation have given their death a second thought? "That day," she writes, "being a man was no protection, hence the world's response."[268]

For MacKinnon, 9/11 highlighted the hypocrisy of framing the fight against terrorism as war, and a just war at that, while doing nothing to address violence against women. Violence against women isn't seen as a war because the state isn't held responsible for it. Violence against women doesn't meet the criteria of the Geneva Conventions: the combatants aren't in uniform, women aren't usually armed, many of the weapons used against women aren't considered weapons, and women in general don't defend themselves (and, when they do, they aren't seen as combatants, but found guilty of having themselves committed a crime).

"The battle of the sexes," MacKinnon writes, "simply does not look the way a war is supposed to look ... There are no rules of engagement, no rules of combat ... instead of being regarded as war crimes ... Acts of violence against women are regarded not as exceptional but inevitable, even banal."[269] Violent crime against women is of course judged in the context of national laws. MacKinnon holds that, if violence against women were considered civil war, a significant portion of what happens to women every day around the world would be prohibited by the Geneva Conventions.[270]

The victims of 9/11 were immediately perceived as innocent; it is the nature of terrorism to target civilians rather than soldiers. Are women not innocent victims, MacKinnon asks? Or not innocent enough? "What happens to women is either too particular to be universal or too universal to be particular, meaning either too human to be female or too female to be human."[271] The supposedly private situation of women is still seen as separate from the political sphere, whereas when some men are victims of violence, the cause becomes political, and even a human rights issue.[272] In the end, says MacKinnon, violence against women is a form of terrorism in the same way the 9/11 attacks were:[273] "After a century of increasing convergence in status and numbers between the civilian casualties of war and the noncombatant casualties of peace, it is time to ask: what will be done for the women all over the world whose own September 11th can come any day?"[274]

• • •

What interests me in MacKinnon's argument is once more the invisibilization of men – in this case, violent men, and more specifically men who are violent towards women in the United States, a social category that tends not to be the focus of attention, unlike those identified as terrorists (that is, who are of Arab origin, from the Middle East, Muslim, and so forth).

MacKinnon quotes Benjamin: "The tradition of the oppressed teaches us that the 'state of emergency' in which we live is not the exception but the rule."[275] Benjamin's words are echoed by Agamben's on civil war:

> In the stasis [civil war], the killing of what is most intimate is indistinguishable from the killing of what is most foreign. This means, however, that the stasis does not have its place within the household, but constitutes a threshold of indifference between the oikos and the polis, between blood kinship and citizenship.[276]

There lies the real meaning of the feminist slogan "The personal is political" (proposed by Carol Hanisch),[277] which also comes up in *Munich*. The opposition between the naked hired assassin and the clothed and armed Mossad commandoes is analogous to the opposition between zōē and bios, between a naked life that can be taken without consequence and the state, between the biological body and the body politic. The woman's nakedness contrasts with the men's clothes, just as her slumped posture in the armchair is a counterpoint to theirs as they loom over her. It's a scene that has been replayed over and over through the ages – men, alone or in a

The Boys' Club: The Many Worlds of Male Power

group, dominating a woman in a position of vulnerability. In our world, naked life, a life ended with impunity, is most often that of women, among others. The naked life, the life sacrificed and stripped of all humanity, depersonalized, depoliticized, is that of so many women raped and murdered without any justice, or not quite, which is to say with justice that is always inadequate.

The case of Missing and Murdered Indigenous Women and Girls in Canada, regarding which a report was published in June 2019, was properly called genocide.[278] A genocide is indeed unfolding, not only under the definition of the instigation of discrimination by the colonial state, but because it is still being allowed to happen, and because nothing is being done to protect Indigenous communities. The inquiry's final report raises a number of failures:[279]

> In actuality, genocide encompasses a variety of both lethal and non-lethal acts, including acts of "slow death," and all of these acts have very specific impacts on women and girls. This reality must be acknowledged as a precursor to understanding genocide as a root cause of the violence against Indigenous women and girls in Canada … not only because of the genocidal acts that were and still are perpetrated against them, but also because of all the societal vulnerabilities it fosters, which leads to deaths and disappearances and which permeates all aspects of Canadian society today.[280]

The failings of the police, the blindness of the government, and general indifference are all part of disappearances and killings that are permitted and even sanctioned by various boys' clubs: governments and police bodies, authorities who have the power to abuse the existence of those who represent no more than a biological, animal body, and who see no trace of the vanished.

On the one hand, there are serial girls, made invisible by serial femicides; on the other, there are boys' clubs, comprised mostly of white men in suits and ties, who are invisible in the power they wield.[281]

CHAPTER FIFTEEN

Clothes Make the Man

In her book *Where Are the Women Architects?*, Despina Stratigakos recounts the arrival of Architect Barbie at the New York Toy Fair in 2011 and reminds us that the genesis for the doll was in 2006, at the University of Michigan, and that it was political. At a time when state affirmative action measures were being abolished in the United States, Stratigakos was a researcher at the university, reflecting on the ways architecture was increasingly gatekeeping who did and didn't belong. For starters, there was that idealized image of the architect, which dominates the profession and is reinforced by popular culture, an image that suggests that architecture and women do not mix. Stratigakos tackled the issue from a new angle. She remembered Architect Barbie having been proposed during a survey on what Barbie could be, but Mattel had decided not to market the architect doll, saying that the word wasn't part of children's vocabularies. Stratigakos asked the faculty and students of the University of Michigan Taubman College of Architecture and Urban Planning to develop prototypes of an architect Barbie. The results, she writes, were astonishing, contrary to her own expectations: she had imagined a Barbie in a black suit with Le Corbusier-style glasses ("architecture would come first, Barbie second"[282]), but some of the students' prototypes flipped the notion on its head and chose to explore the profession from a Barbie-based, ultra-feminine angle:

> In these dolls I was confronted with the "femmenism" or "girl (grrrl) power" of a younger generation that seeks empowerment by playing up femininity in contexts that prohibit it. Inside architecture's hallowed halls, Barbie's "girlie" attributes

were a mark not of oppression but of resistance. These dolls looked you right in the eye and asked, "Why can't architects wear pink?"[283]

In 2010, Mattel launched a new appeal. This time, Stratigakos and her colleague Kelly Hayes McAlonie were invited to collaborate. How to reconcile the worlds of childhood and adulthood? And further, how to reconcile the masculine world not only of architecture, but also the closely connected field of construction, with the feminine world of dolls?

Wearing a coloured dress and black ankle boots (instead of the usual high heels), with black-rimmed glasses, a pink design tube, and a construction helmet, Architect Barbie was both celebrated and mocked – celebrated for feminizing a largely male and misogynistic industry, and mocked for being implausible. The criticism reflected the prevailing misogyny – her helmet was useless since as a woman she wouldn't be allowed to set foot on a construction site, she looked more like a designer than an architect, or she was a failed architect who needed to retrain in design, and so on – and the responses also highlighted architecture's inherent gender issues. Stratigakos quotes a comment posted by the user Sarah on a Nancy Levinson article in *Design Observer*:

> Architect Barbie couldn't wear such a skimpy outfit to the office, which is inevitably full of old men, or to the building site which is full of construction workers. She would wear faded black pants and a shirt that is wrinkled from sleeping under her desk. Her teeth would be bad because she won't have dental insurance, and her stomach would be pouchy from a bad diet hurriedly scarfed down at her desk. Her accessories should include a paycheque that is 30 percent less than the men's, antidepressants, and IBS medication.[284]

Yet workshops held for children – meaning little girls – around Architect Barbie, including, for instance, to get them to reimagine the Barbie Dreamhouse, were hugely successful. Even if little girls didn't know beforehand that women could be architects, those workshops allowed them to design their own plans for their own dream house, without ever questioning their intellectual or creative abilities. We may claim that clothes don't make the man, but Architect Barbie's outfits and accessories allowed little girls to see themselves in front of a drafting table or on a construction site. Because, let's be honest, clothes do make the man; they may even make the woman.

•   •   •

Much has been written in recent years about dress codes and, more generally, about the demands made on women, from corsets and high heels to makeup and cosmetic surgery. Award ceremonies, in particular the Oscars and the Césars, are essentially a parade of gowns draped over more or less naked bodies spotlit and photographed as if each star were unique. There are just as many suits crowded around the women, with tuxedoed men standing around as if they were one and the same. Some actors have ventured into bolder colours and materials: at the 2019 Oscars, Billy Porter went so far as wearing an elaborate tuxedo dress.[285] But by and large, the men's uniform remains the same: suit and tie, or tuxedo and bow tie. The suit makes the man.

Masculinity is a costume, but unlike dresses and other garments that make women ornaments first and foremost, men's suits are the uniforms that signify belonging to clubs where business is conducted. Ornamental women, like models, are reduced to silence (remember the protests of actresses demanding red-carpet journalists ask them about something other than what they were wearing), while men's suits give them access to speech. The suit is the skin of power; there is a metonymic relationship between men's uniforms and their domination. Men's invisibility is achieved by a multiplication of their appearance, while the extreme figuration of women has the effect of erasing them. On the one hand, there is the omnipresent, transparent male, and on the other, the Technicolor female; the invisibility of the former, which abets his domination, and the showiness of the latter, which is part of her subordination.

•   •   •

Businessmen, civil servants, and soldiers – those who walk in step with institutional precepts, those who have influence, authority, money, and power – are known as "the suits." The suit is a stand-in: a single garment can sum up everything that a man embodies – his role, his social position. His suit replaces him; it says it all.

Suits is also the title of an American television series [286] about a commercial-law firm, with "suits" in this case being short for lawsuits. The series is about a gifted young man, Mike Ross, who works as a bicycle courier but moonlights writing law school entrance exams for applicants, who pay him handsomely. From one episode and one misunderstanding to another, he winds up faking it as an actual lawyer in a real firm. The lie rests not only on his legal knowledge and his ability to pass himself off as a lawyer, but on the suit he wears. The suit standardizes the male body by erasing details, forms, and distinguishing characteristics of its wearer. [287]

Men's suits have been around for ages, but the golden age of the suit and tie was undoubtedly the 1980s. Richard Gere's Armani suit in American Gigolo [288] not only contributed to the Italian designer's rise in popularity, it also launched the fashion trend of the power suit: a suit, striped or not, with broad padded shoulders, worn over a white shirt, with pleated pants, suspenders, and an impressive amount of hair gel. [289] In the 1980s, the power suit was the uniform of greed, after the mantra of Gordon Gekko, the Michael Douglas character in Wall Street: "Greed is good." [290]

The suit is part of the sartorial lineage of armour and military uniforms: it "makes power visible"; [291] it is the uniform of male authority. Clothes make the man; they are the man, as Brenden Gallagher writes [292] of Gere, whose role as an escort in American Gigolo is shaped by what he wears: the film is less about its hero,

Gallagher suggests, than about his clothes, the Armani suit that will soon become a Wall Street trademark. The suit thus shifts from functional to elegant and even sexy. Wall Street wanted to look like Gere (Armani's popularity skyrocketed after the film's release), and suddenly the average man wanted to look like the wolves of Wall Street, wearing suits that oozed money, and the ability to make it or steal it.

Suits are the mainstay of any political wardrobe. Then minister Cécile Duflot was cat-called at the French National Assembly in 2012 for wearing a floral dress,[293] and two years later Ségolène Royal, who was ecology minister, was told that the colour of her outfit suited her.[294] Florence Parly quickly realized that it was better to wear a pantsuit to the National Assembly to stay out of trouble.[295] The suit may be the most important item of clothing in politics, yet paradoxically it is depoliticized, its strictly political dimension erased thanks to the anonymity it confers. Suits thus become a suit of armour, as the designer Tom Ford says,[296] a cloak of invisibility[297] and impunity. It is the psychological armour needed to survive in the trenches of the stock-market world as in the arena of parliament, a garment that is "the primary psychological exoskeleton by which the professional man ... may protect his image, declare his status, and potentially intimidate those in his purview into obedience and submission."[298]

● ● ●

Another character who wears the power suit gloriously[299] is Patrick Bateman, the antihero of Bret Easton Ellis's novel *American Psycho*.

Patrick Bateman, serial murderer and first-rate psychopath, is a fashion statement, an emblem of 1980s style. Unlike Jordan Belfort, played by Leonardo DiCaprio (who was also considered for the role of Bateman) in Martin Scorsese's *The Wolf of Wall Street*,[300] Bateman has no redeeming qualities. He's simply a villain. While *The Wolf of Wall Street* shows us Belfort's rise from a shoddy suit, cut too long and with too-broad shoulders, to a bespoke suit complete with silk tie, gold Rolex, and Gucci loafers, the character is defeated: he cooperates with the FBI and rats out his colleagues, his brokerage firm shuts down, and he ends up behind bars. Patrick Bateman's fate is quite different, which tells us something about the boys' club.

The novel and its film adaptation were misunderstood, perceived as misogynistic and extremely violent,[301] so much so that several of the people involved received death threats. Yet, as Ellis points out and as director Mary Harron and the feminist screenwriter Guinevere Turner show in their film, it is indeed a critique of masculinity. The spotlight is on men: their behaviour is under scrutiny in a comedy of manners set in the 1980s, the Wall Street and Reagan years, the era of yuppie financiers.

The film features a group of colleagues who all look alike, real serial men who skip from meal to meal in New York City's fanciest restaurants, talk clothes between two lines of cocaine, debate how to wear a cardigan, and compare business cards as if they were dicks. The men are so alike that they are interchangeable. The whole story revolves around the disappearance of one Paul Allen, a Wall Street broker and Bateman's doppelganger and victim. Some people claim to have met Paul Allen after he was in fact already dead, and his body disappears, so that we no longer know whether that murder, and all the others, really took place. That is the crux of the story: the hero's ultimate impunity.

Bateman is the distillation of those men who are so often seen together in restaurants, bars, and private clubs, sitting side by side, looking so much alike that they seem like mirror images of each other, not unlike the twin towers shown side by side on the screen. Bateman embodies all the common denominators, with the added bonus of pushing the trope to its most morbid and violent limits. Patrick Bateman is a psycho, a serial killer and a psychopath, and as such he is perfectly in tune with a culture that thrives on that sort of masculinity, a masculinity we now describe as toxic. His minimalist black-and-white apartment looks straight out of a decorating magazine. His multi-step morning routine for ageless skin, his indoor-tanning regimen, and the exercise program he follows are all part of a desire to sculpt his body into a timeless work of art. His perfectly pressed shirts and suits, the limousine he drives in, and his accessories and jewellery are all devices that reinforce his character as a true wolf of Wall Street, in a pack where everyone wants to howl loudest. Mary Harron's film cracks the veneer and rips the mask off, like the beauty mask Bateman peels off his face at the start of the film. We never see him working. All he does is organize his next meal. His hypermasculine, misogynistic friendships conceal a homoeroticism that Harron brings to light. The world of *American Psycho* is a superficial one in which work is idleness, wealth is moral poverty, love is convention, male friendship is a beard, and so on. Everything is fake, counterfeit, right down to the hero's crimes. Bateman's face unravels over the course of the film, from an initial gel mask to the sheen of sweat that covers his face from the moment he can no longer control his impulses and accelerates the pace of his murders. Eventually, he leaves a long message for his lawyer in which he confesses to his many crimes, but the lawyer doesn't believe it. So, unlike the hero of *The Wolf of Wall Street*, whose downfall we observe and which makes him a hero whose humanity allows the audience to identify with him, nothing saves Patrick Bateman in our eyes precisely because he is safe and sound at the end of the film. He is an anti-antihero, a pathetic villain, the protagonist of a black comedy (and of events that may or may not be real), whose character says a lot about what men can get away with.

The end of the film, which Harron said she regretted because it suggested that Bateman might have imagined it all,[302] breaks down male impunity. In a metonymic transfer for men's place in the world, particularly when they are part of the boys' club, the suit orchestrates their disappearance, that is, their profound invisibility and perfect impunity. Although *American Psycho* is a work of fiction, it left a powerful mark on the imagination, and on Western culture. As Ezinne Ukoha writes, "American psychos are being harvested in our own backyard."[303] Donald Trump, whom Patrick

Bateman idolizes, is infamously the American president who wears the worst suits. They are far too big for him, the sleeves are too long and the legs too wide, and the jacket seems to be stuffed with shoulder pads (which works well with his hair, as Luke Leitch points out [304]). Trump's blue suits and that ever-present red tie say something about the way he speaks to the people. The Brioni suits, sewn from very fine wool, are expensive (between \$6,000 and \$17,000 each), but they make Trump look like a president who is wearing his father's clothes, a uniform he's playing in. His clothes also say a lot about the way he ran the country: he doesn't care about details. He's got the suit, he was handed the position, and that's good enough. His first lady Melania's clothes were strangely reminiscent of *House of Cards* [305] first lady-turned-president Claire Underwood. The echoes between Melania Trump's wardrobe and Underwood's are "quite remarkable," costume designer Johanna Argan points out. [306] Every detail of the characters' clothing is calculated, just as every detail of a first lady's or a president's outfit is calculated, and it's almost impossible not to notice the similarities between two first ladies' clothes, as well as the way they evoke military and colonial dress. While Melania Trump's time in the White House was marked by sartorial faux pas, [307] one constant remains: whether in support of or in opposition to her husband, the first lady, in a power suit of her own, gave the impression of being at war. [308]

CHAPTER SIXTEEN

White Men

Suits are a uniform that allows men to fade into the background, to disappear into the crowd of others like them – the group, the collective, the category to which they belong. Suits, to which we might also add briefcases and shoes, haircuts, and even a particular make of car, are among the mechanisms that ensure that masculinity remains an invisible attribute, a way of slipping unnoticed in the name of and for the benefit of that power that every man in a suit partakes in. In the boys' club formed by the most powerful men, clothing plays a huge part: the more power a man has, the more he sticks to his uniform in order to concentrate on more important things. Facebook billionaire Mark Zuckerberg, for example, sticks to a grey T-shirt and a pair of jeans: "I really want to clear my life to make it so that I have to make as few decisions as possible about anything except how to best serve this community."[309] When Barack Obama was in power, he chose to wear only grey or blue suits because he had too many decisions to make. And of course Steve Jobs will always be remembered for his black turtleneck and dad jeans.[310] Their efforts to go unnoticed raise the question: do we really see these men? Do we really see men in general? Do we know how to look at them? And how can we stop the boys' clubs from fading into the background?

• • •

Harron's adaptation of *American Psycho* can be said to be feminist – she presents Ellis's novel not as misogynistic, but as feminist – because the lens is a woman's: the boys' club is shown in all its mediocrity and misogyny, with the constant sacrifice of women who are worth less than even the quality of a tan,[311] in their eyes; and the camera subjects Christian Bale, who plays Patrick Bateman, to the treatment usually reserved for film actresses.

We're used to seeing the camera strip and parse women's bodies in order to reinforce the audience's identification with the masculine point of view of the heroes (who are not only male, but also more often than not white).[312] In *American Psycho*, the camera caresses the body of the serial killer, who is shown naked on several occasions. The film underscores the extent to which appearances can be deceiving – Bateman's beauty is a mask for his cruelty – and highlights and even condemns the way women are treated in cinema. In general the camera, in its framing of those it's watching, is itself something of a psychopath, not unlike the video camera Bateman points at the prostitutes with whom he films himself having sex, as if he fancies himself a bodybuilder, or a cowboy in mid-rodeo, looking first at himself and enjoying the sight of his own image more than anything. Harron unmasks the narcissism of (male) cinema, which takes pleasure in looking at itself, hence the predominance of white male heroes.

Christian Bale, in the role of Patrick Bateman, was able to work with the director's vision to bring to life a hollow antihero. Bale remembered watching Tom Cruise (whom he physically resembled at the time of shooting.) on *David Letterman* and noting "what Bale called a very intense friendliness with nothing behind the eyes,"[313] which inspired his portrayal of Bateman, a character he played without trying to save him. Harron's view of her hero, meanwhile, is both humorous and merciless, its effectiveness derived from what she calls the "minutiae of success"[314] – for example, the scene where Bateman and his colleagues compare business cards, or when Bateman moonwalks behind Paul Allen's back just before killing him. The attention to detail is important: it is one of the keys to defusing the male gaze.

The journalist Lili Loofbourow proposes the opposite of the male gaze – or "its narrative corollary" – as the male glance,[315] a look that glides furtively over something without taking the time to stop because it knows from the outset what to expect. Nothing can surprise those eyes; their mind is made up. Loofbourow contrasts that absent glance with the gaze, which lingers in order to penetrate. She points out that we pick apart women's faces much more than we do men's: we look for details, wrinkles, grey hair, for details to subtract, in a clever calculation, from the sum total of beauty. But whereas we tend to dwell on the details of a face perceived as feminine, to scrutinize it, when we look at a woman's work (that is, made by a person identified with or identifying with the so-called feminine gender), we, as the public who have adopted the supposedly neutral male gaze, operate in the opposite way: we glide over it quickly, as if we know from the outset what it was all about, based on a collection of snapshots. Our habits prevent us from seeing the complexity of work by women: we're quick to dismiss it as intimate, autobiographical, sensitive, emotional, and obviously without any universal weight [316] ... Unlike the way we look at a woman's face, when we look at a text or a film made by a woman, we jump to conclusions, whereas we immediately project quality onto the work of men, because we expect success, we don't look for mistakes, we don't try to drag down the percentage of beauty, we don't dwell on details. We assume complexity, intelligence, and talent, without feeling the need to check if it's true.

Following Loofbourow's logic, we have to unlearn the male gaze in order to be able to focus on the works of women. That unlearning must furthermore go hand in hand with practising the female gaze – taking the time to linger over works made by men, looking for details, digging deeper. Refusing that apparently male neutrality. Acknowledging that maleness is not "the sex that isn't" [317] because it is universal. Reveal that the boys' club is in fact inflected.

• • •

The boys' club, and the masculinity within it, the masculinity it constructs through its allegedly neutral state, the fact that it is unremarkable, is based on the same blindness as whiteness, the state of being white. The members of that "tribe," as Grayson Perry writes, [318] "are among us and hide in plain sight":

> They dominate the upper echelons of our society, impos-
> ing, unconsciously or otherwise, their values and preferences
> on the rest of the population. With their colourful textile
> phalluses hanging round their necks they make up an over-
> whelming majority in government, in boardrooms, and also
> in the media. They are of course white, middle class, hetero-
> sexual men, usually middle-aged. And every component of
> that description has historically played a part in making this
> tribe a group that punches far, far above its weight. [319]

Perry calls the members of that group "default men" – the shortcut, in other words, the version that results from a habit or a reflex, a choice that seems to have made itself.

Default Man is what spontaneously comes to mind, the man who represents everyone. Default Man, like the browser that opens automatically when you turn on your computer, is the face that appears right away, a category of human being that includes all others. Default Man, as Caroline Criado Perez shows in *Invisible Women: Data Bias in a World Designed for Men*, has always been part of our construction of the present and of history. The category of "male unless otherwise indicated" contaminates ethnographic research. Criado Perez gives the example of cave paintings, which, because they often depict game, have been assumed to have been created by men, following the classic narrative that men were the hunters; yet recent analyses of handprints in caves in France and Spain suggest that the majority of the images were in fact made by women. [320] Or consider the usual definition of the Renaissance as beginning in the sixteenth century: as Carol Tavris pointed out in 1991, that era was the Renaissance for men, but not for women, who were largely excluded from intellectual and artistic life. Or Greece, which is touted as the cradle of democracy, even though more than half the population, including women, didn't have the right to vote.[321] Based on these and other similar assumptions, Criado Perez points out that the use of the universal masculine has the effect of making the figure of a man appear more often than woman in people's minds. Job postings are a case in point: if a posting is written in using a default-masculine language, men will feel like it applies to them, and women will be less likely to apply.[322]

The manifestations of this invisible discrimination are innumerable, since the history of humanity, of art, of literature, of music, and of evolution itself, as Criado Perez reminds us, have always been presented based on fact, from a supposedly objective point of view, yet that factuality is undermined as soon as the veil on the myth of "masculine universality"[323] is lifted. If masculinity and whiteness are never named, it is because they are taken as self-evident, and do not need to be questioned; they exist by default.

Grayson Perry remembers realizing, while working on a documentary series on identity, that the most elusive, ephemeral identity was Default Man because his view of the world coincides so well with the dominant narrative. He is "like a Death Star hiding behind the moon," his thoughts and feelings inextricable from the "proper, right-thinking" attitude.[324] When Perry asked Chris Huhne, a sixty-year-old, white, heterosexual man from Westminster, whether he thought he benefited from belonging to that group, Huhne said no: Default Man will not recognize, or even realize, the benefits that come from belonging to that category because, according to the capitalist project in which he is fully embedded, he is first and foremost an individual. If he is successful, it is thanks to his merit alone. In fact, as Perry points out, identity only counts when it is threatened; as long as Default Man isn't facing an existential threat, his identity goes without saying.

Identities and communities exist only in the eyes of Default Man as beholder, as subcategories, smaller subsets of individuals. Communities are other people, whereas Default Man belongs to society. Default Man looks down on society – he is a henchman of Big Brother's from *1984*, or The Eyes in *The Handmaid's Tale*. He dominates, from the vantage of the supposed neutrality conferred by his grey suit: "The business suit is the uniform of those who do the looking, the appraising. It rebuffs comment by its sheer ubiquity."[325] Default Man is Teflon, unchangeable and "unreasonable": the man who adapts to the world is reasonable, Perry suggests, quoting George Bernard Shaw, while the man who expects the world to adapt to him is not.[326]

Default Man may be on the way down, but in the meantime he reigns, unseen and unknown.[327]

• • •

The whiteness of skin, Ross Chambers writes, like all supposedly blank categories, that is, categories perceived as neutral, affirms invisibility by othering those who are "examinable."[328] The act of examining, which distinguishes between those who are examined and those who are not, is a form of scapegoating, a way of separating the world between those who are "in(di)visible" – individuals whose whiteness is simultaneously invisible and indivisible – and the others: those who are (di)visible, that is, divided or set apart as othered and visible, and therefore examinable. White individuals as a group are invisible, and even transparent, and in that group each person has the luxury of existing individually, thanks to the presence of others they have invented by relegating them to a marked group, which must therefore be examined ... by white people, obviously.

Throughout his article "The Unexamined," Chambers plays himself, the white Australian university professor in the United States, diagnosing his own behaviour and preconceptions in order to show how whiteness goes unnoticed because it cannot be examined, either in the likelihood of it being subjected to an examination or as an object to be examined. If blackness or the "dark continent" (what Freud called the feminine[329]) represents an object so opaque and therefore exotic that it is impossible to know, then "blank whiteness"[330] evades examination because it is the norm. Between those two extremes lies a set of categories that can be scrutinized and which must be examined. Chambers suggests that we need to relinquish the categories of the examinable and the practices of examination and replace them with the notion of legibility and of different ways of reading: reading is a relational practice which instead of denying the other in favour of an (illusory) self recognizes a mutual dependence between subject and object and the importance of context, mediating through the codes and conventions required for sociality.[331] For social relationships to be truly mutual, instead of perpetuating a system in which some people are marked and others are not, we need to take the gamble of relating to each other.

• • •

Replace whiteness with masculinity. Recognize that, in the West, men are most often, most commonly and most routinely considered ungendered, unmarked by their sex, whereas women are their sex and essentially their sex. By endorsing forms of speech and communication that defer to the masculine,[332] we perpetuate that marking, we maintain the masculine in its state of neutrality, of universality, and we preserve the figure of Default Man, allowing the masculine to continue to be absent, to distract from its own gender.[333]

We need a reversal. As George Yancy suggests with regard to skin colour, we need to oppose the warning that calls attention to a Black person's skin colour, which contributes to the stigmatization of Black men as dangerous, with "Look, a White!" to reflect instead on the threat of whiteness.[334] Similarly, the idea would be to say, "Look, a man!," or "Look, a boys' club!," or better yet, "Look, a white boys' club!," to reveal the system in which masculinity is manufactured, to make it visible[335] and thus undermine the illusion of a neutrality that, as Alice Coffin writes, constitutes "the subjectivity of the dominant."[336] Is that why, in April 2021, French senators adopted an amendment that allows the government to dissolve associations that exclude "a person or group of people on the grounds of their skin colour, origin, or membership or non-membership in a particular ethnic group, nation, race, or religion"?[337] Though the move would seem to be an indirect admission of defaulting, by banning non-mixed groups, it's not so much white supremacist groups that are under attack as groups considered to be exclusionary because they organize discussions on discrimination; the amendment had the effect of once more deflecting the conversation, once more jeopardizing traditionally marginalized groups in favour of those who represent the majority, in this case white people, whose privileged position will not be seen or made visible.

As the mass shootings keep happening, relentlessly, in the United States, including in recent years in Las Vegas and Orlando, that kind of awareness is urgently needed: in those two instances, as in so many others, the killers were young men, rabidly misogynist white supremacists.

Whiteness is invisible to those who embody it, and so is masculinity. Just as Yancy highlights the importance of the non-white gaze in analyzing whiteness, we need the non-male gaze, the gaze of the excluded, in order to understand the boys' club.

CHAPTER SEVENTEEN

On Government

In 1991, the sociologist Iris Young borrowed from Jean-Paul Sartre's notion of seriality as a way of thinking about a feminist coalition, to see how women might organize themselves as feminists without excluding each other, defining themselves neither by a common identity nor by shared attributes, but by the fact that they shared constraints and relationships to objects.[338] The boys' club is the privileged, powerful, cruel, and often perverse version of that seriality; it is also one of the mechanisms through which privilege is manufactured, established and maintained, and defended and protected. The costume is the badge, the armour, and even the camouflage.

● ● ●

Thinking about masculine power through the formulation of the boys' club means trying to see what can't be seen, focusing on what has been unmarked (as we say of police cars), what dominates, controls, subjugates, and directs, all completely unnoticed. The masculine, like the skin we identify as white, is unmarked, draped in invisibility. Like date-rape drug assaults, where the victim has no memory of the assault, the masculine usually acts without us being aware of it. There's also a collective tendency to refuse to identify it, hence, for example, the importance, as Jackson Katz points out, of not using the passive voice when we talk about violence against women, because it erases the subjectivity of the perpetrator: don't say that women are beaten; since they are beaten by men, say that men beat them.[339] Don't say that women are sexually assaulted, say that men have sexually assaulted them; in that way, men are made to bear the responsibility.

108   The Boys' Club: The Many Worlds of Male Power

In his lectures on governmentality, Michel Foucault, rereading Machiavelli's *The Prince*, reflects on the problem of government. He looks at European treatises written between the sixteenth century and the end of the eighteenth century that deal with self-government, the government of children, and state government by princes. "How to govern oneself, how to be governed, by whom should we accept to be governed, how to be the best possible governor?"[340] Those are questions that arise in the shift from feudal systems to territorial, administrative, and colonial states, at a time when spiritual government was being called into question. To govern, in Foucault's words, has to do with managing individuals, property, and wealth, and doing it properly. How can we introduce a quasi-paternal relationship into managing a state? Therein lies the question of governmentality. The paterfamilias was the first model of government, which largely disappeared at the end of the eighteenth century, when population study displaced the family as the model of governmentality, and made it its vector: the family was used to exercise the power of the state; it was one of the security mechanisms that produced government, the most important of which was undoubtedly the police.

There are countless films and television series, especially in the United States, that feature a government, and usually its leader, and those who surround them, such as civil servants, but above all the police and security guards. There are endless variations on the theme of power: who has it, who loses it, who is prepared to do anything to protect it or keep it. From behind-the-scenes political manoeuvring and scheming (as in *House of Cards* or *Scandal*) to attacks on the president (in *Designated Survivor*) or the seat of power (*White House Down, Olympus Has Fallen, Air Force One*), via the mundane and not-so-mundane day-to-day of governmentality (*The West Wing, The American President*), the representation of power is at the heart of popular culture, and the US president is its superhero. A number of the examples above depict a president in search of justice (*The West Wing*), a human, even feminist, anti-racist, and humanist character (*Designated Survivor*[341]). In some, the White House is used as a pretext to tackle sensitive issues, such as abortion: in *Scandal*, we see the Black heroine with her feet up in stirrups, waiting to terminate a pregnancy after having sex with the white president.[342] Others show the darker, crueller, murderous political side of a man who wants to hold on to power at any cost: the boys' club must win. When women occasionally take centre stage, like in the final season of *House of Cards*,[343] they keep the system in place: the one who's holding the stick keeps it for herself.

In real life, even while the number of women in politics has increased, their position remains precarious,[344] as numerous studies have shown, including Pascale Navarro's *Femmes et pouvoir*,[345] which decries the illusion of equality: as long as there is no parity between men and women (and, more broadly, diversity and true heterogeneity) within a government, we cannot truly speak of gender equality.[346] Drawing on the work of Françoise Collin, Navarro points out that new citizens always lead to a redefinition of citizenship and of the sociopolitical space.[347] In 1990, Collin wrote:

> The resistance of structures and men to the advancement of women and the creation of a shared world is such that it sometimes seems that it can only be overcome by a systematic policy of quota for equality, which would replace the silent policy that has prevailed so far and which has ensured that men (who make up 50 percent of the population) hold 70 percent to 90 percent of leadership positions, under the pretext of a principle of competence that looks more like a system of privilege.[348]

There is a boys' club in politics because women and individuals who are not men (and, in the West, white and predominantly heterosexual) remain perpetual newcomers in government. Much space is given over to how governmentality is exercised over women's bodies, through reproduction (and particularly the right to abortion) and sexual health, care (provided for the most part by women who are the primary caregivers), and issues surrounding sexual assault (especially in a legal system that largely fails to prosecute sexual crimes). In each one of those policy areas there is the exercise of biopower, those power technologies that call life into question, as Foucault proposed, and which Agamben revisits: we are "citizens whose very politics is at issue in their natural body." [349]

What happens to politics and the political when what is assumed to be their natural body, which is only one type of body, has a voice, is listened to and represented? What happens to women's rights, or to trans rights, for instance, when a group of men restricts abortion access or refuses to allow a change of gender on a birth certificate? What kind of citizenship is that? On the eve of the 2016 elections in the United States, Katha Pollitt reminded us that feminists who demanded more women in Congress were referred to as "vagina voters," [350] though there was never any mention of penis voters, she pointed out, and men were never accused of identity politics. Pollitt quotes Bernie Sanders, who said, as he and Hillary Clinton faced off for the Democratic nomination in 2016, "'No one has ever heard me say, *Hey, guys, let's stand together – vote for a man. I would never do that, never have.*'" "Oh, Bernie, Bernie, Bernie," Pollitt replies,

> I'll work my heart out for you if you win the nomination, but let's be serious: When the whole system has been set up by men for men since the founding of the Republic, and when men are still 81 percent of Congress, 75 percent of state legislatures, 88 percent of governorships, and 100 percent of US presidents over the past 230 years, there is no need to mention your unmentionables. [351]

Having more women in government is obviously good for women. It is thanks to women that laws have been passed against harassment, discrimination, and sexual violence. But while "women legislators," Pollitt points out, "tend to be clustered in the more progressive parties and to promote 'women's issues' – health, education, childcare, fighting discrimination and violence against women – more than male legislators do,"[352] they need to be equally present in every sector. How? Well, why not establish quotas to finally put an end to the political boys' club?

Obviously, quotas will only have a real impact if the mentality also changes and people stop saying things like what then French secretary general Marc Guillaume said: "It's rare for a woman to think ... and it's beautiful too, especially when she's wearing a skirt."[353] For parity to really count, maybe we need to start by tackling political science programs, where, if #SciencesPorcs,[354] the field-specific version of the MeToo hashtag, and the testimonies of female students are anything to go by, an endemic rape culture persists. As Anna Toumazoff tweeted acerbically, "let's not be surprised by the state of our political class given what they are taught."[355]

●　●　●

The first season of the television series *Jessica Jones* features a female superhero who stands up to an antihero named Kilgrave, a one-man representation of governmentality. The series reveals the inextricable link between governmentality and male domination.

Jessica Jones[356] has been described as a lesson in consent and sexual assault and how they are discussed. The series sets up a debate that we can't escape: What is rape? What does it mean to be raped? What is consent? How does it get overlooked? How can it be deliberately ignored? How do survivors of sexual assault go on? What motivates those who assault them?

But there's more: the series makes a connection between sexual violence, bullying, hegemonic masculinity, misogyny, and government: what viewers are witnessing is the representation of a governmental maleness, of governmentality as profoundly masculine.

Unlike series like *Game of Thrones*, *Mad Men*, *Scandal*, or *Downton Abbey*, where scenes of sexual assault are snuck into the plot, *Jessica Jones* makes rape, both literal and figurative, its main theme. There is an almost pedagogical dimension in the dialogue between Kilgrave and Jones. When Kilgrave pretends not to understand how he is a rapist, Jones explains:

"It's called rape."

"What? Which part of staying in five-star hotels, eating in all the best places, doing whatever the hell you wanted, is rape?"

"The part where I didn't want to do any of it! Not only did you physically rape me, but you violated every cell in my body and every thought in my goddamn head."

"That's not what I was trying to do –"

"It doesn't matter what you were trying to do …"

"How am I supposed to know? … I didn't have this. A home, loving parents, a family."

"You blame bad parenting? My parents died! You don't see me raping anyone!"[357]

Kilgrave, in his attempt at seduction, summons up heterosexual couplehood, family home, married life, and childhood memories to subjugate Jones, to strip her of her subjectivity. She is the chosen one; he chooses her in an attempt to govern her. She is the only woman in the world of men that he stands as the essence of, and he is the only man, the antihero Übermensch, representing all men. That kind of government.

• • •

Jessica Jones is ungovernable because she can't be tamed, feminized, forced to take on particular roles – those of the domestic and sexual worker responsible for production and reproduction, for increasing the population (that is, the production of new workers), and for men's sexual relief (in alignment with Silvia Federici's discussion of in the rise of capitalism in the late nineteenth century[358]). As the series progresses, Jessica Jones's apartment disintegrates, the windows, doors, and walls break down, the bed is never made, there's no food in the fridge, and the only thing the heroine consumes is alcohol. She sleeps all day, fully clothed. She resists romantic relationships, sticking to casual sex with the unbreakable Luke who, like all the men she associates with, is not white. Jones is a woman who rejects the trappings of femininity, and she never changes her look, her uniform of jeans, T-shirt, boots, and leather jacket. And she never smiles.

In our world, women are first and foremost objects to be contemplated, while Jessica Jones, private detective, looks without being seen. The women she looks at are first and foremost other women she wants to defend and protect, the sleeping beauties Kilgrave lulls almost telepathically, sleepwalking, remote-controlled women who will have everything taken away, dolls he can rape without compunction (in a modern version of what Federici describes as domesticated sexual labour in the late nineteenth century, and which women have always found ways of resisting, from hysteria or migraines to fainting[359]), housewives who look after meals and cleaning. The universal is masculine and the masculine is neutral, and Kilgrave stands for the masculine, the neutral, and the universal. The series deals with men and power, with the sick relationship that men, and specifically white, heterosexual men, have with power in general and with the power they can wield unseen – because they are not seen, because they protect each other – and over women in particular.

Kilgrave is not just a sexual abuser; he manipulates, conquers, and subjugates. Kilgrave is an elegant man, a white bourgeois with a British accent, but his name reeks of death: "kill" and "grave." Kilgrave is the gloved hand of domination. The invisibilization of men is not trivial; it's part of a powerful god complex, part of men's belief that everything is owed them, and draws its strength from the fact that they can go unnoticed. That's what Kilgrave is all about. Rebecca Solnit suggests "the western world has held up a mirror to [men]"; [360] as Virginia Woolf puts it, "women have … as looking-glasses possessing the magic and delicious power of reflecting the figure of man at twice its natural size." [361] It's time to force those faceless men to come into the light. Reams of feminist theory have sought to defend women's voices and their representativeness, their place in politics, education, the economy, and culture. But *Jessica Jones* tells us that what we need to demand is the appearance of men, we need to make them visible in order to force their identification by those they dominate, to make the boys' club come out to those who are devalued, attacked, enslaved, used up, banished, or eliminated, because they are potentially ungovernable, and because, by being ungovernable, they reveal the face of government.

CHAPTER EIGHTEEN

Everyman

Kilgrave's power in *Jessica Jones* lies in his use of telepathy. He dictates to his victims the violent acts they must carry out, including against themselves, and therefore has the freedom to do nothing. He doesn't do anything, he's not guilty of any violence. The way the series frames violence against women hinges on that unidirectionality, just as Jonathan Kaplan's 1988 feature film *The Accused*[362] did.

The Accused is based on the true story of the gang rape of a young woman by a group of men on a pool table at a tavern called Big Dan's in New Bedford, Massachusetts. At the time of the incident, in 1983, the media also condemned the men who had witnessed and encouraged the rape. Jonathan Kaplan's film takes up the story and invents a sequel: the prosecutor takes the spectators to court. The rape, after all, was a performance in front of an anonymous audience. The prosecution focuses on identifying those who encouraged the crime, who egged on the rapists, just as the audience at a hockey game will incite players to fight, an analogy developed in the film in an early scene when the prosecutor attends a hockey game with her boss shouting next to her to whip up the players on his preferred team.

The Accused has been called a women's movie, made by women – lead actors Jodie Foster and Kelly McGillis,[363] Paramount's production chief Dawn Steel, and Sherry Lansing, co-producer along with Stanley Jaffe – and for women, because it puts the spotlight on rape and shows both the crime and the aftermath for the victims. The film could just as well be about and for men, however. The plot follows the investigation and trial for a rape that we know nothing about except that it happened. Only at the very end of the film, when the crime is shown in flashback, do we see it,[364] as told by the only man who agreed to testify against the others, a student who is a member of a fraternity and whose frat brother is one of the rapists. The rape is shown from his point of view.

Some feminist critics took exception to the choice, arguing that the film re-enacts the crime in question. However, it can also be seen as a challenge to men, an invitation to attend the show, this time not from the rapist's point of view but from that of a man who does not take part and remains on the fringes of the community of men who push each other to rape a woman. We hear them shouting at the rapists to get in there, to hold the young woman back: "Go get her, frat boy! ... Stick it to her ... Hold her down ... Kurt! Go. Fuckin' get her." They go so far as to intimidate the man who resists by accusing him of being gay. Their voices blend together, and it's hard to tell who's who or who's saying what.[365] The rapists all look alike, and the camera shows them from behind, with their pants down, covering the young woman's mouth, suffocating her, spreading her legs and forcibly holding her down on the pool table. The scene is repeated three times, so that the rapists and the spectators become one and the same: in the end, they are one man.

That is the film's strongest accusation: one rapist for all and all for one.[366]

•　　•　　•

Jane Campion's series *Top of the Lake*[367] runs along similar lines. In the first season, Campion immediately places us in a world where men and women inhabit separate spheres. On the one hand, there is the police station and the house where the drug lord lives (and where he notably makes gamma hydroxybutyrate, or GHB, known as the date-rape drug), which are both male worlds; on the other, there is the makeshift commune called Paradise, where women live together in shipping containers set up on a plot of land near a lake. The main characters move between these worlds: a detective, Robin, and the missing girl she is trying to find, Tui. Everything sets these two characters apart except the experience of rape.

Tui, a twelve-year-old biracial (white and Thai) girl, is pregnant, and Robin, the white detective from the village of Laketop, is desperate to find her. Over the course of the episodes, we learn that Robin left Laketop herself shortly after being raped at the age of fifteen by a group of boys. The man she loved witnessed the event, and the rape left her pregnant with a child she gave up for adoption. In the end, Tui keeps her child, and Robin, by finding Tui and helping her look after the baby, reclaims her past.

The two women whose experience Jane Campion centres in *Top of the Lake* resonate beyond their age and ethnocultural identity because of their experience of a gang rape committed by faceless men. We learn at the end of the series that Tui was assaulted after having been given GHB, in one of a series of rapes committed by wealthy businessmen – suits – against teenage girls, but Jane Campion's ultimate message is far more serious. When, during their first meeting at the police station at the start of the series, Robin asks Tui who did this to her (that is, who got her pregnant), the girl writes two words in reply on a piece of paper: "No one." The phrase has multiple meanings: no one, not one person, not one person all alone, not one person in particular. And those people who are no one are men.

•   •   •

Men who rape children are also the subject of the second season of the sequel *Top of the Lake: China Girl*.[368] Campion paints a pitiless portrait of a group of technogeeks, who are indistinguishable from one another. She shows them sitting around a table in a café comparing the Asian prostitutes whose services they pay for through a clandestine network linked to sex and human trafficking. Campion's choice of those particular young men, who like video games, social networks, forums, and virtuality, is not haphazard. Even today, that world is primarily masculine, one in which men work together to imagine our technological future.

In *Brotopia: Breaking Up the Boys' Club of Silicon Valley*, Emily

Chang attacks the homogeneity of the technology industry.[369] Based on interviews with women who have spent time in Silicon Valley, Chang profiles that boys' club, replete with the next Bill Gates, Steve Jobs, and Mark Zuckerberg, notably looking at former Facebook COO Sheryl Sandberg, one of the few women to have made it.[370] From the use of a *Playboy* photo of Lena Söderberg as a test for digitization (dubbed the "original sin" of the industry, and the first step towards the exclusion of women[371]) to the distribution of pornography on electronic platforms and social networks, the place of women in the world of high technology is far from assured. In the wake of #MeToo, dozens of women have spoken out against sexual violence committed by well-known Silicon Valley men, including inventors, CEOs, and investors. The fact that a group of men from the same schools are helping themselves to the same knowledge and power necessary for the development of the tech sector has implications for what lies ahead, for example, with regard to gender and sexuality issues as well as to artificial intelligence and robotics.

Although women pioneered the practice of coding, from Ada Lovelace to the female engineers and mathematicians who were central to the programming for the Apollo 11 mission in 1969[372] – they have been sidelined in so many ways, through rampant sexual harassment and mansplaining, but also by the macho culture fostered in these industries:[373] the endless working hours, alcohol, gambling, Las Vegas, strippers, the absence of family and children, the sex parties[374] – all of it serves to keep women away, deliberately or not, making it clear to them that they have to be one of the boys or leave. But there's more: as Chang shows, Silicon Valley was built on the myth of meritocracy and the rejection of diversity.[375] Citing the founders of PayPal, Chang looks at the positions taken by these former Stanford students on the multiculturalism promoted by American universities in the early 1990s. Writing in the *Stanford Review*, they accuse professors of imposing an anti-Western and anti-patriarchal curricular bias. They also attack feminism, and some of the men who went on to found PayPal even opposed the anti-rape awareness campaigns on university campuses at the time.

Chang focuses on PayPal because several members of the original team went on to launch some of the world's biggest companies, namely Tesla, SpaceX, LinkedIn, and YouTube, the same men *Fortune* magazine featured on their cover in 2007, cigars and glasses in hand, playing cards. There are no women in the photo. Nonetheless, the boys' club that started Silicon Valley has succeeded to a large extent in making people believe in the gospel of technological meritocracy, a myth that supports the good conscience of companies who, as a result, feel no obligation to take into account differences in gender and sexuality, among other things. Nothing could be further from the truth, Chang says: there is no meritocracy; what there is, is a boys' club.

What about trolls and their endless online harassment, particularly on 4chan, X (formerly Twitter), and Reddit, all founded by white men? While hashtags have been important tools for feminist mobilization since social media was invented, they've also been used in online violence against women and feminists. Anita Sarkeesian's experience of #Gamergate is one of the most telling examples: Sarkeesian was subjected to sexist attacks and death threats following her series on female stereotypes in video games, *Tropes vs. Women in Video Games*[376] broadcast on her YouTube channel, Feminist Frequency. In recent years, many women, people referred to as racialized, and people who identify as not men have left X (formerly Twitter), and sometimes social networks in general, because of the violence of bullying, humiliation, and rape threats. Cyberbullying victims are most often girls, and feminists are most often subjected to cyberharassment.[377] We imagine idle boys and men fuelled by hatred on the other side of the screen. We might also imagine network managers suspending certain accounts, such as Rose McGowan's in October 2017, when she was speaking out against Harvey Weinstein as part of the #MeToo movement, while they leave others to broadcast freely, regardless of content. More recently, Alice Coffin was the victim of what was dubbed an "army of medals," [378] a reference to a recent cyberharassment strategy that attributes medal emojis in lieu of verbal insults on some posts, although the objective remains the same – to harass, intimidate, and hunt down leftists with the aim, in that case, of "defending France by attacking the political correctness that is destroying it from within." [379] The emoji attacks consist of awarding medals to reward left-leaning commenters for being so-called snowflakes. Greg Toussaint and his trolls substitute medals for insults in an attempt to hide their true faces and avoid accusations of harassment – a cyberstalker system in which not only do men hide, but for whom the emoji, an apparently harmless symbol, is a way of expressing hatred.

That unbridled hatred is precisely what Florence Hainaut and Myriam Leroy decry in their documentary *Sale pute* [380] ("dirty whore") – the unbridled hatred women suffer on the web: women appear on screen, sometimes using humour to say something that makes sense, and then they are put through hell. In addition to run-of-the-mill sexism and sexual harassment, women online are threatened with rape, torture, and kidnapping. The web is one big saloon, a place for men only, for all men. The French social entrepreneur Alice Barbe testified that, after an interview that was shared by a far-right website, she received four hundred death and rape threats in the space of two hours. [381] Those who threatened her, she pointed out, were four hundred Everymen. [382] What's more, Hainaut and Leroy say, if you add up all the men who attack women on the internet around the world, it always seems to be the same man insulting the same woman. The problem is systemic: these men aren't lunatics; they're not morons. They're not anomalies in the system: "They are the system." [383]

• • •

Jane Campion shines a spotlight on that kind of system in the second episode of *Top of the Lake: China Girl*, where we see the group of run-of-the-mill café nerds engaged in competitive misogyny, vulgarity, and violence in front of their screens: they objectify the young Asian trafficking victims, commenting on their online "performance."[384] Proportionately speaking, those men embody what Hannah Arendt, after Adolf Eichmann's trial in Jerusalem, called "the banality of evil."[385] Reflecting on the nature of a totalitarian government, and wondering whether that totalitarianism is not in the nature of all bureaucracy, Arendt considers the way men become civil servants, "cogs in the machinery"[386] and, as a result, dehumanized: "One can debate long and profitably on the rule of Nobody, which is what the political form known as bureaucracy truly is. Only one must realize clearly that the administration of justice can consider these factors only to the extent that they are circumstances of the crime."[387]

Is it possible to imagine the participation or complicity of men, or even their complacency, in the injustices and crimes of all kinds to which women are subjected as part of the male domination that is the backdrop – the "circumstances," to use Arendt's word – of our society? Male domination, which looks so bureaucratic because it's so standard, erases the conscience of individuals and replaces it with ready-made ideas, clichés that are essentially a refusal to think. The ordinary, interchangeable young men portrayed by Campion in *Top of the Lake: China Girl* are representations of Arendt's "Nobody," young men who refuse to be accountable, and drop their conscience in order to reproduce a system, an Everyman's boys' club that is guilty of banality.

CHAPTER NINETEEN

The Hunt

In the film *The General's Daughter*,[388] Lieutenant General Joseph Campbell, the father of Captain Elisabeth Campbell, is found guilty by a military tribunal of attempting to cover up the gang rape of his daughter during training, a decision the film suggests was made to protect the school's recent co-ed status and give the impression that women were welcome at the academy. The film was made in the late 1990s, at the height of affirmative action.

In the film, which is based on a 1992 novel by Nelson DeMille, the rape takes place during night training in the forest at West Point Military Academy, the recruits dressed in camouflage. Elisabeth Campbell was among the first women admitted to West Point, and to punish her for being among the best students, and simply for being there, her colleagues catch her in the middle of the night during military training. They force her down in the mud and leaves, spread her limbs apart, tie her wrists to tent pegs, strip her naked and take turns raping her, leaving her for dead. Much like the *Munich* scene in which the Dutch assassin is killed, the naked body of the young white woman, blond and blue-eyed, lights up the dark night, while the group of men is hard to make out in the darkness: it's almost impossible to tell how many there are, blurred by the night and by their uniforms – a military uniform reminiscent of what hunters wear to hide in the wilderness and escape detection by their prey.

The General's Daughter follows the investigation of a military policeman (played by John Travolta) and a rape detective (played by Madeleine Stowe). The detective confronts one of the only men whose name appears in the victim's medical records in the military base locker room. "You're just a guy who's gotten by on his smile and his charm," she tells him, "but you could never lead a rape."[389] The man, essentially confessing, replies that he didn't do anything, he tried to stop them, but the others "hated her so much."[390] His words echo those spoken by female students at military colleges such as Saint-Cyr-l'École in the Yvelines. In a survey published in *Libération* in 2018, female military students denounced the sexist violence to which their classmates were subjected by their male classmates, and on which their future regimental commanders did not comment, thus encouraging "disruptive elements": "Fraternities are formed, it's just that there are no sisters."[391]

Women make up 16 percent of the French army, though major efforts have been made over the years to increase the gender mix. However, while the French Ministry of Armed Forces is keen to increase the number of women in senior positions as quickly as possible through a proactive policy, which aimed to double the proportion of women generals by 2025, the policy hasn't gone over well with the rank and file, where there is an attachment to tradition, a fear of setting a precedent, and, above all, concern about promoting women who lack the required skills.[392] The feminization of the army, particularly its upper echelons, is not going smoothly: it's not just a matter of joining an old boys' club, but of being accepted by men who, through their strength and physical appearance, their embodiment of order and authority, are the very definition of masculinity.

• • •

"I hate feminists," Marc Lépine cried before opening fire on a group of female engineering students at the University of Montréal's École Polytechnique. His words came at the height of a backlash against feminism, a backlash which in Lépine's hands turned deadly. "Backlash" implies something sudden and violent, a retreat, the act of being whipped sharply backwards. With regard to feminism, Lépine's message couldn't have been clearer: feminists had to be silenced, and he was going to do it with his semi-automatic, a weapon allegedly intended for hunting.[393] Not only were the students Lépine targeted supposed to be quiet, with death the ultimate silencing, but the Polytechnique massacre on December 6, 1989, was an attack on all women and all feminists. The journalist Sue Montgomery, during the commemoration ceremony in 2014, recalled the backlash of the 1990s: "The F-word – feminism – became a bad word ... They didn't want to hear that men hated us."[394]

Hate is the bullet that pierces a woman's body, it is the blows that rain down on her; it is also, as Francine Pelletier has called it, a grey area of domestic and sexual violence,[395] the purpose and effect of which is to make us "just a little less free."[396] Hatred is a game of cat and mouse, Günther Anders writes,[397] which delights those who despise, who are eager to chase down the mouse and eat it. That eagerness, that hunger is partly a perverse and cruel form of love, and partly genuine hatred, since the pleasure of the catching lies in its postponement. Hate is a love that wants to annihilate the other, to make them disappear by absorbing them – consuming them, assimilating their body, owning them, and becoming them. Taking their flesh into themselves after the hunt, the kill, just as game hunters take the lives of animals even while they claim to be conservationists – a familiar refrain, as Anders points out.[398] Portraying the other as an animal is not just about dehumanizing them; it's about expressing the hatred that is a love of hate, hatred as love.

The Isla Vista killer in California in 2014, the Roseburg killer in Oregon in 2015, the Yonge Street killer in Toronto in 2018, and the Tallahassee yoga studio killer in Florida in 2018, to name only a few, are all linked to incels, "involuntarily celibates."[399] Incels are men who complain that they don't have girlfriends because some men have them all, but mostly because of feminists and what they describe as a culture of anti-masculinity.[400] While the incel movement is mainly web-based, it literalizes the link between hunting and that other form of hunting, courtship: women who have been hunted are killed for sexual purposes, without having been caught. Sex is replaced by murder, and sexual intercourse by the murderous, terrorist use of a weapon or vehicle.

The more you hunt, the more you hate, Anders writes, and the closer we are to the victim, the more we experience hatred,[401] hence the need to look at the new ways of waging war, to think about what it means to kill when the distance between self and other becomes ever greater, when victims become an increasingly indistinct mass and their faces a pale memory of distant humanity. If we have to be close in order to hate, if proximity engenders hate, what becomes of hate when war is waged from a distance? To compensate for the distance and to feed the hatred, Anders explains, there must be the illusion of a close fight by demonizing a type or group, "preferably a defenceless minority. Most of the time, that group has nothing to do with those who are to be fought or eradicated,"[402] and exists only as the target of hatred to justify taking action against the enemy. "If you want your people to fight or eradicate an element A unknown to them," according to Anders, "unperceived by them, equally impossible to perceive and hate, you engender in them, by means of language or caricature, hatred of an element B they think they know."[403] A dialogue he imagines with the fictional "President Traufe" ends as follows:

"What does this remind you of?"

"The GIs who, in the evening, after a day's work, used to
get excited with the help of mighty sexy pinup girls so that
they could take the uninspiring girls at their disposal and ..."

"Shoot them with live ammunition?"

"You said it, buddy."[404]

It's not the image or pinup as opposed to real women that is of interest here so much as the fact that the relationship with women serves as an example, and that combat and sexuality are suddenly fused: the soldiers described as firing with live ammunition, just as misogynist killers do. The gesture in both cases is of taking women and feminists – those who refuse to accept them and bend to male domination – by force, and turning them into prey.

• • •

The title of Amy Ziering and Kirby Dick's documentary about sexual assault on college campuses is on the nose: *The Hunting Ground*.[405] The team's previous documentary, *The Invisible War*,[406] was an exposé of the unchecked and unpunished sexual assaults committed in the army:[407] between 2010 and 2012, just the estimated number of sexual assaults increased by 35 percent.[408] *The Invisible War* shows how in the army, which is often described as a family, the victims, as in the case of incest, are ordered to remain silent for the sake of the cohesion of the group, which of course is made up of mostly men. Furthermore, given the hierarchical structure of the army and the fact that crimes are tried behind closed doors by court martial, it's almost impossible for a victim to file a complaint without being ostracized, humiliated, and punished. Despite the documentary, and the publication of numerous studies on sexual assault in the army, the *New York Times*, citing the 2018 *Report on Sexual Assault in the Military*, announced a 38 percent increase in cases of "unwanted sexual contact" with women in uniform compared with the previous survey in 2016.[409] While women make up 20 percent of the military workforce, they are the victims of 63 percent of assaults, with younger and lower-ranking women most at risk. Similar statistics have been recorded in military academies, where future soldiers are trained.

In *The Hunting Ground*, colleges, and fraternities in particular, are the focus of the investigation, reminiscent as they are, like the army, of a veritable hunting ground. A group of female students first approached Dick and Ziering about making the film at a time when sexual assaults on American college campuses were highly visible: a large number of cases had been reported in the media, and at least fifty colleges were under investigation under Title IX, which guarantees education free of sex discrimination for any program or activity that receives federal subsidies. [410]

Title IX requires schools to take preventive action, to investigate allegations of sexual assault promptly whether or not the police are involved, and not to resort to mediation after the fact. Title IX is supplemented by the Clery Act, [411] which concerns the obligation to inform the public about crimes committed on campus and the danger they represent, as well as by the Campus Sexual Violence Elimination Act, an amendment to the Clery Act, which increases protection for survivors of sexual assault. In 2014, the Obama administration launched "It's On Us," a social movement that aims to radically change the way sexual assault is considered in order "to create an environment in which sexual assault is unacceptable and survivors are supported." [412] The program focuses to a significant extent on environment, since college campuses are a veritable hunting ground for sexual assaults.

• • •

The Invisible War shows the inner workings of the military boys' club, while The Hunting Ground unmasks the culture surrounding sexual assaults on campus, and especially in fraternities. The documentary focuses on two groups: the women (students, professors, friends, and managers who have left the college because of its failure to act) and the men (students, athletes, coaches, managers, and lawyers), two relatively closed groups, with the serial victims pitted against serial aggressors, who in fact even sometimes attack together, who help each other, and who always look out for each other. The whole thing, and every single case, should be considered gang rape, because the term not only refers to rape committed by several people, but to an act that depends on a community, and on an entire system. One scene shows a map of the United States pinned to the wall of one of the activists' rooms, linking the different cases, cities, and colleges. Campus rape is not the exception but the norm, a kind of sport that values non-consensual sex, and in which women are prey, from whom a trophy must be taken, often in the form of images disseminated on social media.

The Hunting Ground has been described by *New York Times* film critic Manohla Dargis as an example of cine-activism,[413] in which the director and filmmaker pull out all the stops to make their voices heard, to highlight the system itself and the complicity of administrations that turn a blind eye to what goes on behind fraternity walls: between these administrations and the fraternities there is a tacit contractual – economic, political, and of course gendered – relationship.

At the start of the documentary, a grey-haired man in purple regalia greets students at the start of the school year: "As your parents learned when they dropped you off today, what happens in college stays in college – most of the time."[414] We don't know who the man is or what his job is exactly, other than a representative of male power. He's joking, but he's not: the complicity of adults in campus rape culture is sadly true, and particularly the complicity of white men who, by protecting boys accused of sexual violence, whether they are wealthy frat boys or famous athletes, uphold a culture of privilege.

As Jessica Valenti points out, one in five women will be sexually assaulted in the four years they spend on a college campus, and women in sororities are 74 percent more likely to be sexually assaulted.[415] Fraternities are particularly dangerous because alcohol flows freely, GHB is in common use, and the masculine culture fraternities promote is eminently toxic. The boys act together and mimic each other in a climate of competition coupled with a demand for loyalty: the fraternity is a family and everything must be done to protect it. Elizabeth A. Armstrong, a professor at the University of Michigan and the author of major studies on fraternities and frat culture, explains that there is a big difference between Black, multicultural, or co-ed fraternities and white, single-gender fraternities, which bring together boys from wealthy families.[416] Fraternities are organized around the notion of a network, which extends its tentacles, from the boys who live together during their studies or the athletes who are part of the same team, to the politicians, lawyers, financiers, and entrepreneurs who work in the White House, on Wall Street, and in Silicon Valley.[417] Some would say that fraternities have helped generations of men grow up.[418] There are 400,000 men in fraternities in the US today, and most of them, according to a frat advocate, are leaders in their communities. They raise millions of dollars for charitable foundations, they volunteer, they get top grades. They also do better after college and are successful all their lives.

Fraternities have created something that's fairly unique in the modern world: a place where young men spend three or four years living with other men whom they have vetted as being like them and able to "fit in." What do you expect to happen at a club where women are viewed as outsiders, commodities, or worse, as prey, and where men make the rules? It should be no surprise they end up recreating the boys' club – and one that isn't all great for the boys, either.[419]

• • •

In September 2014, Tulane University alumna Valenti called for the closure of fraternities, following an investigation at the University of Wisconsin-Milwaukee; women had found Xs painted in red and black on their hands after being hospitalized for memory loss due to intoxication during a fraternity party.[420] Three sexual assaults were also reported at a Texas fraternity in just one month, and an email message entitled "Luring your rapebait" was circulated at Georgia Tech.[421] A Wesleyan fraternity was branded a "rape factory,"[422] and members of a Yale fraternity had strolled across campus shouting, "No means yes, yes means anal."[423]

Since the 1980s, fraternities have come under fire. These guylands, to use Michael Kimmel's word,[424] must abandon a testosterone-fuelled culture, where men dominate women, in favour of co-ed fraternities that are more likely to encourage young people to see each other as equals. Based on a five-year study she conducted with Laura Hamilton on the campuses of an anonymous university in the American Midwest, Elizabeth Armstrong describes fraternities as a public health problem, encouraging administrations to reform them by banning alcohol, preventing students from living in frat houses, and forcing socialization between students of different genders, backgrounds, and social classes.[425]

Fraternities first came into being in the early nineteenth century as secret societies aimed at getting around prohibitions against fun[426] (at a time when women were forbidden to attend university); they now seem anachronistic. They half-disappeared in the 1960s and 1970s in the wake of the sexual revolution and the civil rights movement, but since the 1980s they have made a comeback of sorts, and with that has come an epidemic of alcohol- and drug-related accidents (falls, hypothermia, serious injuries, and so on[427]) and, above all, sexual violence.

In his 1969 book *Men in Groups*,[428] the anthropologist Lionel Tiger sought to demonstrate that men are naturally dominant and violent and that their primitive mode of being is as part of a pack. Within those groups, close relationships are born, and there is a need to be together that explains, according to Tiger, the hierarchy in single-sex structures such as the church, the army, and the government, from the Palaeolithic era to the rise of feminism (when Tiger published his book). Although Tiger criticizes the violence of fraternity hazing, he nonetheless excuses it by describing male aggression as not only natural, but positive: the sexes are essentially different and, in this sense, each plays its role: men protect women, who in turn protect children. This way of conceiving of sexual binarism, and of essentializing gender, heterocentrism, and reproduction, and the reference to prehistory and to a certain male animality in order to keep things as they are, haunts the fraternity system to this day.

To that primitive scenario we might add themes that run through fairy tales, as Kelly Oliver does in the book *Hunting Girls: Sexual Violence from* The Hunger Games *to Campus Rape*.[429]

Oliver quotes a student at George Washington University: "At frat parties, it's more of a hunting ground. Not all guys are like this, of course, but sometimes it feels like the lions standing in the background and looking at the deer. And then they go in for the kill."[430] Contrary to the American myth that Black men are a threat to white women, here, as Oliver points out, the vast majority are white men, well dressed, among the best students and athletes, boys next door who rape middle-class girls, the girls next door who are their peers. There is only one step between the prehistoric man hunting women as he does animals and a woman waiting for the prince who will wake her up. On university campuses, both tropes are brought to life in the scenario where fraternity members extend party invitations to young women, who arrive in their best clothes and find themselves in a dirty, dangerous environment where the men drug them: a cliché of a masculine setting (by men and for men) reminiscent of the harshness of actual hunting camps.

● ● ●

Laura Wade's play *Posh* premiered in 2010,[431] less than a month before the general election in the United Kingdom. Four years later, on the eve of another round of elections, Lone Scherfig's film adaptation of the play, *The Riot Club*, hit the big screen,[432] thumbing its nose at David Cameron, George Osborne, and Boris Johnson,[433] all members of the Bullingdon Club on which the film is thought to be based.

Laura Wade began writing her play after the publication of a photo of a young David Cameron in a tailcoat with some of his Oxford mates, including the then mayor of London, Boris Johnson. In December 2005, members of the club smashed seventeen bottles of wine, all the crockery, and a window in a fifteenth-century pub near Oxford.[434]

Scherfig's film, released a year after *The Wolf of Wall Street*, presents the same excesses, extravagance, and vice of the rich, much like Scorsese, with the difference that while *The Wolf of Wall Street*, based on the story of Jordan Belfort, presents us with the point of view of a hero, *The Riot Club* leaves the audience on the outside, alongside the director. There is no pleasure in watching this film; quite the contrary. Wade and Scherfig uncompromisingly denounce the cruelty of the privileged, their impunity, and the toxicity of the masculinity they invent and live out together.

The club in the film was created in memory of a certain Lord Ryot, a renowned seventeenth-century Oxford scholar who was killed by his mistress's husband. The members follow the motto "Eat till we are sick at the full table of life."[435] The film portrays the club and its members, tracing lineages from father to son, and showing how privilege is passed down from generation to generation. The camera takes us right up close to the debauchery, with its concomitant racism, misogyny, and classism. Wade and Scherfig depict the selection of future members and their initiation, which includes drinking a cocktail of urine, spit, maggots, and boogers, and finding the walls of their room covered in sperm: "You did bukkake on my room!" cries Miles, the young Oxford student who has been invited to join the Riot Club. These various stages of the initiation are part of what Lauren, the film's female character, describes as "massively homoerotic."[436]

Most of the action takes place at the Bull's Head Pub, which hosts the annual meal of Oxford's banned Riot Club. Club members arrive at the pub, dressed in tailcoats and armed with vomit bags, and take up residence in a private room where they eat and drink and do endless amounts of drugs. "We are legends!" proclaims one young man. During the evening, the pub owner and his daughter are subjected to unbridled condescension, and the only member of the club whose parents are not white (he is of Greek origin) is the butt of racist jokes. They ask the sex worker whose services they have booked to crawl under the table and perform oral sex on each of them. "I'm not just a live version of the sock you wank into!" she replies before walking away. To Lauren, Miles's girlfriend whom they've tricked into thinking he's written her to come and join them, they offer £27,000 to replace the sex worker: "We've got the finest sperm in the country in this room, you should be paying us to let you drink it!" After threatening her with sexual assault, they let her go and then set about demolishing the pub room. When the landlord makes it clear that they can't demolish everything and just "buy your way out of everything," calling them spoiled brats, they beat him savagely. "News for you," one says, "you fucking love me. You'd like to be me." After the attack, recovering from his injuries in the hospital, the pub owner is asked to identify who hit him. He couldn't say, he replies: "They all look the same." Which of the men will bear the heinousness of the crime? Each man shies away, blaming his neighbour, until the club president agrees to turn himself in to the police on behalf of everyone. After his departure, another member takes over the club and sets about finding recruits. To quote one of the club's elders, a prominent lawyer of aristocratic background, "People like us don't make mistakes."[437]

• • •

The Riot Club is a compendium of the attributes of the boys' club and its impact on society. Privilege and impunity, arrogance and unbridled hatred, misogyny and racism, rivalry and solidarity ... The boys are together, in coattails, around a table, bound together by an overabundance of food and alcohol and, above all, by the certainty that the world belongs to them. They all look the same and they have every right to anything them want, they can commit any crime and always get away with it. Nothing can touch them, nothing can ever stop them.

As the character of Miles puts it, getting into Oxford is like being invited to a hundred parties at once. The party to which Wade and Scherfig invite us is as much about the raid on boys' clubs as it is about the fear their spectacle arouses. The writer Amy Woolsey draws a link between the British club and the American political boys' club:

On September 27, Supreme Court nominee Brett Kavanaugh sat in front of a Senate committee – and a national television audience – to refute Christine Blasey Ford's assertion that he sexually assaulted her at a high school party in the '80s. During the hearing, as well as the weeks of media coverage that preceded it, I thought about *The Riot Club* a lot. It's not like real-life circumstances suddenly made the movie relevant. Rather, they crystallized what made the movie relevant all along, lending immediacy to its somewhat esoteric critique of British higher education. Although cinema history is littered with stories of careless rich people, from *Citizen Kane* to *The Wolf of Wall Street*, few depict with such brutal intricacy the way privilege cultivates and shores up toxic masculinity. [438]

CHAPTER TWENTY

Boys Will Be Boys

In its August 2015 special issue on sex, *Les Inrockuptibles* magazine devoted an article to bukkake, [439] that subgenre of porn in which a group of many men are filmed masturbating together and ejaculating onto the chest and face of a woman in their midst. The article describes the participants as amateurs: some want to offer themselves a "special treat," while others say they are looking to "let loose, nothing calculated, just enjoy." The journalist notes the words of one of the participants as he arrives in the parking lot a few minutes before the shoot: "I can't take it anymore, man, I just got out of the gym. I'm on fire. I hope the girl has good health insurance, because she's gonna pay! She's gonna shit bricks!"

The men gather around. The shoot takes place in a garage, away from prying eyes. Everyone watches each other in silence. "I thought we were here to fuck," says one man, "but it feels more like we're getting ready for a boxing match." The men clean themselves with wipes provided by the director. They down a bottle of booze, grope their crotches, and put on balaclavas to hide their faces.

The Japanese practice of bukkake, which means "to splash with liquid," dates back to a punitive feudal method in which women who were judged guilty of infidelity were sprayed with sperm by the village men. Bukkake was popularized by Japanese pornography and revived in the West in gonzo porn. The bukkake in the *Inrockuptibles* piece ends up turning into a gangbang, which in fact it tends to: viewers virtually enjoy the gang rape of a woman who is ostensibly acting.

Yet being paid five hundred or a thousand Euros to take part in a shoot like that, according to the French porn star Anna Polina, is "akin to slavery." The former porn actress Angell Summers adds, "You get the feeling the girls in these videos don't know where they are, they don't know what they're going to go through."[440] That's the scene: a circle of masked men with one woman in the middle, unconscious in one form or another, waiting.

• • •

Numerous studies show that when men rape together, during a gangbang, or collective rape, what's at stake is not only their power of domination, and the objectification of a woman, but the relationship between the men themselves. Taking turns raping as others watch, showing off, choosing to display an erect penis, talking about what's happening, commenting on the "catch," the pleasure, the performance, performing sexual and violent acts collectively, watching each other do it ... These aspects highlight the importance of men being together. Gang rapes were the subject of much discussion in the French suburbs a decade or so ago, and in college fraternities and sports teams, without forgetting that the trope is common in porn, mainstream cinema (think of *L'Été meurtrier*[441] or *The Accused*), and prostitution culture (the Carlton Affair in Lille, in which Dominique Strauss-Kahn was involved,[442] comes to mind). In gang rape, whether it's a violent assault committed by several men or what's known as a running a train or training (when several men take turns on the same woman), the act has everything to do with homosociality, not to say homoeroticism, the touchstone of which is spectacle: you have to be watched by others who are the same as you.

"They're happy to be together," Virginie Despentes writes in *Baise-moi*, "they trade good jokes, they have a common activity, a common enemy. How far do they intend to go to prove to each other that they are together?"[443] In *King Kong théorie*, she describes the rape she suffered with a friend, an assault committed by three boys:

We are the sex of fear, of humiliation, the foreign sex. Manhood
is founded on that exclusion of our bodies, their famous male
solidarity, this is what it's forged in. It's a pact based on our
inferiority. The laughter of men, men with other men, the
laughter of the loudest, in numbers. [444]

While Despentes writes that "it was the project of rape that remade
[her] into a woman, someone essentially vulnerable," [445] she also
demands that we think about how the project of rape remakes men:
"Rape, the condemned act that must not be spoken of, synthesizes
a set of fundamental beliefs about virility." [446]

● ● ●

Gang rape is a well-known weapon of war used to occupy territory
and affirm political, cultural, and religious power through the domination of women; it was used by nazis in Auschwitz, Dachau, and
Buchenwald; in countless unspeakable crimes committed in Bos-
nia, Rwanda, and Syria; during the riots in Cairo's Tahrir Square;
in India on the street and on buses; in Texas, where around twenty
men raped an eleven-year-old child; in Steubenville, Ohio, where
football players raped an unconscious young woman ... the list
goes on and on. Rape is a weapon of war in the ordinary, everyday war that is the war on women, to come back to Catharine A.
MacKinnon, a war that has as much to do with putting women in
their place as it does with men's need to perform their gender for
other men, in their presence, and for their recognition. They have
to belong to the group, to the team: "Those who raped me didn't
squeal," Hélène Duffau remembers in *Trauma*; "they shouted. They
were hollering. Like fans at a match. Like coaches on the pitch.
To encourage each other. To give themselves the strength to excel.
To not hear the shamelessness." [447]

• • •

The Steubenville High School rape, in 2012, was widely reported: a young woman was repeatedly raped by peers, who filmed the assault and shared it on social media, where it went viral. The sixteen-year-old victim, who was heavily intoxicated, was described by her attackers as looking like a dead body: "They peed on her. That's how you know she's dead, because someone pissed on her."[448] In Delhi, Jyoti Singh, a physiotherapy intern, was gang raped and tortured by six men and left for dead; she died thirteen days later from her injuries.[449] These two cases not only attracted worldwide attention, but also sparked significant feminist social commitment.[450]

What interests me here are the words used to refer to these two women: "living corpse" in the case of Jyoti Singh,[451] and "dead girl" in the case of the young woman from Steubenville. In a video filmed on the night of the Steubenville attacks by one of the witnesses and later circulated by Anonymous, a man is heard saying, "she is so raped right now ... You don't need any foreplay with a dead girl ... She's deader than O.J. [Simpson]'s wife ... She's deader than Caylee Anthony ... They raped her harder than that cop raped Marsellus Wallace in *Pulp Fiction*."[452]

Rapes filmed and broadcast on social networks are legion, and so are young women's suicides. Shortly after Steubenville, two eighteen-year-old football players from Torrington, Connecticut raped two thirteen-year-old girls. "Young girls acting like whores there's no punishment," their classmates tweeted, "young men acting like boys is a sentence."[453]

The number of boys in the Steubenville case was questioned, as was the description of what had really happened. Since the victim was unconscious, could we really know what had happened? And if a young woman is unconscious, it is really rape?[454] But there were videos and witnesses, and, at the trial, one of them testified that he couldn't tell whether or not the young woman was participating in the sexual acts to which she was subjected. He also said he wasn't concerned when he saw his friend masturbating on the girl's inert body: "They were texting,"[455] and what his friend was doing to the girl seemed acceptable in light of that virtual relationship.

The Crown prosecutor in the case, Jane Hanlin, who withdrew because her son was a friend of one of the accused, made the following comment:

> The narrative that goes through these stories is: there are doz-
> ens of onlookers; she's taken from party to party; she's raped
> at multiple locations. Understandably, people are outraged
> when they read that, because it makes it look as though there
> is a whole group of kids here who watched and heckled and
> laughed and participated. That's not true: there are five that
> behaved very badly. But five is less than eighty.[456]

How many men make up a group? What is the minimum number of rapists required for an assault to count as gang rape?

Hundreds of thousands of text messages, photos, and videos have circulated showing the attack on the girl, the young girl who became "the dead girl." "Is she dead?" asks a boy standing in front of the camera during the assault. "She's as dead as you can get ... What if she was pregnant and gave birth to a dead baby too? ... She's dead."[457]

She's a dead girl: that's the expression that comes up time and time again in a video that has been posted and shared thousands of times, showing the girl unconscious on a bed, surrounded by a group of young men, aggressors and witnesses, enjoying themselves.

• • •

The trial of Brock Turner has also been much talked about. The Stanford University student and top athlete was found guilty of sexually assaulting a young woman in January 2015 while she was passed out behind a dumpster. Turner was caught by two students who happened to be passing by at the time, but to the end he denied assaulting his victim; he used other words instead of assault, claiming alcohol abuse or sexual promiscuity. He went so far as to claim in court that there had been consent, despite the fact that the medical examination had revealed vaginal lesions, that the half-naked young woman was dirty, with pine needles in her hair, that she had woken up in the hospital with no memory of what had happened to her, and that she had learned of the attack on the news. [458]

On June 2, 2016, a year and a half after the incident, Turner was sentenced to six months' jail time and three years' probation. [459] A longer sentence, the judge explained, would have had a serious impact on his life. At the sentencing, the young woman Turner assaulted read a long letter to the court, addressed mainly to Turner. She went back over the facts, and spoke out against Turner's refusal to acknowledge the truth.

> He admitted to kissing other girls at that party, one of whom was my own sister who pushed him away. He admitted to wanting to hook up with someone. I was the wounded antelope of the herd, completely alone and vulnerable, physically unable to fend for myself, and he chose me. Sometimes I think, if I hadn't gone, then this never would've happened. But then I realized, it would have happened, just to somebody else. You were about to enter four years of access to drunk girls and parties, and if this is the foot you started off on, then it is right you did not continue. [460]

Shortly afterwards, Turner's father published a letter in his son's defence. The letter, which he also presented to the judge, describes Turner as the perfect son, underlining his academic and athletic successes, and was intended to convince the judge that Turner did not deserve to go to prison: it was only a misdemeanour, a simple case of alcohol abuse because the young man was having a hard time adapting at Stanford. [461] The father appealed to the judge's sensitivity, invoking an alliance, an ensemble, a group – a boys' club, which ultimately prevailed over the woman standing alone, the young woman Turner had preyed upon.

The same thing happened when Roxane Gay was gang raped as a young teenager, an assault she describes in her autobiography *Hunger*:

> I was twelve when I was raped ... in an abandoned hunting cabin in the woods where no one but those boys could hear me scream ... He just unzipped his jeans and knelt between my legs and shoved himself inside of me. Those other boys stared down at me, leered really, and egged Christopher on ... After Christopher came, he switched places with the boy who was holding my arms down ... All those boys raped me ... I was a toy, used recklessly ... I don't remember their names ... I remember that they enjoyed themselves and laughed a lot. I remember that they had nothing but disdain for me. [462]

The LOL Leagues

The boys who raped her had fun, Roxane Gay recalls; they laughed, a lot, and together – a clear sign of their contempt.

In recent years, we have often quoted the words attributed to Margaret Atwood and echoed, among others, by the heroine of the series *The Fall*, [463] a detective who hunts down serial murderers: men are afraid that women will laugh at them, while women are afraid that men will kill them. But anyone with even the slightest interest in the media, cultural representation, or gender studies knows that women are also afraid of being laughed at by men – before, during, and after killing them.

Atwood's apocryphal words bring to mind another parallel, in a survey on young people's sexual satisfaction carried out by Sara McClelland, a University of Michigan professor. [464] McClelland interviewed young heterosexuals about the notion of bad sex and what they thought an unpleasant, failed sexual encounter was. At the end of the interviews, she noted that, for boys, a failed sexual encounter had to do with a passive, unexciting partner and the absence of pleasure, whereas for girls, failure was associated with physical pain, discomfort, and negative emotions. Girls feared pain; boys feared a lack of pleasure.

Laughter is one of the manifestations of entitlement – the feeling that we are owed something. The feeling too that we are allowed to possess something, and that possession goes without saying. When men laugh together, when they make fun of a woman together, that entitlement is expressed as arrogance. Mocking – to mock, the verb, comes from the Old French "mocquer," meaning to scorn or jeer, possibly from the Latin "muccare," "to blow one's nose" in derision. Mockery is the precursor to violence; it is also its soundtrack.

• • •

On October 11, 2018, the *New York Review of Books* published a lengthy article by former radio personality Jian Ghomeshi in which he complained about his pariah status and about the discomfort that now arose from the mere mention of his name.[465] Ghomeshi's article provoked such ire that the editor-in-chief resigned a few days later despite public support from his staff members. The publication of the piece raised an important question: what does it mean when a respected, world-renowned magazine splashes a text across its front page by a man who's been accused of sexual violence by twenty women, a man partially exonerated in court due to lack of evidence, but who was nonetheless made to publicly apologize to one of his victims? Ghomeshi was a free man, but he had been ostracized: he had lost his job and now wandered around in search of someplace where he might introduce himself to a stranger without them backing away in fear.

But the *New York Review of Books* wouldn't back down, and up went Jian Ghomeshi's name. Ghomeshi, in his plaint, quotes a friend who jokingly told him that he should be recognized as a pioneer of the #MeAlso movement. "There are lots of guys more hated than me now," Ghomeshi writes, "but I was the guy everyone hated first!" That joke alone, Ghomeshi openly mocking his victims, sums up the whole article.

Around the same time, on September 27, 2018, Professor Christine Blasey Ford was describing her assault at the age of fifteen by future Supreme Court Justice Brett Kavanaugh, who was seventeen when the assault took place. Testifying before the US Senate Committee, Blasey Ford described every detail of the event: how he threw her on the bed, tried to take off her clothes, ran his hands all over her body, and, when she screamed, covered her mouth to stop her; how she was convinced that he was going to rape her, how she was terrified that he would kill her by suffocating her.[466] Above all, she says she remembers Brett Kavanaugh laughing with his friend Mark Judge during and after the events: "Indelible in the hippocampus is the laughter. The uproarious laughter between the two, and their having fun at my expense."[467]

The boys' club coalesces around multiple objects and practices, from the economy to sports, politics, and sex. What we tend to forget is that, as well as the looks and words that men exchange when they're together, there's also laughter: the laughter of old members of a private club in New York over a private joke in *Patrick Melrose*; the laughter of traders making fun of women over a meal in a top restaurant in *American Psycho*; the intellectual humour of the architects of in *An Eye for Beauty* on the patio of their artful house; Donald Trump's laughter in 2016 as he boasted of his sexual prowess to Billy Bush before his *Access Hollywood* interview; and the same laughter Trump encouraged during the Brett Kavanaugh United States Supreme Court nomination hearings, when he openly mocked Christine Blasey Ford, caricaturing her testimony by mocking the fact that Blasey Ford said, on a few occasions, "I don't remember."[468] At the rally at which he made the comments, Trump was cheered on by a jubilant crowd, just as men cheer each other on during a gang rape. "I don't know. I don't know. What neighbourhood was it?" he said, in an apparent impression.

I had one beer, right? I had one beer ... How did you get home? I don't remember. How'd you get there? I don't remember. Where is the place? I don't remember. How many years ago was it? I don't know. I don't know. I don't know. I don't know. What neighbourhood was it in? I don't know. Where's the house? I don't know. Upstairs, downstairs, where was it? I don't know ... But I had one beer. That's the only thing I remember.[469]

A Yale classmate of Kavanaugh's, Deborah Ramirez, also remembers him laughing as he dropped his pants and waved his penis in her face, with his friends laughing around him – as if it were necessary to play up heterosexuality to combat any appearance of homosexuality.[470]

In high schools, in colleges, at law schools, and in the halls of Washington, men perform for one another and ascend to positions of power. Watching it happen is a deadening reminder, for victims of sexual assault and harassment, that, in many cases, you were about as meaningful as a chess piece, one of a long procession of objects in the lifelong game that men play with other men. [471]

• • •

Many films feature scenes of a group of boys making fun of one or more girls. In a typical scenario, friends might make a bet about a woman they consider plain, if not ugly, and try to seduce her, only to humiliate her by revealing that she was just a pawn in their game. Neil LaBute explores that structure in *In the Company of Men*, [472] in which two colleagues, on the pretext of getting revenge against women who have treated them badly, and against the socially prevailing feminism of which they feel they are the victims, [473] choose as their prey a deaf employee they both try to seduce. When she falls in love with Chad, the subterfuge is revealed to her by Howard, who against all odds has actually fallen in love with her. Although the young woman leaves them both, hurt by their game, the perversity of the bet takes on a whole new dimension when we learn that Chad, the more attractive of the two, who ultimately seduced the girl, lied to his friend: he led Howard to believe that he was heartbroken when he wasn't at all. The idea for the game was just a cruel, misogynistic whim. Howard, meanwhile, is in love with the woman he was just supposed to fool, and ends up losing everything. In despair, he asks the friend he so admired why he did it, to which Chad replies, "because I could." [474]

LaBute's film, released in the nineties at the height of anti-feminist backlash, is a critique of the companionship men find in each other as a pretext for misogyny. Lili Loofbourow writes about Brett Kavanaugh with regard to that model of male homosocial toxicity: pleasing other men often involves a comedy of cruelty towards women. [475]

We know the thick, heavy, loud laughter of men slapping their thighs, laughing at inside jokes only they understand, growing ever closer by making fun of somebody, most often a woman or someone who represents a marginalized group, and who in any case they consider beneath them. Laughter is a way of imposing domination at the expense of others, laughter that's often referred to as just locker-room banter, though it's far from confined only to that space; it's a way of taking up all the space.

• • •

In 2017, in the wake of the spate of allegations against Hollywood film producer Harvey Weinstein (by more than fifty women, for sexual harassment and assault), the list of media and public men accused of sexual violence grew and grew. Among them was the comedian Louis C.K., who masturbated in front of women (young comedians themselves), or while they were talking to him on the phone, without their consent.

Louis C.K. had been considered a feminist ally, though rumours had been going around even before the accusations were made public, Emily Nussbaum wrote in the *New Yorker*, citing four incidents of the comedian masturbating in front of women, albeit after asking them, he contended, if he could do it, a question to which, his victims point out, it was impossible, given the comedian's power, to say no. [476]

Nussbaum refers to the episode "American Bitch" from the last season of the television series *Girls*, which seems to allude to the rumours surrounding Louis C.K. Hannah, the show's heroine, confronts a famous writer, who is reminiscent of both Philip Roth and Chuck Palahniuk, who's been accused of abuse by a student. [477] The writer asks to meet Hannah after she publishes an article online that included allegations. He arranges to meet her at his home. Throughout their conversation, he defends himself and tries to convince her that he has not abused the student. He admits that, yes, he had a sexual relationship with her, but that what he is guilty of, if anything, is not of having slept with her, but rather of not having pursued the relationship; the allegations are unfounded, he says. Hannah wants him to understand that the student had no choice but to say yes if he, a famous writer, handsome, charming, talented, well-known and well-connected, powerful, an authority figure, invites a young woman who wants to become a writer to have a drink in his hotel room. In his presence, the young woman feels like she exists, and it's impossible to say no. And if in that hotel room the great writer pulls his penis out of his pants and instructs her to perform oral sex on him, it will be just as impossible for her to refuse. She's trapped, afraid of what might happen to her if she doesn't comply, not just now but in the future, in her possible future as a writer. Given the power he represents, he can't expect her to consent, and that's where the violence comes in.

In the second half of the episode, it's Hannah, herself an emerging writer, who finds herself caught up in the web of the admiring writer. Standing in front of a bookshelf, the two of them are talking about a Philip Roth novel, the original title of which was rumoured to have been *American Bitch*. The camera moves and we realize that they're in the writer's bedroom. Out of the blue, he lies on the bed and asks Hannah to lie down beside him: it's been a long time, he says, since he's felt this close to someone. Hannah hesitates, uncomfortable, but he's just given her reason to trust him, and she lies down beside him. The next instant, he's pulled out his penis, turns towards her, and rubs it against Hannah's leg. Shocked, she holds it in her hand for a split second before jumping to her feet. "You pulled your dick out and I touched your dick! ... And now it's still out. You didn't even put it away! I can see your dick!"[478] Her anger is palpable, as is her shame, while he, a mocking smile on his lips, is visibly proud. At the end of the episode, Hannah leaves the building as a series of women gather at the front door: more potential fodder.

• • •

Louis C.K. left the comedy circuit, and then, in August 2018, less than a year after the allegations, he came back, "in control of the narrative," as Roxane Gay points out, [479] as if he had paid for his transgressions, as if he had been forgiven. He should have waited, Gay suggests, and spent as much time offstage as the assaulted women had to stay away, as much time as they suffered because of his actions. And he should pay financial compensation to the victims, to help them make up for what they lost professionally because of him, he should pay for their psychological care, he should donate to non-profits ... Male humour isn't innocent, as the case of comedian Aziz Ansari, denounced on *Babe* by a young woman, [480] reminds us. In Québec, Gilbert Rozon, founder of the Just for Laughs comedy festival, was accused of rape and indecent assault by fourteen women in 2017 and was the subject of a class action suit brought by those who call themselves Les Courageuses, the brave ones. [481]

Humour, mockery, sarcasm, and subsequent humiliation bind together the members of boys' clubs; France's Ligue du LOL, which came to media attention in February 2019, serves as a prime example.

La Ligue du LOL was a Facebook group, created in 2010, of about thirty Parisian journalists and various communications professionals with dazzling careers. In February 2019, they were accused of harassing and humiliating feminist activists, students, bloggers, and journalists. At the time, racist, sexist, and homophobic insults, pornographic photomontages, anonymous emails and threats were flying on X (formerly Twitter), largely unnoticed by the majority of the population, but leaving their mark on the lives of those who were targeted, in this case women and homosexuals, who were thus kept off the web, their work curtailed and their private lives shaken by violence passed off as humour. The feminist activist Daria Marx describes having "spent many years on Twitter feeling like I was running from a sniper, lucky to escape the virtual bullets of an army gone mad." [482] The journalist Mélanie Wanga, for her part, described the Ligue du LOL as "a pyramid scheme where shit-eaters harassed people to show their bosses how valuable they were."[483]

Several members of the group, described as "trendy, clever, bearded, white thirtysomethings,"[484] posted online apologies after being outed in the newspaper *Libération*, while others were suspended, including Alexandre Hervaud, who was web editor at *Libération*, Vincent Glad, a *Libération* freelancer who was also laid off by *Brain Magazine*, and David Doucet, *Les Inrockuptibles* editor-in-chief.[485] These "Twitter kingpins," as group founder Vincent Glad called them, have done enough damage to slow down, if not completely halt, the rise of women in magazine and web journalism. As Olivier Tesquet explained in *Télérama*, in the wake of the #MeToo and #BalanceTonPorc movements: "The web is made by men, for men. Or by older teenagers, for older teenagers who are still growing up ... All of which gives substance to the sexist figure of the 'brogrammer,' who is incapable of designing a tool that protects women and men who don't look like him."[486]

In May 2019, the feminist collective Prenons la Une ("Take back the front page") referred the matter to the Paris public prosecutor and asked for an investigation to be opened into the Ligue du LOL in order to "shed light on the alleged facts of cyber harassment, sexist, racist, and homophobic insults, and incitement to racial or sexist hatred."[487]

Shortly afterwards, another private group surfaced in France, Le Divan des Médecins ("the doctors' couch"), made up of more than eleven thousand medical practitioners. The group's posts included photos of patients, sometimes along with mockery, racist and sexist insults, dirty jokes, and comments that were classist, fatphobic, homophobic, and transphobic. The closed medical in-group was a place for letting off steam at patients' expense, which sometimes went as far as potentially criminal comments. While most Divan members didn't take part in these kinds of exchanges, the group was dominated by small hard-core bunch of about twenty white, heterosexual men, says one member of the group: "They think they're better than everyone else"; "They act like a boys' club that's very much aware of its privileged status but refuses to question it, and spends its time bashing those who don't have the same privilege."[488] Anyone who dared criticize the group's posts quickly became a target themselves: who said that, and how can they be shut up and shut down? Because, as they acknowledged, "let's not kid ourselves, this group will eventually be discovered and it'll be the Ligue du LOL all over again."[489]

● ● ●

These LOL leagues are all about the exclusion and even the expulsion of women from certain circles through mockery and insult. The boys' clubs thus maintain their ascendancy over the world, by ridiculing, devaluing, and humiliating those who dare try to join them and who, by their very presence, might contribute to dismantling them. In her documentary *Je ne suis pas une salope, je suis une journaliste*[490] ("I'm not a slut, I'm a journalist"), the French journalist Marie Portolano interviews female sports presenters and journalists and highlights the sexism and even the sexual harassment they face – a not-so-subtle way of making sure they know they're not welcome in the boys' club of sports journalists. That harassment is also a way of reminding women that they are first and foremost pretty faces, and about as relevant as potted plants. Female sports journalists get greeted with bouquets of flowers, described as "fresh talent" or the "charm," or as providing the "feminine touch" to a program; they are objectified, reduced to their status as mere women in a man's world that wants at all costs to remain unchanged.

Portolano's documentary aired a year after Clémentine Sarlat published an article exposing the sexism she suffered during her time at France Télévisions.[491] Around thirty journalists from the L'Équipe channel came out in support of Sarlat, and the head of France Télévisions, Delphine Ernotte, launched an investigation. Sarlat left France Télé because of this sports-journalism #MeToo moment, and Portolano's documentary more than confirms that women in the field get bullied by their colleagues and by trolls. In the film, nearly a dozen female journalists speak about their poor treatment off-screen, during meetings, backstage, and in the office: they are harassed by colleagues, victimized by sexist jokes, accused of sleeping their way to the top. They are debased in innumerable ways both on-camera and off – cut off, prevented from speaking, and begrudged any misstep. As for the online peanut gallery, they send messages by the thousands, with insults, malice, humiliation, and even rape and death threats.

The Ménès affair blew up in the wake of *Je ne suis pas une salope*. Excerpts from Portolano's documentary were allegedly censored by French television channel Canal+ management, who removed all passages in which men were interviewed, so that outtakes of the disgraced sports journalist Pierre Ménès wouldn't stand out. When Marie Portolano showed her images of star commentator Ménès forcibly kissing his colleague Francesca Antoniotti on set, and when she recalled the time he lifted her skirt off-camera but in front of the audience, Ménès downplayed the incident, claiming that he "gives his male colleagues a hard time" too. Commenting on the events, Ménès explained that this was all before #MeToo, that you can't say anything anymore, you can't do anything. The edited excerpts circulated online, provoking a flood of reactions – tens of thousands of tweets, for instance, hashtagged #PierreMenesOut. Although Ménès tried to make amends on the set of *Touche pas à mon poste!*, he couldn't escape the legal consquences, or a suspension from Canal+.

The day after Marie Portolano's documentary was broadcast, 150 journalists and journalism students signed an article in *Le Monde* demanding that women be better represented in sports media – in other words, that the doors to the boys' club of sports journalism be thrown wide open.

● ● ●

In December 2018, following the success of her comedy *Nanette*, the actor and stand-up comic Hannah Gadsby delivered a monologue at the *Hollywood Reporter*'s 2018 Women in Entertainment morning gala in which she criticized those she called "the good men," in this case, her peers: the set of late-night "Jimmys."[492] The good guys don't have to get up early, as Gadsby herself had that morning; "for their opportunity to monologue their hot take on misogyny, they get primetime television and the late shows."[493] These guys are great: the Jimmys and the Davids are smart and funny, but the last thing Gadsby needs is to listen to men going on about what other men are doing wrong. The problem, she says, is that for the Jimmys, there are only two types of "bad men": the Bill Cosby/Harvey Weinstein type, who are almost a species apart, and Jimmy's friends, the "consent dyslexics," who've just misread the rules. The problem is that when the good guys talk about the bad guys, it's the good guys who draw the line of what's acceptable. That's the line we need to talk about, because the good guys draw a different one depending on the circumstances:

> They have a line for the locker room, a line for when their wives, mothers, daughters, and sisters are watching, another line for when they're drunk and fratting, another line for non-disclosure, a line for friends and a line for foes. You know why we need to talk about this line between good men and bad men? Because it's only good men who get to draw that line. And guess what? All men believe they are good. We need to talk about this because guess what happens when only good men get to draw that line: this world – a world full of good men who do very bad things and still believe in their heart of hearts that they are good men because they have not crossed the line, because they moved the line for their own good.[494]

Gadsby finishes by saying that it is up to women to set that limit, and that it is non-negotiable. She invites the audience to listen to her monologue again from the beginning, replacing the word "man" with the words "white" or "straight" or "cis" or "able-bodied" or "neurotypical," highlighting all the limits that we set for all sorts of reasons in order to be sure of being good.

Gadsby is not the only woman who's made a place for herself in the world of comedy, but there aren't many who have taken on what has always been the prerogative of men, the "few good men" who are sure they're on the right side of things because together they can laugh at others. [495]

•   •   •

"A few good men" was the slogan of the US Marines in 1985. Their recruitment ad shows a sword being made, which will become part of the soldier's uniform by the end of the clip: "You begin with raw steel. Shape it to fire, muscle, and sweat. Polish it to razor-sharp perfection. We're looking for a few good men with the mettle to be Marines." [496]

A Few Good Men is also the title of a hit film [497] about the military trial of two white soldiers, who killed another, who was Latino, during an "extrajudicial punishment." We witness the confrontation between Tom Cruise, who plays a lawyer, and Jack Nicholson as a ruthless, authoritarian colonel, yet it is Demi Moore, the only woman in the cast, a lawyer and captain, who stands for the law. Moore essentially plays a version of the lawyer Catharine A. MacKinnon describes in *Butterfly Politics: Changing the World for Women*, talking about her own path to law school: she didn't want to be the kind of lawyer who enjoyed "their godlike position of saying 'no, that's impossible' to most things women wanted law to do," [498] who choose

> argument over feeling, interrogation over receptivity, combativeness over cooperation, grandstanding over self-expression, smokescreening over openness, "just being careful" ... over trust, tact over sensitivity, self-control over self-mastery, and always being right over self-change. [499]

Demi Moore, the only woman among a few good men, plays the Smurfette.

CHAPTER TWENTY-TWO

The Smurfette Principle

The boys' club, past and present, both in its stereotypical form and in its more subterranean manifestations, has left its mark on the imagination. There are countless representations of groups of men working together for a common cause, glorious or not, in the arts, in film, and on television. We are as though collectively haunted, inhabited by the image, in a sort of daydream.

I am thinking of Charlotte Beradt's work collated in *The Third Reich of Dreams*, after she collected three hundred dreams between 1933 and 1939, during the rise of Hitler's party. Beradt wanted to try to "help describe the structure of a reality that was just on the verge of becoming a nightmare": [500]

> Regardless of how, in their "slumberings upon the bed," these dreamers follow the thread they have seen winding through the labyrinth of political reality and which threatens to strangle them, their power of imagination ranges far. The nazi official who maintained that people could lead a private life only in their sleep certainly underestimated the power of the Third Reich. Our dream authors, the soon to be totally subjected whose dreams are recorded here, saw it all with greater clarity, "in a dream, a vision of the night." [501]

In his afterword to the book, [502] Reinhart Kosellek writes, "the dreams bear witness to an initially open terror that then turns insidious, and they even anticipate its violent crescendo ... This perversion, dictated upon the body, had to be suffered in order for a person to be liberated from it." [503]

In the same way, scenes from films or television series are

also dictated to our bodies, moving images as hauntings that play a part in our way of thinking. The scene in *Munich* described earlier disturbs me in the same way as all those scenes in which men gang up around a woman who somehow turns them on. A woman who represents all of us. It is a scene endlessly repeated, replayed, re-presented, and always updated. Katha Pollitt, writing in the *New York Times*, identified that stock scene as the "Smurfette principle": [504]

> A group of male buddies will be accented by a lone female, stereotypically defined. In the worst cartoons ... the female is usually a little-sister type, a bunny in a pink dress and hair ribbons who tags along with the adventurous bears and badgers. But the Smurfette principle rules the more carefully made shows, too. Thus, Kanga, the only female in *Winnie-the-Pooh*, is a mother. Piggy, of *Muppet Babies*, is a pint-size version of Miss Piggy, the camp glamour queen of the Muppet movies ... The message is clear. Boys are the norm, girls the variation; boys are central, girls peripheral; boys are individuals, girls types. Boys define the group, its story and its code of values. Girls exist only in relation to boys. [505]

Most of the time, Smurfette is white. She is Hollywood-beautiful. From one film to the next (in series like *Star Wars*, for example), the actress changes, but they all look the same.

• • •

The world of *The Smurfs* is a world of men with clearly defined roles in which a female troublemaker has been placed, like a virus in a healthy body. Smurfette was created by the sorcerer Gargamel in a pastiche of Genesis. Made of clay, Smurfette has to infiltrate the Smurf community to stir up trouble. The description of the elements used by Gargamel to make her appear is worthy of the most misogynistic discourse:

A sprig of flirtatiousness ... a solid layer of non-objectivity ... three crocodile tears ... a bird brain ... powder of viper's tongue ... a carat of sneakiness ... a handful of anger ... a dash of lying tissue, transparent, of course ... a bushel of greediness ... a quart of bad faith ... one thimbleful of recklessness ... a stroke of pride ... a pint of envy ... some zest of sensitivity ... a bit of foolishness and a bit of cunning, lots of volatility and lots of obstinacy ... a candle burned at both ends ... [506]

Although a footnote in the original comic book ironically states that "this text is the sole responsibility of the author of the spellbook *Magicae Formulae*, 'Beelzebub Editions,'" [507] the overarching misogyny cannot be ignored. The wizard's creation of a failed Smurfette – she's too ugly – gives way to her transformation, in a before-and-after worthy of women's magazines, into a Smurfette with long eyelashes and blond hair, who will certainly do the trick. She'll know how to turn the Smurfs' heads, playing on their rivalry as they try to win her affections. But Smurfette, who is aware of the trouble her presence is causing, flees the village, leaving the men to fend for themselves. In any event, the Smurfs are happiest when they are alone together, when they celebrate and dance in circles, or when they are in a circle.

Smurfette's primary role remains to be seen. At first, she goes unnoticed. None of the Smurfs is interested in her; none of them wants her. Once she has become blond, sexy, and high-heeled, not only does she attract attention, but the Smurfs also find themselves bound by their shared desire for the same object. Based on a Girardian reading of the scene, Smurfette, who leaves the Smurf village to preserve the community of men, plays into the trope of the scapegoat: it is clear that the woman's role is sacrificial. Left to their own devices, the Smurfs resume their lives. What they need is to be able to stay together to ensure the transfer of power, [508] as in this scene from the film *Donnie Darko*, [509] where Smurfette comes up:

Sean Smith: We gotta find ourselves a Smurfette ... Like this cute little blond that will get down and dirty with the guys. Like Smurfette does.

Donnie Darko: Smurfette doesn't fuck.

Smith: That's bullshit. Smurfette fucks all the other Smurfs. Why do you think Papa Smurf made her? Because the other Smurfs were getting too horny ...

Darko: First of all, Papa Smurf didn't create Smurfette. Gargamel did. She was sent in as Gargamel's evil spy, with the intention of destroying the Smurf village. But the overwhelming goodness of the Smurf way of life transformed her. And as for the whole gangbang scenario ... It just couldn't happen. Smurfs are asexual. They don't even have reproductive organs under those little white pants. That's what's so illogical, you know, about being a Smurf. What's the point of living if you don't have a dick? [510]

More than a quarter of a century after Pollitt's short Smurfette piece was published, little has changed: the trope is just as present and still so common that, more often than not, we don't notice it, we don't stop to consider the image, we forget to take into account who is represented. We're distracted, shuffling around in our slippers.

•   •   •

As Manohla Dargis suggests, [511] "movies get into our bodies" – the narrative, the visuals; their ideas and ideologies leave a mark.

Cinema is certainly no "pastime for miserable, illiterate creatures, bewildered by work and worries;" [512] it plays a part in shaping our imagination. As Erwin Panofsky put it in 1934: "Whether we like it or not, it is the movies that mould, more than any other single force, the opinions, the taste, the language, the dress, the behaviour, and even the physical appearance of a public comprising more than 60 percent of the population of the earth." [513] Benjamin, like Panofsky, described cinema as the instrument best suited to the exercise of reception through distraction,[514] and as a means of mobilizing the masses.

I don't know if film today has the power to mobilize the masses, but I do know that it has the power to mobilize me, as a feminist. It has taught me and continues to teach me. I can't ignore the fact that, even today, we still find ourselves watching movies that feature mainly white male heroes whose quest or survival we stand witness to at the end of terrible ordeals, ending with the warrior's return to a waiting woman.

The 2021 report on the representation of women in film and television published by the Center for the Study of Women in Television and Film at the University of San Diego shows that 31 percent of films had a woman as the main character, a slight increase from the previous high in 2019.[515] Hollywood remains weighed down by stereotypical practices, continuing to invest the bulk of its millions into films with male protagonists:

> The percentages of females in speaking roles and as major characters declined slightly, while the percentage of films with female protagonists increased slightly. An astounding 85 percent of films featured more male than female characters, but only 7 percent of films had more female than male characters … In 2021, females accounted for 35 percent of major characters … This represents a decline of 3 percentage points from 38 percent in 2020. Males comprised 65 percent of major characters.[516]

The percentages of major Black, Latina, and Asian or Asian American female characters increased substantially, though largely from a few films.[517] Finally, 57 percent of films directed or written by women had a female protagonist, compared to only 29 percent for male directors or writers.[518]

As the study's author, Martha Lauzen, has pointed out in previous reports, it's hard to change things when the field in question has no desire to change them. In 2018, for instance, 20 percent of the

250 highest-grossing films included a female director, screenwriter, producer, editor, or photographer, which is only a 1 percent increase from 2001, and only 8 percent of films were directed by women in 2018, which is 1 percent less than in 1998.[519] The celluloid ceiling, Lauzen writes, belies a number of preconceived ideas about women in Hollywood, including the idea that their situation has improved. If Hollywood really did want to increase the number of women in important roles behind the camera, that could be achieved in just a few years and bring about a radical transformation in what we see on screen:

> Filmmakers' visions are necessarily shaped by their experience as women or men and by their position in society. Greater equity for women directors would necessarily bring a diversity of viewpoints, stories, and characters, and the richer cinematic landscape that would result would benefit the population as a whole.[520]

Reacting to a 2018 announcement that the Société de développement des entreprises culturelles, Québec's cultural development agency, was achieving parity and funding film projects written or directed by women, Isabelle Hayeur, of the feminist directors' association Réalisatrices équitables, spoke to the same need for a sea change: "The more women there are going to be making films, the more the conventions are going to change. It's going to change the collective imagination, to open doors for diversity."[521] In France, the organization Collectif 50/50 has been fighting for more egalitarian and inclusive representation. In the words of Fabienne Silvestre, co-founder and director of the Lab Femmes de cinema think-tank, women "evaporate" between film school, where they make up almost half of graduates, and the professional field, where their numbers dwindle to one in three: "women are less subsidized, less rewarded, less programmed. That ecosystem has an impact on their representation on screen. It's a double bind."[522]

• • •

Movies have taught me that most women are alone; that there is one and only one chosen one on whom the camera shines, and, with the camera, the desire of men. As they did *New York Times* film critic Dargis; they have taught me that women exist to be kissed, that they deserve to be punished, that they should be shown taking a shower, that we like to see them in their underwear, with their breasts and buttocks bare, and that they are more often than not mothers or passionate lovers whose role is to make men look good.[523] Virginia Woolf was already on the case at the beginning of the last century:

> Suppose, for instance, that men were only represented in literature as the lovers of women, and were never the friends of men, soldiers, thinkers, dreamers; how few parts in the plays of Shakespeare could be allotted to them; how literature would suffer! We might perhaps have most of Othello; and a good deal of Antony; but no Caesar, no Brutus, no Hamlet, no Lear, no Jaques – literature would be incredibly impoverished, as indeed literature is impoverished beyond our counting by the doors that have been shut upon women.[524]

Today, a large proportion of blockbusters, action movies, political films, teen comedies, and action flicks are based on the Smurfette principle. The list is endless, from the early days of cinema to today, including cartoons and video games:[525] always a group of boys or men in front of a woman or girl, a pretext for the hero's action. Following that pattern, female characters never exist as subjects, but as the boys' club's foils.[526]

· · ·

Dargis admits that it took her a long time to accept the fact that films are complex and paradoxical, and that they must be considered critically, refusing complacency about movies and the sexism they reproduce, or guilt about the pleasure we take in watching them: "the greatest thing I could learn from them is to refuse to let them or my equally messy pleasures off the hook." [527]

As a film critic, Dargis says she is torn between her love of cinema and the sexism it perpetuates; we love the movies even though they hurt us. Dargis wonders what it means to be a film critic after #MeToo: it's not that sexism has become clearer to her since the Weinstein affair, she writes, but now she refuses to ignore it. Whereas before she had to accept a certain amount of sexism in order to continue enjoying films and not be angry all the time, now she calls a spade a spade and states clearly that the film industry treats women essentially as inferiors, subalterns. Hence the importance of being indignant. Hence the need to continue to love the movies even while we point out what the industry doesn't see – the women whose domination is perpetuated by the films they watch – and as we are called upon to watch from her point of view.

I tell myself that we have to refuse the idea of doing to film what film does to the women it has its eye on: get closer, widen the shot, watch carefully, taking our time to detail the sexism. Keep loving the movies, but love them as feminists, read cinema as feminists. We have to refuse to be blinded by the spotlight and wait for the end credits, shuck off that state of distraction, and think critically. We won't see everything, but we can at least try to see what it is that we're used to turning away from. We can be like Kate Macer in *Sicario*: [528] the one who sees, who knows because she sees, and who threatens resistance. When she is made to understand that she has no right to defend her principles because the boys' club will annihilate her if she does, she speaks out anyway.

That's the power of the boys' club at its most sociopathic: they stand together, no matter the cost, no matter what lives are at stake.

The men in *Sicario* guard their place, and in the process they sacrifice a woman. Kate Macer, an FBI agent, works on a team of men who use her to cover up their actions by forcing her to endorse them. Macer's character was almost rewritten as a man at one point, [529] adding a layer of significance to how accountability is addressed in the film: Emily Blunt plays Macer as a woman who refuses the part she is told to play; a woman is cast as the lead in a film, and becomes the heroine in a violent saga about the American war on drugs, a role the director defends despite the film's backers' insistence that the part be played by a man.

The role remained about resistance, in the end, in every way, as if the film were admitting, in spite of itself, that the battle to secure a place for women, both on-screen and off, is far from being won.

CHAPTER TWENTY-THREE

Butterfly Effect

We can make them feel strong or weak. We know them that well.
We know their worst nightmares. And, with a bit of practice, that's
what we'll become. Nightmares.
—Margaret Atwood, *The Handmaid's Tale*

But what butterflies together – sometimes even one – can set in
motion cannot be stopped.
—Catharine A. MacKinnon, *Butterfly Politics: Changing the
World for Women*

I began this book by describing the boys' club as an apparatus.
I now propose [530] that the apparatus must be desecrated: returned
to common use, stripped of what remains of its sanctity. [531]

If an apparatus is a machine that generates subjectivities, which
is why it's a government machine and a mechanism of governmentality, then desecration is a required gesture of citizenship.
Desecration here means making the effort to think about the structure of the boys' club, the system – its homogeneity, its wealth, its
heterosexuality, its whiteness ... there are so many rungs on the
ladder of privilege. Desecration means turning to, seeking out,
imagining, encouraging, and maintaining counter-structures, or
anti-boys' clubs, configurations of men who deviate, images that
allow us to think about masculinity when it escapes the structure
of the boys' club, or that engage in and reinvent the figure by taking issues of class, sexual preference, skin colour, cultural identity,
and gender into consideration; male groups that don't fit into the
boys' club norm, or refuse it. Those groups overwhelm the image,
distorting it, shattering it. The following examples come to mind,

some of them mentioned elsewhere in this book: the character of Patrick Melrose, who was abused by his father and became a drug addict and a critic of the boys' club, and the gay characters in *London Spy*, for their critical discourse on the boys' club and its existence in politics and espionage; the trans women in the fashion world in *Paris Is Burning*;[532] the tenderness of boys and men in *Moonlight*;[533] the activism of the characters in *Dallas Buyers Club*;[534] the wrongly convicted Central Park Five whose story is told by Ava DuVernay in *When They See Us*; the soldiers tasked with mine clearance in *The Hurt Locker*,[535] and those who build something like a family unit in *Fury*;[536] and the engineers, firefighters, soldiers, and miners in the *Chernobyl* series, whose lives were sacrificed to the party.[537] I'm thinking too of the non-binary character of Taylor Mason in *Billions*, who not only upsets the balance of the boys' club, but also reveals its darker side;[538] the importance ascribed to female masculinity in Ben Churchill's *Drag King*;[539] the documentary filmmaker André-Line Beauparlant's look at the world of hunters in *Antlers*;[540] Neil LaBute's uncompromising look at male friendship in *Your Friends & Neighbors*;[541] the critique of fraternities in *Goat*;[542] *Mad Men*, the machismo in which has been eroded over the years;[543] the history of colonization and the resurgence of repressed feelings around Indigenous Nations in relation to Molson stadium and a football team in François Girard's *Hochelaga, Land of Souls*;[544] and the relationships between Atikamekw men in *Before the Streets* by Chloé Leriche.[545]

I won't go into the many possible on-screen and real-life anti-boys' clubs here – that would be another book – but I can dream of what comes next. "The more apparatuses pervade and disseminate their power in every field of life, the more government will find itself faced with an elusive element, which seems to escape its grasp the more docilely it submits to it"; Agamben writes, "Nothing looks more like a terrorist than the ordinary man."[546]

Or an ordinary woman.

A threat lurks beneath the docility; beneath the apparent tranquility, a disturbing quiver.

• • •

When private men's clubs appeared in London, women's clubs also sprang up. Every effort had been made to exclude women from private clubs, and every effort was made to prevent them from forming their own. Women, it was said, had no natural inclination for social life:

> As shy creatures, they did not possess the savoir faire that men embodied. Furthermore, women did not value solidarity; they were not capable of a wider view and, therefore, had little sense of class, or group, allegiance. Even more damning, conventional wisdom saw women as inherently competitive. [547]

The *Saturday Review* insisted, in 1874, that "the very dress of a woman is a non-clubable element." [548]

Barbara Black describes the various women's clubs in her epilogue to her book, "A Room of Her Own": some of them are elitist, and some are mixed, with attributes similar to those of men's clubs. The most notable and ambitious club in London, she writes, was the Lyceum, founded in 1903 by Constance Smedley, who believed that young professional women needed a place to meet, do business, and socialize. Smedley dreamed of a club that would allow women to enjoy their right to a professional life by pushing back social boundaries. [549] The Lyceum was attended by women of wealth and modest means, women of letters, artists, scientists, university graduates, writers' wives and daughters. Debates were held so that women could develop their public speaking skills, Smedley said, and develop the ability to express themselves as if they were people of influence in the public square. There were book and art exhibitions, as well as balls. Within a year, membership had doubled.

Smedley's vision of a "worldwide sisterhood" [550] was to create an international club, a "commonwealth of women travelling and communicating that moved beyond nation and beyond politics."[551] These ideals borrowed little from the formula of boys' clubs, which were fuelled by hierarchy and domination, and from which women were automatically excluded. Black quotes Bernard Darwin, who, writing in 1903, continued to recycle essentialist arguments about their ineligibility, although he considered the creation of women's clubs inevitable:

> Clearly such clubs have supplied a much felt want, but at the same time it may be suggested that women are not, or perhaps it is merely that they have not yet had time to become, quite as clubbable as men. It may be merely that they are less fond of good things to eat and drink, and less given to sitting on their shoulder blades in deep armchairs. It is almost certain that they are as a whole more economical in the matters of solid, lazy comfort. Whatever the cause, the male visitor is apt, very ungratefully, to find something of aridity in a ladies' club and to miss the atmosphere of his own jealously guarded castle.[552]

• • •

I want nothing to do with any jealously guarded castle. And why do we need to eat and drink in leather armchairs by a roaring fire as people are dying of hunger and shivering in cold and in fear out in the street, beneath the castle windows and in front of its closed doors? But I still believe in what we can do.

Just as men who refuse the machine of privilege get booted out of the boys' club and are even in some ways demoted from their status as men, I wonder what kind of women we would be if we refused to settle for scraps. What kind of feminists would we be if we gave up our dreams of boys' clubs, of being part of them or of founding them, to imagine a whole different movie, with different characters, and different ways of doing things? Who knows what our desires, our ideas, and our rage might have the power to provoke?

The truth is, I don't know how to end this jaunt as a traumatized flâneuse in the land of the boys' clubs. I stopped when I thought it was time to call it a day and go home, but I could have gone on wandering for a long time yet, forever even, the subject is so vast. There is so much yet to cover – the links between the boys' club and capitalism, thinking about the future of our planet in terms of the relationship between the boys' club, power, money, and the environment ... The question remains: what awaits us if the accumulation of privilege by a tiny proportion of the population continues, and the gap between the rich and the poor, between dominant boys' clubs and dominated populations, becomes ever wider? What kind of a future can we hope for?

We would have had to unfold and unfold again the many facets of what looks like a virus, a living organism reproducing constantly. What can we do to slow it down? How can we treat our social body?

I'm not sure that we should oppose the boys' club with its inverse; I'm not convinced that, instead of a group of men sitting around some form of power, there is anything to be gained by imagining a group of women. Instead of imitating a structure that has always done us harm, I want to believe that we can continue to invent the place of bodies.

● ● ●

I would have preferred not to have written this book, not to have had any reason to do so.[553] I would have preferred never to feel the need to come back to this after thinking, for a little while, that maybe it wasn't necessary anymore. I would have preferred not to feel like all these images fit together so easily because something needs to be brought to light.

I've spent the last few years thinking about, collating, collecting, and analyzing the various manifestations of the boys' club, as a structure that underpins, enables, and fuels the domination of those who live as women, whether they want to or not, whether they choose to or not. I've written this in my office at a university, and at my desk, where I also write novels and stories – hybrid books that read like an autopsy of life lived as a woman.

I wrote this book with the joy of putting words and ideas together; I wrote it against my will. I write hearing your voice in my head. Anticipating what you might say to me from your seat at the back of the room: your dismissals, your questions, your denials, your threats. With such intensity, for the first time, no doubt because I'm taking the risk of telling you what I see from where I stand. In return, I thought I might suffer something other than the setbacks I've already experienced: the mediocre, pathetic phrases that replay the same script we've heard over and over again for centuries, words that attempt to trivialize and infantilize. No: this time I imagined real threats to my body, death threats.

I've pushed forward, as many of us do in books and in life, by fighting back against fear.

I made progress by reading women who had done what I've done before myself – writing in spite of everything, refusing to be repressed, exhausted, annihilated. Refusing to be silenced. Women who carried the words of other women, who had maybe given up, one day, after trying so hard, slipping some stones into their pockets before stepping into a stream or wrapping a scarf around their neck to choke their words.

You're always announcing a backlash, like a sword permanently dangled over our heads, which will drop when you've had enough of hearing us talk. The backlash is always there, ready to be let loose, and we know it all too well. We're intimately familiar with the frenzied back-and-forth of one hand, and the enraged thrusting, the voice that rises up to bury ours, our sentences interrupted over and over again, our conversations derailed. We know the face of your attacks and demolitions, your mockery and humiliation. How you undermine what we're trying to build. We know all that, and every time we forget, just enough. Like I forgot again this time.

A strategic forgetfulness, needed to keep thinking and writing. And, always, to start again. That's how this book ends. I haven't got to the bottom of the boys' club, but I've skimmed the tip of the iceberg, and I've been able to put my own fear at half-mast. I can only close by vowing that I will continue to say what I am convinced needs to be said, as delicately and clearly as possible, but also as firmly as necessary. Against the thousand admonishments to silence, large and small, that permeate our days, I will continue to speak out. I will continue to fight. We will continue to fight, and to document, question, organize, assert, insist. And we will continue to oppose invisible, insidious power with our own empowerment—creative, luminous, persistent.

Acknowledgments

I am grateful for financial support from the Réseau québécois en études féministes, without which this book would have had a much harder time coming into being. My thanks to Gabrielle Doré, Jennifer Bélanger, and Jean-François Lebel for their research and their passion.

Thanks to Mélodie Drouin and Laurence Pelletier for their patient support and their eagle eyes.

Thanks to Patrick Harrop for a million discussions about architecture and, of course, about people.

Finally, thank you to Valérie Lebrun for her generous, precise, exacting, and invaluable contributions to this book; thank you for staying so close.

Endnotes

Please note that URLs have been provided whenever possible. In citations of French texts where a translator is not credited, the translation is by Katia Grubisic.

INTRODUCTION

1   First published in 2019 by Éditions du remue-ménage (Montréal) and reprinted in 2021 by Éditions Payot & Rivages (Paris).

2   Suzanna Danuta Walters, "Why Can't We Hate Men?," *Washington Post*, June 8, 2018, www.washingtonpost.com/opinions/why-cant-we-hate-men /2018/06/08/f1a3a8e0-6451-11e8-a69c-b944de66d9e7_story.html.

3   To echo Silvia Federici's categorization, the term "women" is used throughout this book as a collective identity, traversed by struggles, "a particular place, a particular function in the capitalist division of labor, but also, at the same time, a battle cry, as fighting against that definition also changed its content ... 'Woman' is not a static, monolithic term but one that has simultaneously different, even opposite and always changing significations. It is not just a performance, an embodiment of institutional norms, but also a contested terrain, constantly being fought over and redefined"; Silvia Federici, *Beyond the Periphery of the Skin: Rethinking, Remaking, and Reclaiming the Body in Contemporary Capitalism* (Oakland, CA: PM Press, 2019), 48. Women are thus a "political subject ... contested but also constantly redefined in ways that are important for constructing a vision of the world we strive to create"; Federici, 3. I would also add, following Catherine Malabou, that "women" identifies a category of subjects overexposed to a particular type of violence, to symbolic and actual discrimination, to the exclusion, rejection, defeat, erasure, and disappearance that touches women in particular; Catherine Malabou, *Changing Difference: The Feminine and the Question of Philosophy*, trans. Carolyn Shread (Malden, MA: Polity Press, 2011), 2.

4   Ashley Burke, "Crisis on Ice: What You Need to Know about the Hockey Canada Scandal," CBC, July 29, 2022, www.cbc.ca/news/politics/hockey -canada-sexual-assault-crisis-parliamentary-committee-1.6535248.

CHAPTER ONE: MEN ASK ME QUESTIONS

5   An earlier version of the French original of this chapter first appeared in *À bâbord!* 79, May 2019.

6   Rebecca Solnit, *Men Explain Things to Me* (Chicago: Haymarket Books, 2014).

7   Jacques Derrida, *The Truth in Painting*, trans. Geoffrey Bennington and Ian McLeod (Chicago: University of Chicago Press, 2020), 260.

8   Marguerite Duras, *Practicalities*, trans. Barbara Bray (New York: Grove Press, 1992), 39.

9   Simone de Beauvoir, *The Second Sex*, trans. Howard M. Parshley (New York: Vintage Books, 1989), xxi.

10   Virginia Woolf, *A Room of One's Own* (London: Penguin, 2019 [1929]), 20.

11   Woolf, 21–22.

12   Virginia Woolf, *Three Guineas* (Penguin Books, 1977 [1938]), 228.

CHAPTER TWO: FROM SERIAL GIRLS TO BOYS' CLUBS

13   Gilda Williams, "What Are You Looking At? The Female Gaze," Tate Etc. 2 (Autumn 2004), www.tate.org.uk/tate-etc/issue-2-autumn-2004/what-are-you-looking.

14   Williams.

15   "The Way We Live Now: 7-4-99; What They Were Thinking," *New York Times Magazine*, July 4, 1999, 16, www.nytimes.com/1999/07/04/magazine/the-way-we-live-now-7-4-99-what-they-were-thinking.html.

16   Translator's note: Somewhat ironically, recent research suggests that Duchamp's famously iconoclastic work may in fact have been the work of Elsa von Freytag-Loringhoven; Dalya Alberge, "'This was his revenge on art': is Marcel Duchamp's greatest work a fake?," *Guardian*, October 15, 2023, www.theguardian.com/artanddesign/2023/oct/15/conceptualist-art-fountain-is-fake-say-historians-marcel-duchamp.

17   "There is a circle effect. Men attend to and treat as significant only what men say. The circle of men whose writing and talk was significant to each other extends backwards in time as far as our records reach. What men were doing was relevant to men, was written by men about men for men. Men listened and listen to what one another said. This is how a tradition is formed"; Dorothy E. Smith, "A Peculiar Eclipsing: Women's Exclusion from Man's Culture," *Women's Studies International Quarterly*, 1 (1978): 281.

18   Woolf, *A Room of One's Own*, 28.

19   James B. Twitchell, with photographs by Ken Ross, *Where Men Hide* (New York: Columbia University Press, 2006), 14.

20 Jean-Philippe Uzel, "Le montage: De la vision à l'action," *Cinéma: Revue d'études cinématographiques* 9, no. 1 (1998): 68. Echoing Walter Benjamin, Uzel writes that, by thwarting viewers' perceptual habits, a montage forces them to react: "The distraction (in the sense of diversion rather than entertainment) created by the shock of the montage leads to political praxis," 69.

21 Sergei Eisenstein, *The Eisenstein Reader*, trans. Richard Taylor and William Powell (London: Bloomsbury Publishing, 2019), 35.

22 Jean-Philippe Uzel, "Le montage," 71.

23 Georges Didi-Huberman, *Remontages du temps subi: L'œil de l'histoire*, vol. 2 (Paris: Les Éditions de Minuit, 2010), 149.

24 Didi-Huberman, 146.

25 Quoted in Didi-Huberman, 194.

26 Woolf, *Three Guineas*.

27 The Harvey Weinstein scandal broke the silence around sexual abuse in Hollywood since the beginnings of the industry. How can we think that what was going on behind the camera, behind the scenes, the systematic sexual assault on women at the cost of their health and their careers, had no impact on what was served up onscreen?

28 Numerous studies have been published over the past twenty years on the multiple facets and incarnations of masculinity. See among many others Elwood Watson and Marc E. Shaw (eds.), *Performing American Masculinities: The 21st Century Man in Popular Culture* (Bloomington, IN: Indiana University Press, 2011); R.W. Connell, *Masculinities*, 2nd ed. (Berkeley: University of California Press, 2005); R.W. Connell, *The Men and the Boys* (Berkeley: University of California Press, 2000); Herbert Sussman, *Masculine Identities: The History and Meanings of Manliness* (Santa Barbara, CA: Praeger, 2012); John Stoltenberg, *Refuser d'être un homme: Pour en finir avec la virilité* (Montréal: M editeur, 2013).

29 Michael Kimmel notes something interesting in *Guyland*: "Whenever I ask young women what they think it means to be a woman, they look at me puzzled, and say, basically, 'Whatever I want' ... for men, the question is still meaningful – and powerful. In countless workshops on college campuses and in high-school assemblies, I've asked young men what it means to be a man. I've asked guys from every state in the nation, as well as about fifteen other countries, what sorts of phrases and words come to mind when they hear someone say, 'Be a man!'" Kimmel sums up the answers in a list of clichés that say that boys don't cry, that they get angry, not sad; that they

don't let anyone walk all over them, they get even; that whoever has the most toys wins; that they have to work hard ("just do it!"): "size matters," "I don't stop to ask for directions," "nice guys finish last," "it's all good." Michael Kimmel, *Guyland: The Perilous World Where Boys Become Men* (New York: HarperCollins, 2008), p. 44–45.

30   Michel Foucault, "The Confessions of the Flesh," *Power/Knowledge: Selected Interviews and Other Writings*, ed. Colin Gordon, trans. Colin Gordon, Leo Marshall, John Mepham, and Kate Soper (New York: Pantheon Books, 1980), 194.

31   Giorgio Agamben, "What is an Apparatus?," *What is an Apparatus? and Other Essays*, trans. David Kishik and Stefan Pedatella (Stanford, CA: Stanford University Press, 2009), 14.

32   "There is an important distinction to be made, I would submit, between 'deploying' or 'activating' essentialism and 'falling into' or 'lapsing into' essentialism. 'Falling into' or 'lapsing into' implies that essentialism is inherently reactionary – inevitably and inescapably a problem or a mistake. 'Deploying' or 'activating,' on the other hand, implies that essentialism may have some strategic or interventionary value"; Diana Fuss, *Essentially Speaking: Feminism, Nature and Difference* (New York: Routledge, 1989), 20.

33   Walter Benjamin, "Surrealism: The Last Snapshot of the European Intelligentsia," *Reflections: Essays, Aphorisms, Autobiographical Writings*, ed. Peter Demetz, trans. Edmund Jephcott (New York: Harcourt Brace Jovanovich, 1978), 192.

34   Walter Benjamin, *The Work of Art in the Age of Mechanical Reproduction*, trans. J.A. Underwood (New York: Penguin Books, 2008), 9.

35   Benjamin, 7.

CHAPTER FOUR: ORIGIN STORY

36   We often talk about the invisibility or the invisibilization of women, which is one of the effects of domination, but less often about this other invisibility, which has to do with privilege, with the dominant position. See for instance Caroline Criado Perez, *Invisible Women: Data Bias in a World Designed for Men* (New York: Abrams Press, 2019).

37   Translator's note: "Cleave" is of course contronymic, and refers also, and rather aptly here, to being together.

38   Queen Victoria to Theodore Martin, May 29, 1870, in Jan Marsh, *Gender Ideology and Separate Spheres in the 19th Century* (London: Victoria and Albert Museum, n.d.), n.p.

39   John Ruskin, *Sesames and Lilies: Two Lectures delivered at Manchester in 1864* (New York: J. Wiley & Son, 1865), 109.

40   Ruskin, 90.

41   John Stuart Mill, *The Subjection of Women* (New York: D. Appleton and Company, 1870), 148–150.

42   Amy Milne-Smith, "A Flight to Domesticity? Making a Home in the Gentlemen's Clubs of London, 1880–1914," *Journal of British Studies* 45, no. 4 (2006): 796–808.

43   The phrase "the angel in the house," from the Coventry Patmore poem by the same title, represented a Victorian ideal of femininity. Coventry Patmore, *The Angel in the House*, parts 1 and 2 (London: Macmillan & Co., 1863).

44   Barbara Black, *A Room of His Own: A Literary-Cultural Study of Victorian Clubland* (Athens, OH: Ohio University Press, 2012), 21.

45   Katherine Snyder, quoted in Black, *A Room of His Own*, 14.

46   Snyder, quoted in Black, 18.

47   Black, 19.

48   Snyder, quoted in Black, 20.

49   Snyder, quoted in Black, 21.

50   Black, 224.

51   Snyder, quoted in Black, 21.

52   Black, 21.

53   Snyder, quoted in Black, 23.

54   Black, 1–2.

55   Black, 12.

56   Black, 11.

57   Black, 12.

58   Black, 14.

CHAPTER FIVE: MEN, TOGETHER

59   Wayne Koestenbaum, foreword to *Between Men: English Literature and Male Homosocial Desire*, thirtieth anniversary ed., by Eve Kosofsky Sedgwick (New York: Columbia University Press, 2015 [1985]), xi.

60   Heidi Hartmann, "The Unhappy Marriage of Marxism and Feminism: Towards a More Progressive Union," *Capital & Class* 3, no. 2 (1979): 1–33.

61 Sedgwick, *Between Men*, 25.

62 Sedgwick, 27.

63 Pauline Verduzier, "Quels sont ces clubs de 'gentlemen' qui n'acceptent pas les femmes?" *Le Figaro Madame*, July 20, 2015, madame.lefigaro.fr/societe /quels-sont-ces-clubs-tres-prives-reserves-aux-hommes-170715-97505.

64 Verduzier.

65 Boris Thiolay, "La guerre des ladies," *L'Express*, March 2, 2006, www.lexpress .fr/monde/europe/la-guerre-des-ladies_482861.html.

66 Thiolay.

67 Verduzier, "Quels sont ces clubs de 'gentlemen'?"

68 Anthony Layden, "Chairman Anthony Layden's Report to Travellers Club Members," *London Evening Standard*, April 9, 2014, www.standard.co.uk /news/londoners-diary/chairman-anthony-layden-s-report-to-travellers -club-members-9248509.html.

69 Layden.

70 Layden.

71 Brice Perrier, "À Paris, plongée dans des clubs au genre très masculin," *Le Parisien*, June 23, 2019, www.leparisien.fr/societe/a-paris-plongee-dans-des -clubs-au-genre-tres-masculin-23-06-2019-8100678.php.

72 Perrier.

73 Perrier.

CHAPTER SIX: THE FAITHFUL

74 *Patrick Melrose*, season 1, episode 1, "Bad News," directed by Edward Berger, written by David Nicholls, aired May 12, 2018, on Showtime.

75 In May 2024, the Garrick Club voted to accept membership applications from women; the vote passed with approximately 60 percent in favour and 40 percent opposed; Amelia Gentleman, "Garrick Club Votes to Accept Female Members for First Time," *Guardian*, May 7, 2024, www.theguardian .com/uk-news/article/2024/may/07/garrick-club-votes-to-accept-female -members-women.

76 Richard Kay, "Fishy politics: Charles's club bans women," *Daily Mail*, October 21, 2012, www.dailymail.co.uk/news/article-2221229/Prince-Charless -Flyfishers-Club-bans-women.html.

77 Abe Hawken, "Mayfair's Savile Club Bends 150-Year-Old 'Men Only' Rule to Allow a Transgender Member to Stay On after a Sex Change to a Woman

(But Don't Get Your Hopes Up Ladies, It Is a One Off Only)," *Daily Mail*, November 5, 2017.

78   Amelia Gentleman, "Time, Gentlemen: When Will the Last All-Male Clubs Admit Women?," *Guardian*, April 30, 2015, www.theguardian.com/news /2015/apr/30/time-gentlemen-when-will-last-all-male-clubs-admit-women.

79   The Savage Club (website), 2024, www.savageclub.com.

80   Percy V. Bradshaw, *Brother Savages and Guests: A History of the Savage Club 1857–1957* (London: W.H. Allen, 1958), np.

81   In January 2018, a woman spoke out against the Winnipeg Squash Racquet Club (founded in 1909), claiming that its exclusion of women prevented her from networking on the same level as men; CBC News, "What about the Squash? Female Player Weighs In On Debate Over Men's Only Winnipeg Squash Racquet Club," CBC News Manitoba, January 17, 2018, www .cbc.ca/news/canada/manitoba/winnipeg-squash-racquet-club-men-only -1.4491162. In a video by the Winnipeg Squash Racquet Club, entitled "Members of the Club," members explain what they enjoy. Several have been going to the club since they were children and are now employed as squash instructors. As with the gentlemen's clubs of bygone years, they gloss over or play down the networking aspect, claiming that they only go to the club to relax; Winnipeg Squash Club, "Members of the Club," video, 2:22, June 12, 2014, www.youtube.com/watch?v=znA6IsDfrGE.

82   Robert Verkaik, "To Drain the Swamp of Men-Only Clubs There Must Be a Public Register of Members," *Guardian*, January 27, 2018, www.theguardian. com/commentisfree/2018/jan/27/to-drain-the-swamp-of-men-only-clubs -there-must-be-a-public-register.

83   Marie-Béatrice Baudet, "Affaire Olivier Duhamel: Le Siècle, club de l'élite et temple de la bienséance, aimerait continuer à dîner en paix," *Le Monde*, February 10, 2021, www.lemonde.fr/societe/article/2021/02/10/affaire-olivier -duhamel-le-siecle-club-de-l-elite-et-temple-de-la-bienseance-aimerait -continuer-a-diner-en-paix_6069387_3224.html.

84   François Denord, Paul Lagneau-Ymonet, and Sylvain Thine, "Aux dîners du Siècle, l'élite du pouvoir se restaure," *Le Monde diplomatique*, February 2011, www.monde-diplomatique.fr/2011/02/DENORD/20132.

85   Denord, Lagneau-Ymonet, and Thine.

86   Denord, Lagneau-Ymonet, and Thine.

87   Marie-France Baudet, "Affaire Olivier Duhamel."

88   *Les nouveaux chiens de garde*, directed by Gilles Balbastre and Yannick Kergoat (Paris: JEM Productions, 2012).

89   Balbastre and Kergoat.

90   Sciences-Po Ad-Hoc Students' Collective, "Affaire Duhamel: 'Nous, étudiantes et étudiants, demandons la démission du directeur de Sciences -Po Frédéric Mion,'" *Libération*, January 13, 2021, www.liberation.fr/debats /2021/01/13/affaire-duhamel-nous-etudiantes-et-etudiants-demandons-la -demission-du-directeur-de-science-po-frede_1815892.

91   *London Spy*, season 1, episode 3, "Blue," directed by Jakob Verbruggen, written by Tom Rob Smith, aired November 23, 2015, on BBC Two.

92   As Gabriel Tate put it in the *Guardian*, "that Whitehall members' club felt just right: a bunch of hypocritical, emotionally neutered old husks mired in a game of mutually assured destruction: Scottie effectively sealed his own fate by raising the stakes unacceptably high. I can only assume James (James Fox, yet more on-point casting, and already distancing himself from Scottie before the favour was asked) had his own gay skeleton rattling around a closet, allowing Scottie some leverage to extract that absolute rib-tickler. 'An awful shame,' indeed. Unlike Danny, Scottie knows exactly what they're up against, but is still persevering. There's something very admirable about that." Gabriel Tate, "London Spy Recap: Episode Three – 'I knew you'd make a lot of mistakes,'" *Guardian*, November 23, 2015, www.theguardian. com/tv-and-radio/tvandradioblog/2015/nov/23/london-spy-recap-episode -three-danny-mistakes-nightmare.

CHAPTER SEVEN: GOOD OLD BOYS

93   Generally speaking, the words for "boy" – the Italian ragazzo, the French garçon, the Greek pais, the Middle English knave, the ecclesiastical Slav отрокъ – mean servant or employee across the Indo-European map. The meaning of a Black male slave or Asian servant of any age dates from around 1600. The form "boyo" was first coined around 1870. The expression "oh, boy" dates back to 1892. "Boy meets girl," that archetype of conventional romance, dates from 1945. "Boy-crazy," meaning eager to socialize with males, dates from 1923. The meaning "male child" dates from after 1400. In modern English, "boy" evokes a mixture of an onomatopoeia meaning evil spirit ("boi") and a child's word meaning brother ("bo"). See Anatoly Liberman, "The Etymology of *boy, beacon* and *buoy*," *Journal of Germanic Linguistics* 12, no. 2 (2000): 201–234.

94   In *Guyland*, Kimmel denounces the latter expression. Citing Christina Hoff Sommers' *The War Against Boys*, an antifeminist essay that defends the idea of masculinity in crisis (a notion debunked by, among others, Francis Dupuis-Déri in *La crise de la masculinité: Autopsie d'un mythe tenace* [Montréal: Remue-ménage, 2019]), Kimmel writes that they are "the four

most depressing words and educational policy discussions today. They imply such abject rejection: boys are such wild, predatory, aggressive animals that there is simply no point in trying to control them" (Kimmel, *Guyland*, 72). He goes on to suggest that the saying "boys will be boys" not only allows boys to do what they want, it encourages them to do so (82).

95 Kimmel, 82.

96 Yann Moix explained himself in an episode of the French talk show *On n'est pas couché*: "I'm not able to desire women my own age ... I can't be held responsible for my own inclinations, my tendencies, and my tastes"; *On n'est pas couché*, aired January 13, 2019, on France 2, youtu.be/Iy3-1YrCqyY.

97 Michel Foucault, "The Confessions of the Flesh," 198.

98 Pierre Bourdieu, *Masculine Domination*, trans. Richard Nice (Stanford, CA: Stanford University Press, 2001), 53.

99 Quoted in Michael S. Kimmel, *The Gender of Desire: Essays on Male Sexuality* (Albany, NY: State University of New York Press, 2005), 33.

100 Emmanuel Levinas, *Totality and Infinity: An Essay on Exteriority*, trans. Alphonso Lingis (Pittsburgh: Duquesne University Press, 1969), 87.

101 Giorgio Agamben, *Remnants of Auschwitz: The Witness and the Archive*, trans. Daniel Heller-Roazen (New York: Zone Books, 1999), 105.

102 Liane Tessier, "Gossip Within the Male Dominated Workplace," Disappointing the Boys' Club (blog), July 18, 2015, lianetessier.wordpress.com/2015 /07/18/gossip-within-the-male-dominated-workplace.

103 Lili Loofbourow, "The Year of the Old Boys," *Slate*, December 21, 2018, slate.com/human-interest/2018/12/old-boys-trump-kavanaugh-moonves -epstein-childish-masculinity.html.

104 Loofbourow.

105 See the documentary *Beyond Boundaries: The Harvey Weinstein Scandal*, directed by Jordan Hill (London: Entertain Me, 2018).

106 Loofbourow, "The Year of the Old Boys."

107 *The Good Fight*, created by Michelle King, Robert King, and Phil Alden Robinson, produced by Scott Free Productions, King Size Productions, and CBS Studios, aired 2017–2022 on CBS All Access. The show is a spin-off of the series *The Good Wife*, created by Michelle King and Robert King.

108 *The Good Fight*, season 3, episode 1, "The One About the Recent Troubles," directed by Robert King, written by Michelle King and Robert King, featuring Christine Baranski, aired March 14, 2019, on CBS All Access.

109   *The Good Fight*, season 3, episode 1.

110   Donald Trump, "Bring Back the Death Penalty, Bring Back Our Police," advertisement, *New York Times*, May 1, 1989.

111   Trump.

112   Two years before the Central Park crime, Trump announced that he was running for the White House, which was seen as a publicity stunt to promote his book *Trump: The Art of the Deal*. He used the same tactics as in 1989, buying space in newspapers to criticize the government. In 2000, he announced once again that he would run as a presidential candidate for the Reform Party. This time, he paid for anonymous advertising. To bring down a rival, Indigenous-run casino, he took out an ad showing drugs and syringes, asking "Are these the new neighbors we want? The St. Regis Mohawk Indian record of criminal activity is well documented"; Oliver Laughland, "Donald Trump and the Central Park Five: The Racially Charged Rise of a Demagogue," *Guardian*, February 17, 2016, www.theguardian.com/us-news/2016/feb/17/central-park-five-donald-trump-jogger-rape-case-new-york.

113   James C. McKinley Jr., "Killings in '89 Set a Record in New York," *New York Times*, March 31, 1990, www.nytimes.com/1990/03/31/nyregion/killings-in-89-set-a-record-in-new-york.html.

114   Ava DuVernay's series *When They See Us* (premiered on Netflix on May 31, 2019) sheds new light on the events, their impact on each of the boys, and their lives then and since.

115   Ava DuVernay points out that Matias Reyes was known to the police and suggests that he should have been considered the prime suspect at the time. The racism of the police and the detective, who was a woman and a feminist, brought about profiling and discrimination, stigmatizing the group of innocent young men.

116   Laughland, "Donald Trump and the Central Park Five."

117   Jan Ransom, "Trump Will Not Apologize for Calling for Death Penalty Over Central Park Five,' *New York Times*, June 18, 2019, www.nytimes.com/2019/06/18/nyregion/central-park-five-trump.html.

118   Joan Didion, *Sentimental Journeys* (New York: HarperCollins, 1993).

119   Kristen Martin, "Donald Trump's Sentimental Journey to the Top," Literary Hub, March 22, 2016, lithub.com/donald-trumps-sentimental-journey-to-the-top/.

CHAPTER EIGHT: THE DONALD

120   Jill Filipovic, "What Donald Trump Thinks It Takes to Be a Man," *New York*

Times, November 2, 2017, www.nytimes.com/2017/11/02/opinion/sunday/donald-trump-masculinity.html.

121   *Fahrenheit 11/9*, directed by Michael Moore (Midwestern Films, 2018).

122   See notably *Roger & Me* (1989), *Bowling for Columbine* (2002), and *Fahrenheit 9/11* (2004).

123   Donald Trump, interview by Rona Barrett, *Washington Post*, October 6, 1980, www.washingtonpost.com/wp-stat/graphics/politics/trump-archive/docs/rona-barrett-1980-interview-of-donald-trump.pdf.

124   André Carrilho, "American Psycho," *New Statesman* (cover), March 9, 2016.

125   *American Psycho*, directed by Mary Harron (Los Angeles: Edward R. Pressman Productions and Muse Productions, 2000).

126   Dwight Garner, "In Hindsight, an 'American Psycho' Looks a Lot like Us," *New York Times*, March 24, 2016, www.nytimes.com/2016/03/27/theater/in-hindsight-an-american-psycho-looks-a-lot-like-us.html.

127   "Good publicity is preferable to bad, but from a bottom line perspective, bad publicity is sometimes better than no publicity at all"; Donald Trump with Tony Schwartz, *Trump: The Art of the Deal* (New York: Random House, 1987), 176.

128   Donald Trump, interview by Phil Donahue, *The Phil Donahue Show*, aired December 15, 1987, in syndication.

129   Tiffany Markman, "An Analysis of President Donald Trump's Use of Language," Medium, February 9, 2020, tiffanymarkman.medium.com/an-analysis-of-president-donald-trumps-use-of-language-74a76c3d062b.

130   *Trump: An American Dream*, episode 1, "Manhattan," produced by David Glover and Mark Raphael, first aired in the UK on November 2017, on Channel 4.

131   *Trump: An American Dream*.

132   *The Apprentice*, created and produced by Mark Burnett, featuring Donald Trump, aired 2004–2017 on NBC; the show ran for fourteen seasons, with over 100 million viewers.

133   "Democalypse 2016," *The Daily Show*, aired June 16, 2015, on Comedy Central.

134   "Trumptastic Voyage," *The Simpsons*, directed by David Silverman, written by Al Jean (Los Angeles: Gracie Films, 2015).

135   *Trump: An American Dream*, episode 3, "Citizen Trump."

136   "How can I live without it?": David Segal, "What Donald Trump's Plaza

Deal Reveals About His White House Bid," *New York Times*, January 17, 2016, www.nytimes.com/2016/01/17/business/what-donald-trumps-plaza -deal-reveals-about-his-white-house-bid.html.

137   Barbara A. Res, *All Alone on the 68th Floor: How One Woman Changed the Face of Construction* (New York: CreateSpace Independent Publishing Platform, 2013); Barbara A. Res, *Tower of Lies: What My Eighteen Years of Working With Donald Trump Reveals About Him* (Los Angeles: Graymalkin Media, 2020).

138   "Barbara Res on *Tower of Lies*," *Washington Journal*, aired on C-Span, December 26, 2020, www.c-span.org/video/?507537-3/barbara-res-tower -lies#!.

139   "He's terribly sexist. He's a womanizer for sure. He hired me for a specific reason: because I was really good. And he told me, and he believed this, that women had to work harder and be smarter and were willing to work harder than men, and that's what he wanted, and he had a couple of women working for him ... When his business was failing in the early '90s, he blamed it on the fact that his executives did a bad job while he was off, in his words, 'fucking women two and three at a time' – he said that! We were in a limousine the first time he said that, and there were people there we didn't really know very well, you know? And it just, it was very uncomfortable for me ... He wanted it to be believed"; Olivia Nuzzi, "Former Donald Trump Executive: 'He's a Supreme Sexist,'" Daily Beast, updated July 12, 2017, www.thedailybeast.com /former-donald-trump-executive-hes-a-supreme-sexist.

140   Nuzzi.

141   Res, *Tower of Lies*.

142   Nuzzi, "Former Donald Trump Executive."

143   Donald Trump, interview by Nancy Collins, *Primetime Live*, ABC, aired March 10, 1994, www.youtube.com/watch?v=WktcHktNbN8.

144   *Trump: An American Dream*.

145   Trump, interview by Barrett.

146   *Get Me Roger Stone*, directed by Dylan Bank, Daniel DiMauro, and Morgan Pehme (Los Gatos, CA: Netflix, 2017).

147   James Hamblin, "Trump Is a Climax of American Masculinity," *Atlantic*, August 8, 2016, www.theatlantic.com/health/archive/2016/08/trump -masculinity-problem/494582.

148   Hamblin.

149   Jane Mayer, "Donald Trump's Ghostwriter Tells All," *New Yorker*, July 18, 2016,

www.newyorker.com/magazine/2016/07/25/donald-trumps-ghostwriter
-tells-all.

150 David Leonhardt and Stuart A. Thomson, "Trump's Lies," *New York Times*,
updated December 14, 2017, www.nytimes.com/interactive/2017/06/23
/opinion/trumps-lies.html.

151 Eliza Relman and Azmi Haroun, "The 26 Women Who Have Accused
Trump of Sexual Misconduct," Business Insider, updated May 9, 2023, www.
businessinsider.com/women-accused-trump-sexual-misconduct-list-2017
-12.

152 "Transcript: Donald Trump's Taped Comments About Women," *New York
Times*, October 8, 2016, www.nytimes.com/2016/10/08/us/donald-trump
-tape-transcript.html.

153 Trump's explanation seems implausible: "D. Trump: I better use some Tic
Tacs just in case I start kissing her. You know, I'm automatically attracted
to beautiful – I just start kissing them. It's like a magnet. Just kiss. I don't
even wait. And when you're a star, they let you do it. You can do anything.
B. Bush: Whatever you want. D. Trump: Grab 'em by the pussy. You can
do anything"; "Transcript."

154 Moore, *Fahrenheit 11/9*.

155 Jessica Reaves, the author of the report *When Women Are the Enemy: The
Intersection of Misogyny and White Supremacy*, says, "There's a profoundly
anti-woman undercurrent to many white supremacist/alt right online exchanges, and that can easily veer from disrespect into the full-on promotion of
violence, including rape. This is even more evident if you visit incel and
MRA boards, where anger towards and hatred of women is the primary
focus – and participants celebrate and encourage misogynist violence"; quoted
in Maya Oppenheim, "Misogyny Is a Key Element of White Supremacy,
Anti-Defamation League Report Finds," *Independent*, July 26, 2018, www.
independent.co.uk/news/world/americas/misogyny-white-supremacy-links
-alt-right-antidefamation-league-report-incel-a8463611.html.

156 Maggie Astor, Christina Caron, and Daniel Victor, "A Guide to the Charlottesville Aftermath," *New York Times*, August 13, 2017, www.nytimes.com
/2017/08/13/us/charlottesville-virginia-overview.html.

157 "Read the Complete Transcript of President Trump's Remarks at Trump
Tower on Charlottesville," *Los Angeles Times*, August 15, 2017, www.latimes.
com/politics/la-na-pol-trump-charlottesville-transcript-20170815-story.
html.

158 Jonathan Capehart, "'The First White President' Is a 'Bad Dude'" *Washing-*

ton Post, September 18, 2017, www.washingtonpost.com/blogs/post-partisan/wp/2017/09/18/the-first-white-president-is-a-bad-dude.

159 Toni Morrison, "Making America White Again," *New Yorker*, November 14, 2016, www.newyorker.com/magazine/2016/11/21/toni-morrison-trump-election-making-america-white-again.

160 Ed Pilkington, "'Stand Back and Stand By': How Trumpism Led to the Capitol Siege," *Guardian*, January 6, 2021, www.theguardian.com/us-news/2021/jan/06/donald-trump-armed-protest-capitol.

161 Morrison, "Making America White Again."

CHAPTER NINE: CROWN JEWEL OF PALM BEACH

162 I'm thinking here of the Erik Hilgerdt drawing, which appeared in the *New Yorker* in 2007, depicting seven almost identical men posing for an official photo, with the caption: "The Guys Who Look Remarkably Alike Club"; reproduced in Black, *A Room of His Own*, 4.

163 On the racism inherent in Trump's health policies and the dangers they pose to the very people he claims to be defending (i.e., white men), see Jonathan M. Metzl, *Dying of Whiteness: How the Politics of Racial Resentment Is Killing America's Heartland* (New York: Basic Books, 2019).

164 Antonio Fins, "Trump Indictment and Mar-a-Lago: How Much Is Membership, What's It Like Inside, Do You See Melania?" *Palm Beach Post*, June 12, 2023, www.palmbeachpost.com/story/news/trump/2023/06/12/trump-mar-lago-florida-membership-cost-melania-celebrity-photos/70309203007/.

165 Donald Trump, "Executive Branch Personnel Public Financial Disclosure Report, (OGE Form 278e)," United States Office of Government Ethics, May 16, 2016, web.archive.org/web/20190902113525/https://assets.documentcloud.org/documents/2838696/Trump-2016-Financial-Disclosure.pdf.

166 Laurence Leamer, *Mar-a-Lago: Inside the Gates of Power at Donald Trump's Presidential Palace* (New York: Flatiron Books, 2019), 4.

167 Leamer, 5.

168 Nicholas Confessore, Maggie Haberman, and Eric Lipton, "Trump's 'Winter White House': A Peek at the Exclusive Members' List at Mar-a-Lago," *New York Times*, February 18, 2017, www.nytimes.com/2017/02/18/us/mar-a-lago-trump-ethics-winter-white-house.html.

169 "'Mar-a-Lago represents a commercialization of the presidency that has few if any precedents in American history,' said Jon Meacham, a presidential

historian and Andrew Jackson biographer." Confessore, Haberman, and Lipton, "Trump's 'Winter White House.'"

170   Leamer, *Mar-a-Lago*, 250.

171   Leamer, 251.

CHAPTER TEN: XANADU

172   Julia Lechner, "Donald Trump's Favorite Movies," CBS News, December 6, 2016, www.cbsnews.com/pictures/donald-trumps-favorite-movies.

173   NewsHunter29, "Donald Trump Movie Review – Orson Welles's *Citizen Kane*," August 20, 2015, YouTube video, 3:33, youtu.be/aeQOJZ-QzBk.

174   NewsHunter29.

175   See Anthony Audi, "Donald Trump Modeled His Life on Cinematic Loser Charles Foster Kane: What Does a Presidential Candidate's Favorite Movie Reveal?," Literary Hub, October 26, 2016, lithub.com/donald-trump-modeled -his-life-on-cinematic-loser-charles-foster-kane.

176   *Citizen Kane*, directed by Orson Welles (New York: RKO Radio Pictures Mercury Productions, 1941).

177   "Barry: How many times you seen it?

Bobby: This'll be the first.

Barry: Oh, my God, you're in for a treat.

Wags: 'You know, Mr. Bernstein, if I hadn't been very rich, I might have been a really great man.'

Bobby: Wags, man, what are you doing here?

Wags: Apologies for violating the restraining order and entering Xanadu, but I got a pile of documents for you to sign"; *Billions*, "The Good Life," season 1, episode 5, directed by Neil LaBute, written by Heidi Schreck, aired February 14, 2016, on Showtime.

178   Herman J. Mankiewicz and Orson Welles, *Citizen Kane*, screenplay (RKO Radio Pictures Mercury Productions, 1941).

179   Mankiewicz and Welles.

180   Mankiewicz and Welles.

181   Shayne Benowitz, "French Designer Makes a New Mark on Miami," *Miami Herald*, December 14, 2016, www.miamiherald.com/living/home-garden /article120896593.html.

182   Mankiewicz and Welles, *Citizen Kane*.

183   Benjamin, *The Work of Art in the Age of Mechanical Reproduction*, 33–34.

184   *The Architect*, directed by Matt Tauber (Denver: HDNet Films and Sly Dog Films, 2006).

CHAPTER ELEVEN: A WORLD OF THEIR OWN

185   Marylène Lieber, *Genres, violences et espaces publics: La vulnérabilité des femmes en question* (Paris: Presses de Sciences Po, 2008).

186   Dolores Hayden, "What Would a Non-Sexist City Be Like? Speculations on Housing, Urban Design, and Human Work," in "Women and the American City," *Signs* 5, no. 3 (1980): S170–S187.

187   Translator's note: The name of the French feminist activist group La Barbe both translates literally to "The Beard" and references a popular expression meaning "that's enough."

188   Mouna El Mokhtari, "La ville est faite par et pour les hommes," *Le Monde*, March 8, 2018, www.lemonde.fr/societe/video/2018/03/08/la-ville-est-faite -par-et-pour-les-hommes_5267465_3224.html.

189   LDV Studio Urbain, "Saviez-vous que l'urbanité était genrée?," Demain la ville (website), March 8, 2016, www.demainlaville.com/saviez-vous-que -lurbanite-etait-genree.

190   LDV Studio Urbain.

191   Lauren Bastide, *Présentes: Ville, médias, politique... quelle place pour les femmes ?* (Paris: Allary, 2020), 42.

192   Charlotte Willis, "Men Shamed on Tumblr Site for Taking Up Too Much Space on the Train," *Courier Mail*, September 20, 2013, www.couriermail. com.au/entertainment/celebrity/men-shamed-on-tumblr-site-for-taking -up-too-much-space-on-the-train/news-story/8217f0c17486af271fda4d019f- b8fe85.

193   Bastide, *Présentes*, 49.

194   Hayden, "What Would a Non-Sexist City Be Like?"

195   In French, for instance, the original translation of Woolf's book was *Une chambre à soi*, until Marie Darrieussecq rendered it in 2016 as *Un lieu à soi*, literally "a place of one's own."

196   Van Badham, "'Mentrification': How Men Appropriated Computers, Beer and the Beatles," *Guardian*, May 28, 2019, www.theguardian.com/music /2019/may/29/mentrification-how-men-appropriated-computers-beer-and -the-beatles.

197   Names that represent traditionally marginalized communities are likewise in

the toponymic minority, hence the importance, for example, of replacing the name of Montréal's Amherst Street, initially named after General Amherst, with Atateken; Ataté:ken is a Kanien'kéha word that means "brotherhood" and evokes a notion of equality among people, as Hilda Nicolas, long-time director of the Kanesatake Language and Cultural Centre, explains; Verity Stevenson, "Amherst Street becomes 'Atateken,' Symbolizing Fraternity and Peace," CBC News, June 21, 2019, www.cbc.ca/news/canada/montreal/amherst-street-renamed-atateken-symbolizing-fraternity-and-peace-1.5184562.

198   Yves Raibaud, *La ville faite par et pour les hommes: Dans l'espace urbain, une mixité en trompe-l'œil* (Paris: Éditions Belin, 2015), 11.

199   Thanks in part to the Toponym'elles project launched in 2016, the rate increased to 7.3 percent by 2020; Frédéric Lacroix-Couture, "Un peu plus de femmes dans la toponymie montréalaise," *Métro*, March 4, 2020, journalmetro.com/actualites/2425327/un-peu-plus-de-femmes-dans-la-toponymie-montrealaise.

200   Raibaud, 47–48.

201   Jeanne Corriveau, "Au nom des femmes," *Le Devoir*, December 23, 2014, www.ledevoir.com/politique/montreal/427477/toponymie-au-nom-des-femmes.

202   Pierre Sansot, *Poétique de la ville* (Lausanne: Payot, 2015), 88.

203   "Bien cultivés et bien blancs": see Béatrice Delvaux and Joëlle Meskens, "Les Racines élémentaires de Mona Chollet: 'J'ai vu des mecs bien blancs, bien cultivés se comporter de manière horrible,'" *Le Soir*, September 1, 2023, www.lesoir.be/534593/article/2023-09-01/les-racines-elementaires-de-mona-chollet-jai-vu-des-mecs-bien-blancs-bien.

204   Raibaud, *La ville faite par et pour les hommes*, 43.

205   Raibaud, 15.

206   Raibaud, 19.

207   Françoise Collin, *Parcours féministe: Entretiens avec Irène Kaufer* (Brussels: Labor, 2005).

208   *Femme de la rue*, directed by Sofie Peeters, aired July 26, 2012, on Canvas.

209   Hollaback! was a blog founded in 2005 by a group of New York friends to raise awareness about street harassment, which has since become a nonprofit against street and online harassment, now called Right to Be: "We want to build a world that's free of harassment and filled with humanity.

Every day, we train hundreds of people to respond to, intervene in, and heal from harassment." Right to Be (website), righttobe.org.

210 Translator's note: In French, #AgressionNonDénoncée.

211 Woolf, *Three Guineas*, 102.

212 Woolf.

213 Woolf.

214 Woolf.

215 Woolf, 103.

CHAPTER TWELVE: ARCHITECTS OF THE UNIVERSE

216 Sreenita Mukherjee, "Women, Architecture and Education: Experiences of Women in the UK's Architectural Space," Medium, February 9, 2021, medium.com/architectonics/women-architecture-and-education-e44f90cc5b38.

217 Isabelle Regnier, "Stéphanie Dadour: 'Les étudiantes en architecture sont demandeuses de modèles de femmes reconnues par la profession,'" *Le Monde*, June 8, 2020, www.lemonde.fr/culture/article/2020/06/08/stephanie-dadour-les-etudiantes-en-architecture-sont-demandeuses-de-modeles-de-femmes-reconnues-par-la-profession_6042102_3246.html.

218 Quoted in Regnier.

219 Mark Wigley's indictment makes it clear: "The active production of gender distinctions can be found at every level of architectural discourse: in its rituals of legitimation, hiring practices, classification systems, lecture techniques, publicity images, canon formation, division of labour, bibliographies, design conventions, legal codes, salary structures, publishing practices, language, professional ethics, editing protocols, project credits, etc. In each site the complicity of the discourse with both the general cultural subordination of the 'feminine' and the specific subordination of particular 'women' can be identified, often explicitly but usually by way of covert social mechanisms that sustain bias at odds with overt formulations"; Mark Wigley, "Untitled: The Housing of Gender," in *Sexuality & Space*, ed. Beatriz Colomina (New York: Princeton Papers on Architectures, 1992), 329.

220 Florise Vaubien and AFP, "Montpellier: Une enquête ouverte pour harcèlement moral et sexuel à l'École d'architecture," *RTL France*, December 16, 2020, www.rtl.fr/actu/justice-faits-divers/montpellier-une-enquete-ouverte-pour-harcelement-moral-et-sexuel-a-l-ecole-d-architecture-7800941410.

221 Allison Arieff, "Where Are All the Female Architects?" *New York Times*,

December 15, 2018, www.nytimes.com/2018/12/15/opinion/sunday/women -architects.html.

222 *Archigraphie 2022/23: Observatoire de la profession d'architecte* (Paris: Ordre des Architectes, 2023), 20.

223 *Archigraphie 2022/23*, 61.

224 Quoted in Alice Pouyat, "Architectes, faites de la place aux femmes!," WE demain (website), March 8, 2018, www.wedemain.fr/dechiffrer/architectes -faites-de-la-place-aux-femmes.

225 Quoted in Pouyat.

226 See the websites Equity by Design, eqxdesign.com, and Design for Equality, designforequality.org.

227 The OAQ report found that "the number of women architects is rapidly catching up with the number of men: as of March 31, 2013, the Ordre's register showed that women architects outnumbered their male counter-parts. Overall, the profession remains largely male (63 percent compared to 37 percent), but in the twenty-five to thirty-four age group, for instance, the numbers are reversed (58 percent women compared to 42 percent men). Not only is the profession healthy, it's headed straight for equality. Dare we ask for more?"; Ordre des architectes du Québec, *Esquisses* 24, no. 2 (summer 2013), www.oaq.com/esquisses/archives_en_html/balades_au_fil_de_leau /tout_le_reste/portrait_chiffre.html.

228 Robin Pogrebin, "I Am Not the Decorator: Female Architects Speak Out," *New York Times*, April 12, 2016, www.nytimes.com/2016/04/13/arts/design /female-architects-speak-out-on-sexism-unequal-pay-and-more.html.

229 Pogrebin.

230 BIG (website), big.dk.

231 Arieff, "Where Are All the Female Architects?"

232 Denise Scott Brown, "Room at the Top?: Sexism and the Star System in Architecture," in *Gender Space Architecture: An Interdisciplinary Intro-duction*, eds. Jane Rendell, Barbara Penner, and Iain Borden (New York: Routledge, 2000), 261.

233 Quoted in Arieff, "Where Are All the Female Architects?"

234 On the relationship between gender and architecture, see Dörte Kuhlmann, *Gender Studies in Architecture: Space, Power and Difference* (New York: Routledge, 2013).

235 "Identifying manliness with 'genuineness' and femininity with 'artifice,' architects since Vitruvius have associated the ornamented surface with

femininity, not masculinity. Discussing the origins of Doric and Ionic columns, Vitruvius writes: 'In the invention of the two types of column, they borrowed manly beauty, naked and unadorned for the one, and for the other the delicacy, adornment, and proportions characteristic of women'"; Joel Sanders, *Stud: Architectures of Masculinity* (New York: Princeton University Press, 1996), 21–22.

236 "I shall not speak of irrational animals, because they appear to have no certain proportions"; Cennino Cennini, *Treatise on Painting*, trans. M. Merrifield ([orig. Tambroni, 1437], Edward Lumley, 1844), 46.

237 "The 'Modulor' is a measuring tool based on the human body and on mathematics. A man-with-arm-upraised at the determining points of his occupation of space – foot, solar plexus, head, tips of fingers of the upraised arm – three intervals which give rise to a series of golden sections, called the Fibonacci series. On the other hand, mathematics offers the simplest and also the strongest variation of a value: the single unit, the double unit and the three golden sections"; Le Corbusier, *The Modulor: A Harmonious Measure to the Human Scale, Universally Applicable to Architecture and Mechanics*, trans. Peter de Francia and Anna Bostock ([Orig. two vols., 1954, 1958.] Basel: Birkhäuser, 2000), 55.

238 Wigley, "Untitled: The Housing of Gender," 376.

239 White, as per Alberti, in the fifteenth century, who said that any structures erected should be covered with a thin layer of white plaster; Wigley, 379.

240 Wigley, 357.

241 Wigley, 366–367.

242 Wigley, 365.

243 Le Corbusier, *The Decorative Art of Today*, trans. James I. Dunnett (Cambridge, MA: MIT Press, 1987), 188.

244 Le Corbusier, 190, 192.

245 Le Corbusier, 189.

246 Le Corbusier, 188.

247 Mabel O. Wilson and Julian Rose, "Changing the Subject: Race and Public Space," *Artforum*, Summer 2017, www.artforum.com/features/changing-the -subject-race-and-public-space-234352.

248 Wilson and Rose.

249 Sanders, *Stud*, 12.

CHAPTER THIRTEEN: AN EYE FOR BEAUTY

250 *12 Angry Men*, directed by Sidney Lumet (Los Angeles: Orion-Nova, 1957).

251 Tauber, *The Architect*. The film, which went largely unnoticed or got negative reviews, not only features famous actresses like Viola Davis and Isabella Rossellini, among others, it also touches on important issues like racism, sexism, homosexuality, and adolescence.

252 *Jungle Fever*, directed by Spike Lee (Brooklyn, NY: 40 Acres and a Mule Filmworks, 1991).

253 *The Fountainhead*, directed by King Vidor (Burbank, CA: Warner Bros, 1949).

254 Ayn Rand, *The Fountainhead* (New York: Penguin, 1996 [1943]), vii.

255 Sanders, *Stud*, 19.

256 Sanders.

257 *Le règne de la beauté*, directed by Denys Arcand (Montréal: Cinémaginaire, 2014; English version: *An Eye for Beauty*).

258 *Le règne de la beauté* was released to DVD, but nonetheless got a great deal of media coverage.

259 Arcand, *Le règne de la beauté*.

260 Reviews of the film echo that hollowness: a review in *Voir* was titled, "Une belle coquille vide" ("A Pretty, Hollow Shell"; Manon Dumais, *Voir*, May 15, 2014), while another, in *Le Devoir*, was titled "La dictature du vide absolu" ("The Dictatorship of Absolute Void"; Dominique Corneillier, *Le Devoir*, May 24, 2014).

261 Serge Bouchard, "Le boys club ou la théorie du cercle impénétrable," in *C'est fou*, aired September 2, 2018, on Radio-Canada, ici.radio-canada.ca /ohdio/premiere/emissions/c-est-fou/segments/chronique/85446/boys -club-editorial-serge-bouchard-academie-francaise-clubs-prives-quebec.

262 Twitchell, *Where Men Hide*, 37.

263 Quoted in Twitchell, 38.

264 Twitchell.

265 Colomina, *Sexuality and Space*, viii.

CHAPTER FOURTEEN: TERRORISTS

266 *Munich*, directed by Steven Spielberg (Universal City, CA: Amblin Entertainment, Kennedy Marshall, and Alliance Atlantis, 2005).

267 Spielberg.

268 Catharine A. MacKinnon, *Are Women Human?: And Other International Dialogues* (Cambridge, MA: Belknap Press of Harvard University Press, 2006), 274.

269 MacKinnon, 261. "It is hard to avoid the impression that what is called war is what men make against each other, and what they do to women is called everyday life"; MacKinnon, 274.

270 "[The Geneva Convention] prohibits violence to life and the person, especially murder, mutilation, cruel treatment, and torture, and outrages on personal dignity, especially humiliating and degrading treatment"; MacKinnon, 262–263.

271 MacKinnon, 142.

272 MacKinnon, 5. Note also the hesitation in the words of the American philosopher Alison M. Jaggar: "We need an account of terrorism that allows us to think clearly about whether and when occurrences of lynchings, cross-burnings, gay-bashing, and even domestic violence may be terrorist practices"; Alison M. Jaggar, "What Is Terrorism, Why Is It Wrong, and Could It Ever Be Morally Permissible?," *Journal of Social Philosophy* 36, no. 2 (2005): 204.

273 "Military responses to terrorism are disproportionately harmful to women, especially poor women and their children. During the twentieth century, civilians rather than soldiers came to constitute an ever increasing proportion of the casualties of war. The combatants in war are predominantly male but the vulnerable civilians are predominantly women and children, especially women and children in the third world, where most casualties of recent wars have occurred. Women and children also constitute 80 percent of the millions of refugees dislocated by war. Rape is a traditional weapon of war, and military action is usually associated with organized and sometimes forced prostitution"; Alison M. Jaggar, "Responding to the Evil of Terrorism," *Hypatia* 18, no. 1 (2003): 179.

274 MacKinnon, *Are Women Human?*, 278.

275 Quoted in MacKinnon, 274.

276 Giorgio Agamben, *Stasis: Civil War as a Political Paradigm*, trans. Nicholas Heron (Edinburgh: Edinburgh University Press, 2015), 14–15.

277 Carol Hanisch, "The Personal is Political," in *Notes from the Second Year: Women's Liberation*, ed. Shulamith Firestone (1970): 76–77.

278 National Inquiry into Missing and Murdered Indigenous Women and Girls,

"News Release," June 3, 2019, www.mmiwg-ffada.ca/wp-content/uploads /2019/06/News-Release-Final-Report.pdf.

279 "That is, the failure to act"; National Inquiry into Missing and Murdered Indigenous Women and Girls, *A Legal Analysis of Genocide: Supplementary Report of the National Inquiry into Missing and Murdered Indigenous Women and Girls*, 2019, www.mmiwg-ffada.ca/wp-content/uploads/2019 /06/Supplementary-Report_Genocide.pdf, 4.

280 National Inquiry into Missing and Murdered Indigenous Women and Girls, 8.

281 Commissioner Michèle Audette says in the National Inquiry into Missing and Murdered Indigenous Women and Girls press release: "To put an end to this tragedy, the rightful power and place of women, girls and 2SLGBTQQIA people must be reinstated, which requires dismantling the structures of colonialism within Canadian society. This is not just a job for governments and politicians. It is incumbent on all Canadians to hold our leaders to account"; National Inquiry into Missing and Murdered Indigenous Women and Girls, "News Release," www.newswire.ca/news-releases/national-inquiry-calls-for -transformative-change-to-eradicate-violence-against-indigenous-women -girls-and-2slgbtqqia-834022938.html.

CHAPTER FIFTEEN: CLOTHES MAKE THE MAN

282 Despina Stratigakos, *Where Are the Women Architects?* (Princeton, NJ: Princeton University Press, 2016), 40.

283 Stratigakos.

284 Quoted in Stratigakos, 42–43.

285 Christian Allaire, "Billy Porter on Why He Wore a Gown, Not a Tuxedo, to the Oscars," *Vogue*, February 24, 2019, www.vogue.com/article/billy-porter -oscars-red-carpet-gown-christian-siriano.

286 *Suits*, created by Aaron Korsh, produced by Gene Klein, Gabriel Macht, Patrick J. Adams, and JM Danguilan, aired 2011–2019 on USA Network.

287 See Alicia Cornwell, "Making the Man: 'Suiting' Masculinity in Performance Art," *Eagle Feather* 2 (2005): 1–10.

288 *American Gigolo*, directed by Paul Schrader (Los Angeles: Paramount Pictures, 1980).

289 In *White*, Bret Easton Ellis highlights the impact of Richard Gere's image, the gay aspect of his sexualization: in *American Gigolo*, the camera looks at a man's body in a way usually reserved for women, with director Paul Schrader not only taking the time to show Gere meticulously choosing his

clothes, but often filming him half-naked or completely in the buff; Bret Easton Ellis, *White* (New York: Knopf Doubleday, 2019).

290 *Wall Street*, directed by Oliver Stone (American Entertainment Partners and Amercent Films, 1987).

291 "The wardrobe of power was itself a form of power, and thus important to political culture precisely because it embodied social, sexual, political, religious, and economic relations; it gave them shape, materiality, and visibility. By doing so, clothing put power in plain view; it shaped the way in which power was thought, enacted, and reformulated"; David Kuchta, *The Three-Piece Suit and Modern Masculinity: England 1550–1850* (Berkeley, CA: University of California Press, 2002), 7.

292 Brenden Gallagher, "*American Gigolo* and the Rise of the Armani Generation," Grailed, February 27, 2018, www.grailed.com/drycleanonly/american-gigolo-rise-of-armani.

293 Barbara Ellen, "Cécile Duflot: A Woman in a Dress? Mon Dieu, Whatever Next?" *Guardian*, July 22, 2012, www.theguardian.com/commentisfree/2012/jul/22/barbara-ellen-cecile-duflots-dress.

294 A deputy mayor said to then-minister Royal, "Allow me, Madame Minister, to congratulate you on the choice of colour for your suit. Green looks good on you"; "Le maire félicite Ségolène Royal... pour son tailleur," *Le Parisien*, September 11, 2014, www.leparisien.fr/val-de-marne-94/le-maire-felicite-segolene-royal-pour-son-tailleur-11-09-2014-4124999.php.

295 Lison Nicolas, "Florence Parly et le sexisme à l'Assemblée: 'Il valait mieux porter un uniforme tailleur-pantalon,'" *Gala*, March 12, 2021, www.gala.fr/l_actu/news_de_stars/florence-parly-et-le-sexisme-a-lassemblee-il-valait-mieux-porter-un-uniforme-tailleur-pantalon_464832.

296 Tim Lewis, "Tom Ford: 'I Wore a Suit on Set. It's a Uniform ... I Feel Weak in Trainers,'" *Guardian*, October 23, 2016, www.theguardian.com/film/2016/oct/23/tom-ford-suit-set-film-nocturnal-animals-director.

297 cintra wilson, "A Brief History of the Power Suit," Medium, October 11, 2018, gen.medium.com/a-brief-history-of-the-power-suit-544ed4dee095.

298 wilson.

299 Suits are eminently paradoxical, as Anne Hollander writes: "Although male heads of state wear suits at summit meetings, male job applicants wear them to interviews, and men accused of rape and murder wear them in court to help their chances of acquittal, the pants-jacket-shirt-and-tie costume, formal or informal, is often called boring or worse. Like other excellent and simple things we cannot do without, men's suits have lately acquired an irk-

some esthetic flavor, I would say an irritating perfection"; Anne Hollander, quoted in Tim Edwards, *Men in the Mirror: Men's Fashion, Masculinity and Consumer Society* (London: Cassell, 1997), 18.

300 *The Wolf of Wall Street*, directed by Martin Scorsese (West Hollywood, CA: Red Granite Pictures, Appian Way Productions, Sikelia Productions, and EMJAG Productions, 2013).

301 In fact, the number of pages featuring explicit violence is limited, and Mary Harron, in her adaptation, shows the instruments of violence, but leaves the acts off-screen.

302 Bret Easton Ellis, Mary Harron, and Christian Bale, "American Psycho," interview by Charlie Rose, *Charlie Rose*, PBS, aired April 13, 2000, charlierose.com/videos/1102.

303 Ezinne Ukoha, "How *American Psycho* Serves as the White Man's Code for Behavioral Dysfunction," Medium, February 10, 2018, nilegirl.medium.com/how-american-psycho-serves-as-the-white-man-s-code-for-behavioral-dysfunction-acf0eb58abe0.

304 Luke Leitch, "Last Trump for the Suit?" *Economist*, August 4, 2016, www.economist.com/1843/2016/08/04/last-trump-for-the-suit.

305 *House of Cards*, created by Beau Willimon, featuring Kevin Spacey, aired 2013–2018 on Netflix.

306 Vanessa Friedman, "A Primer on Power Dressing From *House of Cards*," *New York Times*, June 8, 2017, www.nytimes.com/2017/06/08/fashion/house-of-cards-power-dressing-melania-trump-claire-underwood.html.

307 "A History of Melania Trump's Most Talked-About Fashion Moments," *Glamour*, August 26, 2020, www.glamour.com/gallery/melania-trump-most-talked-about-fashion-moments.

308 See Marie-Anne Casselot, "L'habillement est un piège pour les femmes en politique," *Le Devoir*, December 22, 2018, www.ledevoir.com/societe/le-devoir-de/544175/l-habillement-est-un-piege-pour-les-femmes-en-politique.

CHAPTER SIXTEEN: WHITE MEN

309 Alex Hawgood, "The Men Powerful Enough to Wear the Same Thing Every Day," *New York Times*, April 3, 2015, www.nytimes.com/interactive/2015/04/02/fashion/mens-style/The-Men-Powerful-Enough-to-Wear-the-Same-Thing.html.

310 Hawgood.

311 *American Psycho*'s co-writer Guinevere Turner said, "I very much think [*American Psycho* is] a feminist film. It's a satire about how men compete

with each other and how in this hypereal universe we created, women are even less important than your tan or your suit or where you summer. And to me, even though the women are all sort of tragic and killed, it's about how men perceive and treat them."; quoted in Trey Taylor, "How American Psycho Became a Feminist Statement," *Dazed*, August 19, 2014, www .dazeddigital.com/artsandculture/article/20751/1/how-american-psycho -became-a-feminist-statement.

312   Laura Mulvey makes the point in her famous article "Visual Pleasure and Narrative Cinema," suggesting that the woman is the image and the man the beholder, and that in the dominant heterosexual economy, the eroticization of women serves the pleasure of men; in *Film Theory and Criticism: Introductory Readings*, fifth edition, eds. Leo Braudy and Marshall Cohen (Oxford: Oxford University Press, 1999), 833–844.

313   Ellis, *White*, 228.

314   Ellis, Harron, and Bale, "American Psycho," interview.

315   Lili Loofbourow, "The Male Glance," *VQR*, Spring 2018, www.vqronline. org/essays-articles/2018/03/male-glance.

316   Marie-Ève Milot and Marie-Claude St-Laurent looked at the vocabulary used in the critical assessment of men's and women's work, in their performance *La place des femmes en théâtre: Chantier féministe*, Montréal, L'ESPACE GO, April 8 to 13, 2019, espacego.com/les-spectacles/2018-2019 /la-place-des-femmes-en-theatre-chantier-feministe.

317   Luce Irigaray, "Ce sexe qui n'en est pas un," *Les Cahiers du GRIF* 5 (1974): 54–58.

318   Grayson Perry, "Grayson Perry: The Rise and Fall of Default Man," *New Statesman America*, October 8, 2014, www.newstatesman.com/long-reads /2014/10/grayson-perry-rise-and-fall-default-man.

319   Perry.

320   Criado Perez, *Invisible Women*, 3.

321   Criado Perez, 13.

322   Criado Perez, 5.

323   Criado Perez, 21.

324   Perry, "Grayson Perry: The Rise and Fall of Default Man."

325   Perry.

326   Perry.

327   Richard Dyer wrote, "One would think that writing about images of male

sexuality would be as easy as anything. We live in a world saturated with images, drenched in sexuality. But this is one of the reasons why it is in fact difficult to write about. Male sexuality is a bit like air – you breathe it in all the time, but you aren't aware of it much"; *The Matter of Images: Essays on Representation* (New York: Routledge, 2013 [1993]), 89.

328   Ross Chambers, "The Unexamined," in *Whiteness: A Critical Reader*, ed. Mike Hill (New York University Press, 1997), 187–203.

329   "The sexual life of adult women is a 'dark continent' for psychology"; Sigmund Freud, *The Question of Lay Analysis: Conversations with an Impartial Person*, trans. James Strachey (New York: W.W. Norton, 1969), 43.

330   Chambers, "The Unexamined," 193.

331   Chambers, 202.

332   Translator's note: For almost three hundred years, normative French grammar held and taught that "the masculine takes precedence over the feminine," which, while nominally intended to be neutral, is of course in fact exclusive, and an everyday example of the masculine-as-default.

333   See Todd W. Reeser, *Masculinities in Theory: An Introduction* (Hoboken, NJ: Wiley-Blackwell, 2013), 9.

334   George Yancy, *Look, a White!: Philosophical Essays on Whiteness* (Philadelphia: Temple University Press, 2012).

335   "Marking whiteness is about exposing the ways in which whites have created a form of 'humanism' that obfuscates their hegemonic efforts to treat their experiences as universal and representative"; Yancy, 7.

336   Thomas Thévenoud, "Alice Coffin: Le neutre, c'est la subjectivité des dominants," *Revue Charles*, December 8, 2020, revuecharles.fr/100-politique /entretiens/femme-d-influence/alice-coffin-le-neutre-cest-la-subjectivite -des-dominants.

337   Cécile Chambraud, "Les sénateurs adoptent un 'amendement UNEF' permettant de dissoudre les associations faisant des réunions non mixtes racisées," *Le Monde*, April 2, 2021, www.lemonde.fr/societe/article/2021/04/02/les -senateurs-adoptent-un-amendement-unef-permettant-de-dissoudre-les -associations-faisant-des-reunions-non-mixtes-racisees_6075311_3224.html.

CHAPTER SEVENTEEN: ON GOVERNMENT

338   Iris Marion Young, "Gender as Seriality: Thinking about Women as a Social Collective," *Signs* 19, no. 3 (Spring 1994): 713–738.

339   Jackson Katz, "Violence Against Women: It's a Men's Issue," Ted, November

2012, www.ted.com/talks/jackson_katz_ violence_against_women_it_s_a_ men_s_issue? language=en-ca.

340 Michel Foucault, *Security, Territory, Population: Lectures at the Collège de France 1977–1978*, trans. Graham Burchell (London: Palgrave Macmillan, 2007), 88.

341 The third season of *Designated Survivor* is particularly interesting in how it tackles a range of sensitive American political and economic issues head-on – pharmaceutical companies, for example, including the opioid crisis, the cost of insulin, etc. – as well as social issues, such as HIV and sex when the virus is undetectable, trans rights, the right to die, etc.; *Designated Survivor*, created by David Guggenheim, featuring Kiefer Sutherland, aired 2016–2019 on ABC and Netflix.

342 *Scandal*, "Baby, It's Cold Outside," season 5, episode 9, directed by Tom Verica, written by Mark Wilding, aired November 19, 2015, on ABC.

343 *House of Cards*, season 6.

344 Manon Massé, long-time Québec Solidaire MNA and the party's former co-spokesperson, spoke out against boys' club culture: "for thirty years, the same clique has been passing the puck of power back and forth"; Manon Massé, "Féministe, puisqu'il le faut encore," *Le Devoir*, March 8, 2018, www. ledevoir.com/opinion/idees/522117/feministe-puisqu-il-le-faut-encore?. Her comments sparked a torrent of protests from various Québec politicians. See Caroline Plante, "'Boys club': des propos de Manon Massé décriés," *Le Droit*, March 15, 2018, www.ledroit.com/2018/03/15/boys-club-des-propos -de-manon-masse-decries-7d88442734551c29d893c92f87984a6b.

345 Pascale Navarro, *Femmes et pouvoir: Les changements nécessaires. Plaidoyer pour la parité* (Montréal: Leméac, 2015).

346 In Québec, after François Legault was elected, it was noted that "the CAQ rhetoric around equality stopped at the cabinet doors ... In all, there are twice as many men as women in cabinet positions: nineteen men (68 percent) compared to nine women (32 percent) ... Since he took over, Legault made twenty-one senior civil service appointments, seven of which went to women (33 percent) and fourteen, twice as many, to men (66 percent) ... The most strategic and best-paid positions in the public service were reserved for men"; Jocelyne Richer, "Le 'boys' club' de François Legault," *Le Devoir*, November 5, 2018, www.ledevoir.com/politique/quebec/540633/les-hommes-aux -commandes-de-l-etat-le-boys-club-de-francois-legault.

347 Navarro, *Femmes et pouvoir*, 26.

348 Françoise Collin, "La démocratie est-elle démocratique?," *Anthologie québécoise, 1977–2000* (Montréal : Remue-ménage, 2014), 73.

349   Giorgio Agamben, *Homo Sacer: Sovereign Power and Bare Life*, trans. Daniel Heller-Roazen (Stanford, CA: Stanford University Press, 1998), 188.

350   Katha Pollitt, "Why We Need Women in Power," *Nation*, March 3, 2016, www.thenation.com/article/archive/why-we-need-women-in-power.

351   Pollitt.

352   Pollitt.

353   See Raphaëlle Bacqué, "En 2018, les conseillères de l'Élysée dénonçaient des comportements misogynes au plus haut sommet de l'État," *Le Monde*, August 6, 2020, www.lemonde.fr/politique/article/2020/08/06/en-2018 -les-conseilleres-de-l-elysee-denoncaient-des-comportements-misogynes -au-plus-haut-sommet-de-l-etat_6048277_823448.html.

354   Translator's note: #SciencesPorcs, a play on words that replaces the abbreviation of "politiques" with "porc," meaning "hog," in the popular informal moniker of the Paris Institute of Political Studies, is an echo of the French version of #MeToo, #BalanceTonPorc, a call to literally "denounce your hog," i.e., sexual aggressor.

355   "#SciencesPorcs: La militante féministe Anna Toumazoff dénonce le 'choix délibéré' des IEP 'de laisser les violeurs dans l'impunité,'" France Info, February 10, 2021, www.francetvinfo.fr/societe/harcelement-sexuel/sciencesporcs -la-militante-feministe-anna-toumazoff-denonce-le-choix-delibere-des-iep -de-laisser-les-violeurs-dans-l-impunite_4291057.html.

356   *Jessica Jones*, created by Melissa Rosenberg, featuring Krysten Ritter, aired 2015–2018 on Netflix.

357   *Jessica Jones*, "AKA WWJD?," season 1, episode 8, directed by Simon Cellan Jones, written by Scott Reynolds, aired November 20, 2015, on Netflix.

358   Silvia Federici, *Le capitalisme patriarcal*, trans. Étienne Dobenesque (Paris: La Fabrique, 2019), 143.

359   Federici, 159. Federici links that resistance by women to the birth of psychoanalysis: "Freud's proposal is for freer sexuality for a healthier family life, for a family where the woman can identify with her function as wife, instead of becoming hysterical or neurotic and wrapping herself in a veil of frigidity after the first few months of marriage, and perhaps being tempted to transgress through 'degenerate' experiments like lesbianism," 164. From Freud to sexual liberation via the Kinsey report, the Masters and Johnson experiments, the existence of the female orgasm and the G-spot, sex has become an imperative, even a job. "The main difference," Federici writes, "is that our mothers and grandmothers saw sexual services in terms of an exchange: you slept with the man you married, in other words, the man

who promised you a certain amount of financial security. Today, on the other hand, we work for free, both in bed and in the kitchen, not only because sex work is never paid for, but because more and more often we provide sexual services without expecting anything in return. The symbol of the liberated woman, moreover, is a woman who is always available but no longer asks for anything in return," 170–171.

360   Rebecca Solnit, "Men Explain *Lolita* to Me," Literary Hub, December 17, 2015, lithub.com/men-explain-lolita-to-me.

361   Woolf, *A Room of One's Own*, 28.

CHAPTER EIGHTEEN: EVERYMAN

362   *The Accused*, directed by Jonathan Kaplan (Los Angeles: Paramount Pictures, 1988).

363   During the promotional tour, Kelly McGillis, who plays the prosecutor in the film, spoke of having been gang raped herself. She insisted on identifying and prosecuting her attackers, even though the police said there was nothing they could do. One of them spent three years in prison; Kelly McGillis, "Memoir of a Brief Time in Hell," *People*, November 14, 1988, people.com /archive/cover-story-memoir-of-a-brief-time-in-hell-vol-30-no-20.

364   At the time of the film's release, the rape scene, which lasts only three minutes, was the longest, most explicit, and strongest cinematic depiction of sexual assault; see Rebecca Ford, "*The Accused*'s Oral History: A Brutal Rape Scene, Traumatized Actors and Producers' Fights to Make a Movie," *Hollywood Reporter*, December 5, 2016, www.hollywoodreporter.com/movies /movie-news/accused-oral-history-a-brutal-rape-scene-traumatized-actors -producers-fights-make-movie-952-952228.

365   Kaplan, *The Accused*. The men's screams reproduce the din during the hockey game McGillis's character attends with her boss, as a way of being one of the boys.

366   Among the testimonials about the shooting, Jodie Foster says she doesn't remember the rape scene as such: "I blanked out," she says. As for the actors who played the rapists, Ann Hearn, who played the waitress, noted, "The boys were incredibly upset. It seemed like nobody had expected how upsetting that would be for them." "The guys were just a mess," Foster corroborated; Ford, "*The Accused*'s Oral History."

367   *Top of the Lake* written by Jane Campion and Gerard Lee, featuring Elisabeth Moss, aired 2013 on BBC UK TV and BBC Two.

368   *Top of the Lake: China Girl*, written by Jane Campion and Gerard Lee, featuring Elisabeth Moss, aired 2017 on BBC UK TV and BBC Two.

369 Emily Chang, *Brotopia: Breaking Up the Boys' Club of Silicon Valley* (New York: Portfolio/Penguin, 2018).

370 Chang, 8.

371 Chang, 1.

372 There were many women in the shadows of "Man's" first steps on the moon, including Margaret Hamilton, JoAnn Morgan, Frances "Poppy" Northcutt, and Jamye Flowers Coplin. The feature film *Hidden Figures*, meanwhile, finally brought to light the Black women mathematicians behind Apollo 11, Kathryn Johnson, Dorothy Vaughan and Mary Jackson; *Hidden Figures* directed by Theodore Melfi (Century City, CA: Fox 2000 Pictures, Chemin Entertainment, and Levantine Film, 2016).

373 Chang, *Brotopia*, 33.

374 Chang, 177–185.

375 Chang, 43–48.

376 Anita Sarkeesian, *Tropes vs. Women in Video Games* (Feminist Frequency, YouTube, 2009–2017).

377 Emily A. Vogels, "Teens and Cyberbullying 2022," Pew Research Center, December 15, 2022, www.pewresearch.org/internet/2022/12/15/teens-and-cyberbullying-2022.

378 Aurore Gayte, "Cyberharcèlement: D'où viennent ces emojis médaille qui inondent des comptes Instagram?" Numerama, February 25, 2021, www.numerama.com/politique/691419-cyberharcelement-dou-viennent-ces-emojis-medaille-qui-inondent-des-comptes-instagram.html.

379 Gayte.

380 *Sale pute*, directed by Florence Hainaut and Myriam Leroy (Brussels: Kwassa Films, 2021); the film was released in English with the title *#FatUglySlut*.

381 Ludivine Ponciau, "Alice Barbe, insultée et menacée pour avoir pris la parole en faveur des migrants: 'Elle doit aimer le vis nègre,'" *Le Soir*, September 6, 2018, www.lesoir.be/177058/article/2018-09-06/alice-barbe-insultee-et-menacee-pour-avoir-pris-la-parole-en-faveur-des-migrants.

382 Isabelle Germain, "'#Salepute': Comment les cyberharceleurs musellent les femmes," *Les Nouvelles News*, June 23, 2021, www.lesnouvellesnews.fr/salepute-comment-les-cyberharceleurs-musellent-les-femmes.

383 *Sale pute.*

384 *Top of the Lake: China Girl.* Campion says of the scene, "I just based the café nerds on art school guys who do go to brothels, who were kind enough

to be honest about their experiences, and not very gross in the way that the people who write the prostitute reviews were"; quoted in Jennifer Vineyard, "*Top of the Lake: China Girl.* Jane Campion on Her 'Ovarian' Series," *New York Times*, September 12, 2017, www.nytimes.com/2017/09/12/arts/television/top-of-the-lake-china-girl-jane-campion.html.

385 Hannah Arendt, *Eichmann in Jerusalem: The Banality of Evil* (New York: Penguin, 2006 [1963]).

386 Arendt, 289.

387 Arendt.

CHAPTER NINETEEN: THE HUNT

388 *The General's Daughter*, directed by Simon West (Los Angeles: Paramount Pictures, 1999).

389 *The General's Daughter.*

390 Susan Faludi looks at the Citadel military academy, which, when her book was published, was still exclusively male. The school refused admission to women to preserve intimacy between men. Some cited the example of showering together: "When we're in the showers, it's very intimate," a senior cadet said. "We're one mass, naked together, and it makes us closer ... You're shaved, you're naked, you're afraid together. You can cry." As one of the teachers puts it, "With no women, we can hug each other. There's nothing so nurturing as an infantry platoon"; *Stiffed: The Betrayal of the American Man* (New York: HarperCollins, 1999), 68.

391 Guillaume Lecaplain and Anaïs Moran, "Lycée Saint-Cyr: Une machine à broyer les femmes," *Libération*, March 22, 2018, www.liberation.fr/france/2018/03/22/lycee-saint-cyr-une-machine-a-broyer-les-femmes_1638211.

392 As the sociologist Camille Boutron points out, "for centuries, the army has embodied masculine values: commanding and defending the nation is a man's job. This mindset is perpetuated by a military elite that is reluctant to make room for women"; quoted in Henri Vernet, "On fournit le même travail qu'un homme: le long combat des femmes dans l'armée," *Le Parisien*, March 8, 2021, www.leparisien.fr/politique/on-fournit-le-meme-travail-qu-un-homme-le-long-combat-des-femmes-dans-l-armee-08-03-2021-8427543.php.

393 Suzanne Laplante Edward, who lost her daughter Anne-Marie in the Polytechnique massacre, said of the gun Lépine used, "it's a weapon for killing people. It's not a gun for killing deer"; quoted in Philippe Teisceira-Lessard, "Des semi-automatiques similaires à celui de Lépine toujours accessibles," *La Presse*, December 2, 2014, www.lapresse.ca/actualites/201412/01/01-4824299-des

-semi-automatiques-similaires-a-celui-de-lepine-toujours-accessibles.php. Sturm, Ruger & Co., which manufactures the Ruger Mini-14 used by Marc Lépine, nevertheless describes its weapon as "rugged, reliable and durable on the farm, ranch or in the deep woods"; Sturm, Ruger & Co., "Mini-14," ruger.com/products/mini14/overview.html.

394 Polytechnique commemoration ceremony, Montréal, Québec, December 6, 2014.

395 Francine Pelletier, "La zone gris foncé," *Le Devoir*, January 20, 2016, www.ledevoir.com/opinion/chroniques/460628/la-zone-gris-fonce.

396 Polytechnique commemoration ceremony.

397 Günther Anders, *La haine*, trans. Philippe Ivernel (Paris: Rivages, 2009), 36.

398 Anders, 38.

399 Zoe Williams, "'Raw Hatred': Why the 'Incel' Movement Targets and Terrorises Women," *Guardian*, April 25, 2018, www.theguardian.com/world /2018/apr/25/raw-hatred-why-incel-movement-targets-terrorises-women.

400 See Francis Dupuis-Déri's description of the movement in chapter six, "La crise aujourd'hui: Quels symptômes et quels discours?," *La crise de la masculinité: Autopsie d'un mythe tenace* (Montréal: Remue-ménage, 2018), 219–292.

401 Anders, *La haine*, 74.

402 Anders, 75.

403 Anders.

404 Anders, 76.

405 *The Hunting Ground*, directed by Kirby Dick (New York: RADiUS-TWC, 2015).

406 *The Invisible War*, directed by Kirby Dick (Los Angeles: Chain Camera Pictures, Independent Lens, Rise Films, ITVS, Fork Films, and Cuomo Cole Productions, 2012).

407 Much ink has been spilled, both in the United States and in Canada, on the issue of sexual assault in the military. Noémi Mercier and Alec Castonguay's investigation in *L'Actualité*, "Crimes sexuels: Le cancer qui ronge l'armée canadienne" (April 22, 2014, lactualite.com/societe/crimes-sexuels -le-cancer-qui-ronge-larmee-canadienne/), won a number of awards. Mercier published several articles, some documenting ex-corporal Stéphanie Raymond's fight to have her alleged assailant retried after he was acquitted by a panel of five male soldiers. The Supreme Court ruled that "there was

no evidence" to support a finding that the accused, André Gagnon, who was Stéphanie Raymond's superior at the time, "had taken reasonable steps to ascertain that the complainant was consenting"; R. v. Gagnon, 2018 SCC 41 (CanLII), [2018] 3 S.C.R. 3. Mercier's work had repercussions across Canada and around the world: in the weeks following the report's publication, more than four hundred articles appeared on the same subject. In 2019, the Canadian government announced that it would pay $900 million to settle multiple class-action lawsuits filed on behalf of victims of sexual harassment, discrimination, and sexual assault in the military; Murray Brewster, "Court clears $900M Settlement for Military and Civilian Victims of Sexual Misconduct," CBC, November 25, 2019, www.cbc.ca/news/politics/national -defence-armed-forces-sexual-assault-settlement-1.5372919.

408 *The Invisible War.*

409 Dave Philipps, "'This Is Unacceptable': Military Reports a Surge of Sexual Assaults in the Ranks," *New York Times*, May 2, 2019, www.nytimes.com /2019/05/02/us/military-sexual-assault.html.

410 Although Title IX in the United States tends to apply to the world of sport, the Civil Code of Québec includes sexual harassment, assault, and sexual violence that hinders a victim's access to education; Québec, Ministère du Travail, de l'Emploi et la Solidarité sociale, "Act to prevent and fight sexual violence in higher education institutions," P-22.1, 2017, c. 2, p. 8.

411 United States of America, "Jeanne Clery Disclosure of Campus Security Policy and Campus Crime Statistics Act," Pub. L. No. 101–542, 20 U.S.C. § 1092, 34 CFR 668.46 (1990).

412 "Take the Pledge," It's On Us, Civic Nation, 2023, www.itsonus.org/get -involved/take-the-pledge.

413 Manohla Dargis, "Review: *The Hunting Ground* Documentary, a Searing Look at Campus Rape," *New York Times*, February 27, 2015, www.nytimes.com /2015/02/27/movies/review-the-hunting-ground-documentary-a-searing -look-at-campus-rape.html.

414 *The Hunting Ground.*

415 Jessica Valenti, "Frat Brothers Rape 300 Percent More. One in 5 Women Is Sexually Assaulted on Campus. Should We Ban Frats?," *Guardian*, September 24, 2014, www.theguardian.com/commentisfree/2014/sep/24/rape -sexual-assault-ban-frats.

416 Valenti.

417 In June 2019, *Le Figaro* revealed that two women had been Photoshopped into a photo of Silicon Valley entrepreneurs showing an all-male meeting

(during a trip to Italy); Harold Grand, "Deux femmes 'photoshoppées' pour rendre une réunion de la Silicon Valley moins masculine," *Le Figaro*, June 13, 2019, www.lefigaro.fr/secteur/high-tech/deux-femmes-photoshoppees-pour -rendre-une-reunion-de-la-silicon-valley-moins-masculine-20190613.

418 Jessica Bennett describes the "fraternity pipeline": "They slide right into the boys club of the business world, where brothers land Wall Street jobs via the 'fraternity pipeline' ... a place where secret handshakes mean special treatment in an already male-dominated field. Fraternities have graduated plenty of brilliant Silicon Valley founders: the creators of Facebook and Instagram, among others. They've also brought us Justin Mateen, the founder of Tinder, who stepped down amid a sexual harassment lawsuit, and Evan Spiegel, the Snapchat CEO, whose apologized for e-mails sent while in the Stanford frat where Snapchat was founded, which discussed convincing sorority women to perform sex acts and drunkenly peeing on a woman in bed"; Jessica Bennett, "The Problem with Frats Isn't Just Rape. It's Power," *Time*, December 3, 2014, time.com/3616158/fraternity-rape-uva -rolling-stone-sexual-assault.

419 Bennett.

420 Valenti, "Frat Brothers Rape 300 Percent More."

421 Erin Gloria Ryan, "Infamous 'Rapebait' Frat Disbanded for Being Entirely Too Rapey," *Jezebel*, April 4, 2014, jezebel.com/infamous-rapebait-frat -disbanded-for-being-entirely-t-1558252895.

422 Jillian Rayfield, "Wesleyan Sued over 'Rape Factory' Frat," *Salon*, October 7, 2012, www.salon.com/2012/10/07/wesleyan_sued_over_rape_factory_frat.

423 Alice Park, "Yale Opts Out of DKE Punishment," *Yale Daily News*, January 17, 2019, yaledailynews.com/blog/2019/01/17/analysis-yales-unmoved -response-to-allegations-at-dke.

424 Kimmel, *Guyland*.

425 In Charlotte Allen, "Of Frats and Men," *Washington Examiner*, August 24, 2015, www.washingtonexaminer.com/weekly-standard/of-frats-and-men.

426 As Caitlin Flanagan, writes, "In 1825, at Union College, in upstate New York ... a small group of young men came up with a creative act of rebellion against the fun-busters who had them down: the formation of a secret club, which they grandly named the Kappa Alpha Society." "These early fraternities were in every way a measure of their time," writes Flanagan, quoting Nicholas Syrett; Nicholas L. Syrett, *The Company He Keeps: A History of White College Fraternities* (Chapel Hill: University of North Carolina Press, 2009); "They combined the secret handshakes and passwords of small boys' clubs; the symbols and rituals of Freemasonry; the new national interest in

Greek, as opposed to Roman, culture as a model for an emerging citizenry; and the popularity of literary societies"; Caitlin Flanagan, "The Dark Power of Fraternities," *Atlantic*, March 15, 2014, www.theatlantic.com/magazine/archive/2014/03/the-dark-power-of-fraternities/357580.

427   Flanagan lists as examples cases of falls in several fraternities, some of them fatal, and others causing paralysis.

428   Lionel Tiger, *Men in Groups* (New York: Routledge, 2017 [New York: Random House, 1969]).

429   Kelly Oliver, *Hunting Girls: Sexual Violence from* The Hunger Games *to Campus Rape* (New York: Columbia University Press, 2016).

430   Oliver, 7.

431   *Posh*, by Laura Wade, dir. Lyndsey Turner, Royal Court Theatre, London, April 2010.

432   *The Riot Club*, directed by Lone Scherfig (London: Blueprint Pictures, Film4, HanWay Films, and Pinewood Films, 2014).

433   On the parallel between Johnson and Donald Trump, see the *New York Times* editorial, "Donald Trump Too Tame for You? Meet Britain's Boris Johnson," *New York Times*, June 29, 2019, www.nytimes.com/2019/06/29/opinion/sunday/boris-johnson-britain-trump.html.

434   "Drinks Club 'Ritual' Wrecks Pub," BBC News, December 3, 2004, news.bbc.co.uk/2/hi/uk_news/england/oxfordshire/4066329.stm.

435   *The Riot Club*.

436   *The Riot Club*.

437   *The Riot Club*.

438   Amy Woolsey, "Total Carnage: The Timely Anger of *The Riot Club*," Film School Rejects (website), November 1, 2018, filmschoolrejects.com/timely-anger-the-riot-club.

CHAPTER TWENTY: BOYS WILL BE BOYS

439   Romain Blondeau, "Sur le tournage d'un bukkake, le X extrême," *Les Inrockuptibles*, July 30, 2015, www.lesinrocks.com/actu/bukkake-89314-30-07-2015.

440   Blondeau.

441   Translator's note: The film's English version is titled *One Deadly Summer*. *L'été meurtrier*, directed by Jean Becker (Paris: Société Nouvelle de Cinématographie, CAPAC, and TF1 Films Production, 1983).

442 "Strauss-Kahn Trial Hears of Lunchtime Sex Parties," BBC News, February 3, 2015, www.bbc.com/news/world-europe-31114468.

443 Virginie Despentes, *Baise-moi* (Paris : Florent Massot, 1994), 53–54.

444 Virginie Despentes, *King Kong théorie* (Paris: Grasset, 2006), 34–35.

445 Despentes, 47.

446 Despentes, 50–51.

447 Hélène Duffau, *Trauma* (Paris: Gallimard, 2003), 115.

448 Jennifer Preston, "How Blogger Helped the Steubenville Rape Case Unfold Online," *New York Times*, March 18, 2013, archive.nytimes.com/thelede. blogs.nytimes.com/2013/03/18/how-blogger-helped-steubenville-rape-case -unfold-online.

449 "What is Nirbhaya case?" *Times of India*, December 18, 2019, timesofindia. indiatimes.com/india/what-is-nirbhaya-case/articleshow/72868430.cms.

450 The role played by Anonymous in the Steubenville affair and the subsequent awareness campaigns about sexual violence among men's sports teams, and the silence surrounding sexual violence, is noteworthy and an interesting example of gender abolition in the context of a gang rape story. Similarly, the rape of Jyoti Singh led to unprecedented protests in India around sexual violence against women in a show of public mobilization against a culture that tends to blame the victims rather than the perpetrators. See the documentary by Nancy Schwartzman, *Roll Red Roll* (New York: Together Films and POV, 2018).

451 See Sharmila Lodhia, "From 'Living Corpse' to India's Daughter: Exploring the Social, Political and Legal Landscape of the 2012 Delhi Gang Rape," *Women's Studies International Forum* 50 (2015): 89–101, www.scu.edu/media /ethics-center/business-ethics/Lodhia-From-Living-Corpse-to-India's -Daughter-Women's-Studies-International-Forum.pdf.

452 "Leaked Steubenville Big Red Rape Video," Don Carpenter, January 2, 2013, YouTube video, 12:28, youtu.be/W1oahqCzwcY.

453 Vivian Yee, "Statutory Rape, Twitter and a Connecticut Town's Divide," *New York Times*, April 4, 2013, www.nytimes.com/2013/04/05/nyregion /generational-divide-in-torrington-conn-over-sex-assault-case.html.

454 I'm thinking too of gynecological exams performed on patients under anesthetic by medical students, a practice permitted in some US medical programs, and which is legal in forty-two US states. The practice has also been denounced in France; see Phoebe Friesen, "Educational Pelvic Exams on Anesthetized Women: Why Consent Matters," *Bioethics* 32, no.

5 (April 2018), www.researchgate.net/publication/324721606_Educational
_pelvic_exams_on_anesthetized_women_Why_consent_matters, and
Lucile Quillet, "Toucher vaginal sans consentement: Une pratique bien
réelle," *Le Figaro*, October 28, 2015, madame.lefigaro.fr/societe/polemique
-touchers-vaginaux-patientes-endormies-non-consententes-050215-94255.

455 Ariel Levy, "Trial by Twitter," *New Yorker*, July 29, 2013, www.newyorker.
com/magazine/2013/08/05/trial-by-twitter.

456 Levy.

457 "Leaked Steubenville Big Red Rape Video."

458 Michael E. Miller, "All-American Swimmer Found Guilty of Sexually
Assaulting Unconscious Woman on Stanford Campus," *Washington Post*,
March 31, 2016, www.washingtonpost.com/news/morning-mix/wp/2016/03
/31/all-american-swimmer-found-guilty-of-sexually-assaulting-unconscious
-woman-on-stanford-campus.

459 Liam Stack, "Light Sentence for Brock Turner in Stanford Rape Case Draws
Outrage," *New York Times*, June 6, 2016, www.nytimes.com/2016/06/07
/us/outrage-in-stanford-rape-case-over-dueling-statements-of-victim-and
-attackers-father.html.

460 Katie J.M. Baker, "Here's the Powerful Letter the Stanford Victim Read
to Her Attacker," BuzzFeed News, June 3, 2016, www.buzzfeednews.com
/article/katiejmbaker/heres-the-powerful-letter-the-stanford-victim-read
-to-her-ra.

461 Victor Xu, "The Full Letter Read by Brock Turner's Father at His Sentencing
Hearing," *Stanford Daily*, June 8, 2016, stanforddaily.com/2016/06/08/the
-full-letter-read-by-brock-turners-father-at-his-sentencing-hearing.

462 Roxane Gay, *Hunger: A Memoir of (My) Body* (New York: HarperCollins,
2017), 35–36.

CHAPTER TWENTY-ONE: THE LOL LEAGUES

463 *The Fall*, created and written by Allan Cubitt, directed by Jakob Verbruggen
and Allan Cubitt, featuring Gillian Anderson, aired 2014–2016 on BBC Two,
RTÉ One, and ZDTneo.

464 Based on Sara McClelland, "Intimate Justice: Sexual Satisfaction in Young
Adults" (Ph.D. diss., City University of New York, 2009); quoted in Lili
Loofbourow, "The Female Price of Male Pleasure," *Week*, January 25, 2018,
theweek.com/articles/749978/female-price-male-pleasure.

465 Jian Ghomeshi, "Reflections from a Hashtag: My Path to Public Toxicity,"

New York Review of Books, October 11, 2018, www.nybooks.com/articles /2018/10/11/reflections-hashtag.

466 Mimi Rocah, Barbara McQuade, Jill Wine-Banks, Joyce White Vance, and Maya Wiley, "Brett Kavanaugh Allegations: Why They Are Not Simply a 'He Said, She Said' Situation," NBC News, September 18, 2018, www.nbcnews. com/think/opinion/allegations-against-brett-kavanaugh-are-not-simply -he-said-she-ncna910771.

467 Jessica Kegu, "Christine Blasey Ford Says She Remembers 'Uproarious Laughter' of Alleged Attackers," CBS News, September 17, 2018, www.cbs-news.com/news/christine-blasey-ford-says-she-remembers-uproarious -laughter-of-alleged-attackers-brett-kavanaugh. After Kavanaugh's testi-mony, Blasey Ford's phrase "indelible in the hippocampus is the laughter" was spraypainted on the ground at Yale University, including in front of the law school; Sammy Westfall and Asha Prihar, "Ford Quotes Spray Painted around Campus," *Yale Daily News*, October 24, 2018, yaledailynews.com /blog/2018/10/24/ford-quotes-spray-painted-around-campus.

468 Maggie Haberman and Peter Baker, "Trump Taunts Christine Blasey Ford at Rally," *New York Times*, October 2, 2018, www.nytimes.com/2018/10/02 /us/politics/trump-me-too.html.

469 Haberman and Baker.

470 Jia Tolentino, "Brett Kavanaugh, Donald Trump, and the Things Men Do for Other Men," *New Yorker*, September 26, 2018, www.newyorker.com/news /our-columnists/brett-kavanaugh-donald-trump-and-the-things-men-do -for-other-men.

471 Tolentino.

472 *In the Company of Men*, directed by Neil LaBute (Los Angeles: Atlantis Entertainment and Company One Productions, 1997).

473 As Chad says to Howard, "We keep playing along ... with this 'pick up the check,' 'can't a girl change her mind' crap ... and we can't even tell a joke in the workplace? There's going to be hell to pay down the line, no doubt about it. We need to put our foot down"; *In the Company of Men*.

474 *In the Company of Men*.

475 Lili Loofbourow, "Brett Kavanaugh and the Cruelty of Male Bonding: When Being One of the Guys Comes at a Woman's Expense," *Slate*, September 25, 2018, slate.com/news-and-politics/2018/09/brett-kavanaugh-allegations -yearbook-male-bonding.html.

476 Emily Nussbaum, "Reacting to the Louis C.K. Revelations," *New Yorker*,

November 9, 2017, www.newyorker.com/culture/cultural-comment/reacting -to-the-louis-ck-revelations.

477   *Girls*, season 6, episode 3, "American Bitch," directed by Richard Shepard, written by Lena Dunham, aired February 26, 2017, on HBO.

478   *Girls*, "American Bitch."

479   Roxane Gay, "Louis C.K. and Men Who Think Justice Takes as Long as They Want It To," *New York Times*, August 29, 2018, www.nytimes.com/2018 /08/29/opinion/louis-ck-comeback-justice.html.

480   Katie Way, "I Went on a Date with Aziz Ansari. It Turned into the Worst Night of My Life," Babe, January 14, 2018, babe.net/2018/01/13/aziz-ansari -28355.

481   Only one of the fourteen criminal charges against Rozon was upheld. In January 2019, Rozon was charged with rape and indecent assault for acts committed thirty-nine years earlier. The civil class action suit, authorized by the Superior Court of Québec, was contested by Rozon's lawyers; Améli Pineda, "Comparution de Gilbert Rozon, accusé de viol et d'attentat à la pudeur," *Le Devoir*, January 22, 2019, www.ledevoir.com/societe/546069 /comparution-de-gilbert-rozon-accuse-de-viol-et-d-attentat-a-la-pudeur.

482   Louis Nadau, "Affaire 'Ligue du LOL': Le crash des journalistes 'caïds de Twitter,'" *Marianne*, February 11, 2019, www.marianne.net/societe/affaire -ligue-du-lol-le-crash-des-journalistes-caids-de-twitter.

483   Nadau.

484   Lâm Hua, quoted in Fabien Jannic-Cherbonnel, "'Ligue du LOL': 'Les mises à pied c'est bien mais on veut des embauches de femmes et de minorités aux postes à responsabilité,'" *Komitid*, February 11, 2019, www.komitid.fr/2019 /02/11/ligue-du-lol-les-mises-a-pied-cest-bien-mais-on-veut-des-embauches -de-femmes-et-de-minorites-aux-postes-a-responsabilite.

485   "Ligue du LOL: 6 journalistes écartés après des accusations de cyber-harcèlement," *Le Monde*, February 11, 2019, www.lemonde.fr/pixels/article /2019/02/11/ligue-du-lol-un-journaliste-de-liberation-mis-a-pied-a-titre -conservatoire_5422027_4408996.html.

486   Olivier Tesquet, "Pour en finir avec la culture web," *Télérama*, November 10, 2017, www.telerama.fr/medias/pour-en-finir-avec-la-culture-web,n5338155. php.

487   "Ligue du LOL: Une association féministe saisit le procureur de Paris," *TF1 Info*, May 20, 2019, www.tf1info.fr/societe/ligue-du-lol-association-feministe -prenons-la-une-saisit-le-procureur-de-paris-2121626.html.

488 Louise Auvitu and Béatrice Kammerer, "'Quand les seins tombent, je refuse la consultation.' Sur Facebook, des médecins violent leur serment," *L'Obs*, January 5, 2020, www.nouvelobs.com/notre-epoque/20200105.OBS23047 /quand-les-seins-tombent-comme-ca-je-refuse-la-consultation-sur-facebook -11-000-medecins-violent-leur-serment.html.

489 Auvitu and Kammerer.

490 *Je ne suis pas une salope, je suis une journaliste*, directed by Marie Portolano and Guillaume Priou (Issy-les-Moulineaux: Canal+, 2021).

491 Charles Bremner, "French TV Rugby Host Clémentine Sarlat Cries Foul over Sexism," *Times*, April 7, 2020, www.thetimes.co.uk/article/french-tv -rugby-host-clementine-sarlat-cries-foul-over-sexism-98365sjbh.

492 Megh Wright, "Hannah Gadsby Calls Out Hollywood's 'Good Men' for Their Hot Takes on Misogyny," *Vulture*, December 5, 2018, www.vulture.com/2018 /12/hannah-gadsby-hollywood-reporter-bad-men-sexism-misogyny.html.

493 Hannah Gadsby, "Hannah Gadsby Full Speech: 'The Good Men' & Misogyny | Women in Entertainment," *Hollywood Reporter*, December 5, 2018, YouTube video, 8:13, youtu.be/OEPsqFLhHBc.

494 Gadsby.

495 Saskia Schuster, head of the British comedy network ITV, has announced that she will no longer produce shows with an all-male scriptwriting team or with only "token woman": "Female writers often don't thrive as the lone female voice in the writing room," she says. She receives only one script written by a woman for every five written by men: "Too often the writing room is not sensitively run. It can be aggressive and slightly bullying"; quoted in "Head of ITV Comedy Drops All-Male Writing Teams," *Guardian*, June 18, 2019, www.theguardian.com/business/2019/jun/18/head-of -itv-comedy-drops-all-male-writing-teams.

496 United States Marine Corps, "We're Looking for a Few Good Men," Television advertisement, 1985, youtu.be/YC82SwuDrcE.

497 *A Few Good Men*, directed by Rob Reiner (Beverly Hills, CA: Castle Rock Entertainment, 1992).

498 Catharine A. MacKinnon, *Butterfly Politics: Changing the World for Women* (Cambridge, MA: Belknap Press of Harvard University Press, 2017), 330.

499 Catharine A. MacKinnon "Political Lawyers: Theories of Their Practice," student paper, 1976; quoted in MacKinnon, *Butterfly Politics*, 330.

CHAPTER TWENTY-TWO: THE SMURFETTE PRINCIPLE

500 Charlotte Beradt, *The Third Reich of Dreams*, trans. Adriane Gottwald (Chicago: Quadrangle Books, 1968), 9.

501 Beradt, 18.

502 Reinhart Koselleck, "Afterword to Charlotte Beradt's *The Third Reich of Dreams*," in *The Practice of Conceptual History: Timing History, Spacing Concepts*, trans. Todd Samuel Presner and others (Stanford, CA: Stanford University Press, 2002), 327–340.

503 Koselleck, 328, 339.

504 Pollitt coined the term; Katha Pollitt, "Hers; The Smurfette Principle," *New York Times*, April 7, 1991, www.nytimes.com/1991/04/07/magazine/hers-the-smurfette-principle.html.

505 Pollitt.

506 Yvan Delporte and Peyo, "The Smurfette," in *The Smurfs 3 in 1 #2: The Smurfette, The Smurfs and the Egg, and The Smurfs and the Howlibird*, no trans. (New York: Papercutz, 2018), 10.

507 Delporte and Peyo.

508 Delporte and Peyo; in "Holt Renfrew," a piece in Nelly Arcan's posthumous collection *Burqa de chair* in the book's section entitled "La honte" ("shame"), the Québec author refers to her appearance on a popular talk show, pointing out the Smurfette principle: she was the only woman among five men on the set, she was the only woman, sitting among five men: "She was the only possible prey on the panel"; Nelly Arcan, *Burqa of Skin*, trans. Melissa Bull (Vancouver: Anvil Press, 2014), 87.

509 *Donnie Darko*, directed by Richard Kelly (Los Angeles: Flower Films, Pandora Cinema, and Newmarket Films, 2001).

510 *Donnie Darko*.

511 Manohla Dargis, "What the Movies Taught Me About Being a Woman," *New York Times*, November 30, 2018, www.nytimes.com/interactive/2018/11/30/movies/women-in-movies.html.

512 Uzel, "Le montage," 66.

513 Erwin Panofsky, "Style and Medium in the Moving Pictures" (1934), in *Aesthetics: A Critical Anthology*, eds. George Dickie and R.J. Sclafani (New York: St. Martin's Press, 1977), 352.

514 Benjamin, *The Work of Art in the Age of Mechanical Reproduction*, 35.

515 Martha M. Lauzen, "It's a Man's (Celluloid) World, Even in a Pandemic Year:

Portrayals of Female Characters in the Top U.S. Films of 2021" (San Diego: Center for the Study of Women in Television and Film, 2022), womenintv-film.sdsu.edu/wp-content/uploads/2022/03/2021-Its-a-Mans-Celluloid-World-Report.pdf, 4.

516   Lauzen 1, 5.

517   Lauzen, 1, 9.

518   With regard to Québec feature film production, Isabelle Hayeur points out that while women account for between 43 and 60 percent of film and television students, as of 2016, they made up only 31 percent of the members of the Association des réalisateurs et réalisatrices du Québec. In the main public funding program, women make between 15 percent and 28 percent of recommended projects accepted and receive between 11 percent and 19 percent of budget allocations. However, the higher the budgets get, the fewer the women directors. Recent measures announced by the NFB in 2016 committed to parity in project grants and budget allocation; the same applies to Telefilm Canada and SODEC; Isabelle Hayeur and Sophie Bisson-nette, addendum, *Enfin l'équité pour les femmes en culture*, brief presented to the National Assembly of Québec June 16, 2016, www.mcc.gouv.qc.ca /fileadmin/documents/Politique-culturelle/Memoires___Metadonnees /REALISATRICES_EQUITABLES_Ajout_au_memoire.pdf. See also Anna Lupien with Francine Descarries and Réalisatrices équitables, *L'avant et l'arrière de l'écran: L'influence du sexe des cinéastes sur la représentation des hommes et des femmes dans le cinéma québécois recent* (Réalisatrices équitables, 2013), annalupien.com/L-avant-et-l-arriere-de-l-ecran. Lupien points out that "lead roles are significantly more often given to a man when a film is directed by a man." Lupien also considers a number of factors, such as the sexualization of characters and the emphasis placed on violence and power relations, in order to assess the impact of the director's gender iden-tity, which leads her to conclude that a greater number of female directors "would necessarily bring a diversity of points of view."

519   Martha M. Lauzen, "Boxed in 2018–19: Women on Screen and Behind the Scenes in Television," (San Diego: Center for the Study of Women in Television and Film, 2019), womenintvfilm.sdsu.edu/wp-content/uploads /2019/09/2018-19_Boxed_In_Report.pdf.

520   Lupien with Descarries and Réalisatrices équitables, 31.

521   Cédric Bélanger, "Place aux réalisatrices," *Journal de Québec*, December 17, 2018, www.journaldequebec.com/2018/12/17/place-aux-realisatrices.

522   Quoted in Clément Arbrun, " La parité dans le milieu du cinéma, une mission impossible?" *Terra femina*, January 6, 2021, www.terrafemina.com

/article/parite-l-egalite-des-sexes-dans-le-monde-du-cinema-est-elle-une
-mission-impossible_a356471/1.

523 Dargis, "What the Movies Taught Me."

524 Woolf, *A Room of One's Own*, 68.

525 Anita Sarkeesian's November 2013 YouTube episode, "Ms. Male Character –
Tropes vs. Male Character – Tropes vs. Women in Video Games," has been
viewed over a million times. Sarkeesian's feminist work, critiquing the world
of video games, among other things, on her *Feminist Frequency* website,
has earned her numerous death threats.

526 Women's roles vary between being the person to be saved (*War of the Worlds*,
Mission Impossible, the Jason Bourne series) and the object of desire (*The
Firm*, *Ocean's Eleven*). In other cases, the heroine is alone and represents
a threat to the boys' club (*Alien*, *Contact*, *The Silence of the Lambs*, *Zero
Dark Thirty*). Sometimes, she is a foreign, worrisome element (*It*, *Stranger
Things*), or else she is part of the group but always as a woman, an exception
in a male environment (*Seinfeld*, *Mad Men*, *Fargo*).

527 Dargis, "What the Movies Taught Me."

528 *Sicario*, directed by Denis Villeneuve (Los Angeles: Black Label Media and
Thunder Road, 2015).

529 Rebecca Keegan, "Why Emily Blunt's 'Sicario' role Role Was Almost Rewritten for a Man and How the FBI Helped Her Get Tough," *Los Angeles Times*,
September 24, 2015, www.latimes.com/entertainment/movies/la-et-mn
-emily-blunt-sicario-20150924-story.html.

CHAPTER TWENTY-THREE: BUTTERFLY EFFECT

530 Following Agamben, of course: Agamben, "What is an Apparatus?"

531 "It's not a simple fix; it takes time, planning, and buy-in. And closed networks can quickly become as toxic and cliquey as any boys' club, so it's
important to keep a focus on subverting that. But it's a power structure that
we *need* to begin creating for ourselves, because the alternative is either to
reify and support their existence by playing along or to be shut out entirely.
Neither is a good outcome. But by building our own systems and our own
structures, we can get around them entirely. And that's good for everyone";
Liz Elting, "How to Navigate a Boys' Club Culture," *Forbes*, July 27, 2018,
www.forbes.com/sites/lizelting/2018/07/27/how-to-navigate-a-boys-club
-culture/?sh=45d1a034025c.

532 *Paris is Burning*, directed by Jennie Livingston (New York: Academy Entertainment, Off-White Productions, and Prestige Pictures, 1990).

533 *Moonlight*, directed by Barry Jenkins (New York: A24, Plan B Entertainment, and Pastel Productions, 2016).

534 *Dallas Buyers Club*, directed by Jean-Marc Vallée (Truth Entertainment and Voltage Pictures, 2013).

535 *The Hurt Locker*, directed by Kathryn Bigelow (Los Angeles: Voltage Pictures, Grosvenor Park Media, Film Capital Europe Funds, First Light Productions, and Kingsgate Films, 2008).

536 *Fury*, directed by David Ayer (Culver City, CA: Columbia Pictures, QED International, LStar Capital, Le Grisbi Productions, and Crave Films, 2014).

537 *Chernobyl*, directed by Johan Renck, created and written by Craig Mazin, produced by Sanne Wohlenberg, aired May 6–June 3, 2019, on HBO and Sky Atlantic, 2019.

538 *Billions*, created by Brian Koppelman, David Levien, Andrew Ross Sorkin, featuring Paul Giamatti and Damian Lewis, aired January 17, 2016–October 29, 2023, on Showtime.

539 *Drag King*, directed by Ben Churchill (Radio Trip Pictures, 2015).

540 *Antlers*, directed by André-Line Beauparlant (Montréal: Coop Vidéo de Montréal and Les Productions 23 Inc., 2007).

541 *Your Friends & Neighbors*, directed by Neil LaBute (PolyGram Filmed Entertainment, 1998).

542 *Goat*, directed by Andrew Neel (New York: Great Point Media, Killer Films, and Rabbit Bandini Productions, 2016).

543 *Mad Men*, created by Matthew Weiner, aired July 19, 2007–May 17, 2015, on AMC.

544 *Hochelaga, Land of Souls*, directed by François Girard (Montréal: Max Films, 2017).

545 *Before the Streets*, directed by Chloé Leriche (Montréal: Les films de l'autre and Telefilm Canada, 2016).

546 Agamben, *What Is an Apparatus?*, 23.

547 Black, *A Room of His Own*, 232.

548 Quoted in Black.

549 Black, 231.

550 Black, 234.

551 Black, 231.

552 Black, 219.

Endnotes

553   There was so much still going on as this book's original French edition was
      being wrapped up: Donald Trump had just openly insulted young female US
      congresswomen from diverse backgrounds. The American financier Jeffrey
      Epstein had just died by suicide after being jailed for sex trafficking and
      abusing a staggering number of underage girls, having been protected for a
      long time by the rich and famous boys' club of which he was a member. In
      the United States and Canada, on the eve of the Canadian 2019 elections and
      as we looked to the American elections in 2020, abortion rights were under
      attack from all sides and in a thousand and one ways. HBO was broadcasting
      the series *The Loudest Voice* about Roger Ailes and his abuse of power and
      sexual assaults, and Hulu had announced the imminent broadcast of the
      documentary *Untouchable*, about Hollywood producer Harvey Weinstein,
      who had by then been accused of sexual violence by over eighty women.
      And Netflix had just aired the documentary miniseries *The Family*, based
      on Jeff Sharlet's investigative books, about an ultra-Christian American
      group called Ivanwald, an all-male organization based on the segregation
      of the sexes and the cohabitation of "brothers," in the manner of college
      fraternities. Ivanwald has everything to do with power, powerful men of
      power in general, throughout the world, and the US Congress in particular:
      its aim is to implant in the minds of young American men the conviction
      that they have been chosen by God to be leaders. The organization, which
      might have been described as a private club called the church, invisibly
      wielded a great deal of undemocratic power... like others before and since.

Works Cited

Agamben, Giorgio. "What is an Apparatus?" *What is an Apparatus? and Other Essays.* Translated by David Kishik and Stefan Pedatella. 1–24. Stanford, CA: Stanford University Press, 2009.

———. *Homo Sacer: Sovereign Power and Bare Life.* Translated by Daniel Heller-Roazen. Stanford: Stanford University Press, 1998.

———. *Remnants of Auschwitz: The Witness and the Archive.* Translated by Daniel Heller-Roazen. New York: Zone Books, 1999.

———. *Stasis: Civil War as a Political Paradigm.* Translated by Nicholas Heron. Edinburgh: Edinburgh University Press, 2015.

Allaire, Christian. "Billy Porter on Why He Wore a Gown, Not a Tuxedo, to the Oscars." *Vogue*, February 24, 2019. www.vogue.com/article/billy-porter-oscars-red-carpet-gown-christian-siriano.

Allen, Charlotte. "Of Frats and Men." *Washington Examiner*, August 24, 2015. www.washingtonexaminer.com/weekly-standard/of-frats-and-men.

Anders, Günther. *La haine.* Translated by Philippe Ivernel. Paris: Rivages, 2009.

Arbrun, Clément. "La parité dans le milieu du cinema, une mission impossible?" *Terra femina*, January 6, 2021. www.terrafemina.com/article/parite-l-egal-ite-des-sexes-dans-le-monde-du-cinema-est-elle-une-mission-impossible_a356471/1.

Arcand, Denys, dir. *Le règne de la beauté.* 2014; Montréal: Cinémaginaire. English version: *An Eye for Beauty.*

Archigraphie 2022/23: Observatoire de la profession d'architecte. Paris: Ordre des Architectes, 2023.

Arendt, Hannah. *Eichmann in Jerusalem: The Banality of Evil.* New York: Penguin, 2006 [1963].

Arieff, Allison. "Where Are All the Female Architects?" *New York Times*, December 15, 2018. www.nytimes.com/2018/12/15/opinion/sunday/women-architects.html.

Astor, Maggie, Christina Caron, and Daniel Victor. "A Guide to the Charlottesville Aftermath." *New York Times*, August 13, 2017. www.nytimes.com/2017/08/13/us/charlottesville-virginia-overview.html.

Audi, Anthony. "Donald Trump Modeled His Life on Cinematic Loser Charles Foster Kane: What Does a Presidential Candidate's Favorite Movie Reveal?"

Literary Hub, October 26, 2016. lithub.com/donald-trump-modeled-his-life-on-cinematic-loser-charles-foster-kane.

Auvitu, Louise, and Béatrice Kammerer. "'Quand les seins tombent, je refuse la consultation.' Sur Facebook, des médecins violent leur serment." *L'Obs*, January 5, 2020. www.nouvelobs.com/notre-epoque/20200105.OBS23047/quand-les-seins-tombent-comme-ca-je-refuse-la-consultation-sur-facebook-11-000-medecins-violent-leur-serment.html.

Ayer, David, dir. *Fury*. 2014; Culver City, CA: Columbia Pictures, QED International, LStar Capital, Le Grisbi Productions, Crave Films.

Bacqué, Raphaëlle. "En 2018, les conseillères de l'Élysée dénonçaient des comportements misogynes au plus haut sommet de l'État." *Le Monde*, August 6, 2020. www.lemonde.fr/politique/article/2020/08/06/en-2018-les-conseilleres-de-l-elysee-denoncaient-des-comportements-misogynes-au-plus-haut-sommet-de-l-etat_6048277_823448.html.

Badham, Van. "'Mentrification': How Men Appropriated Computers, Beer and the Beatles." *Guardian*, May 28, 2019. www.theguardian.com/music/2019/may/29/mentrification-how-men-appropriated-computers-beer-and-the-beatles.

Baker, Katie J.M. "Here's the Powerful Letter the Stanford Victim Read to Her Attacker." BuzzFeed News, June 3, 2016. www.buzzfeednews.com/article/katiejmbaker/heres-the-powerful-letter-the-stanford-victim-read-to-her-ra.

Balbastre, Gilles, and Yannick Kergoat, dirs. *Les nouveaux chiens de garde*. 2012; Paris: JEM Productions.

Bank, Dylan, Daniel DiMauro, and Morgan Pehme, dirs. *Get Me Roger Stone*. 2017; Los Gatos, CA: Netflix.

Bastide, Lauren. *Présentes: Ville, médias, politique ... quelle place pour les femmes?* Paris: Allary, 2020.

Baudet, Marie-Béatrice. "Affaire Olivier Duhamel: Le Siècle, club de l'élite et temple de la bienséance, aimerait continuer à dîner en paix." *Le Monde*, February 10, 2021. www.lemonde.fr/societe/article/2021/02/10/affaire-olivier-duhamel-le-siecle-club-de-l-elite-et-temple-de-la-bienseance-aimerait-continuer-a-diner-en-paix_6069387_3224.html.

BBC News. "Drinks Club 'Ritual' Wrecks Pub." *BBC News*, December 3, 2004. news.bbc.co.uk/2/hi/uk_news/england/oxfordshire/4066329.stm.

———. "Strauss-Kahn Trial Hears of Lunchtime Sex Parties." February 3, 2015. www.bbc.com/news/world-europe-31114468.

Beauparlant, André-Line, dir. *Antlers*. Montréal: Coop Vidéo de Montréal and Les Productions 23 Inc., 2007.

Bélanger, Cédric. "Place aux réalisatrices." *Journal de Québec*, December 17, 2018. www.journaldequebec.com/2018/12/17/place-aux-realisatrices.

Benjamin, Walter. "Surrealism: The Last Snapshot of the European Intelligentsia." In *Reflections: Essays, Aphorisms, Autobiographical Writings*, edited by Peter Demetz, 177–192. Translated by Edmund Jephcott. New York: Harcourt Brace Jovanovich, 1978.

——. *The Work of Art in the Age of Mechanical Reproduction*. Translated by J.A. Underwood. New York: Penguin Books, 2008.

Benowitz, Shayne. "French Designer Makes a New Mark on Miami." *Miami Herald*, December 14, 2016. www.miamiherald.com/living/home-garden /article120896593.html.

Beradt, Charlotte. *The Third Reich of Dreams*. Translated by Adriane Gottwald. Chicago: Quadrangle Books, 1968.

Berger, Edward, dir. *Patrick Melrose*. Season 1, episode 1. "Bad News." Written by David Nicholls. Aired May 12, 2018, on Showtime.

BIG (website). big.dk.

Bigelow, Kathryn, dir. *The Hurt Locker*. 2008; Los Angeles: Voltage Pictures, Grosvenor Park Media, Film Capital Europe Funds, First Light Productions, Kingsgate Films.

Black, Barbara. *A Room of His Own: A Literary-Cultural Study of Victorian Clubland*. Athens, OH: Ohio University Press, 2012.

Blondeau, Romain. "Sur le tournage d'un bukkake, le X extrême." *Les Inrockuptibles*, July 30, 2015. www.lesinrocks.com/actu/bukkake-89314-30-07-2015.

Bouchard, Serge. "Le boys club ou la théorie du cercle impenetrable." *C'est fou*. Aired September 2, 2018, on Radio-Canada. ici.radio-canada.ca/ohdio/pre- miere/emissions/c-est-fou/segments/chronique/85446/boys-club-editorial -serge-bouchard-academie-francaise-clubs-prives-quebec.

Bourdieu, Pierre. *Masculine Domination*. Translated by Richard Nice. Stanford, CA: Stanford University Press, 2001.

Bradshaw, Percy V. *Brother Savages and Guests: A History of the Savage Club 1857–1957*. London: W.H. Allen, 1958.

Bremner, Charles. "French TV Rugby Host Clémentine Sarlat Cries Foul over Sexism." *Times*, April 7, 2020. www.thetimes.co.uk/article/french-tv-rugby -host-clementine-sarlat-cries-foul-over-sexism-98365sjbh.

Brown, Denise Scott. "Room at the Top?: Sexism and the Star System in Archi- tecture." In *Gender Space Architecture: An Interdisciplinary Introduction*, edited by Jane Rendell, Barbara Penner, and Iain Borden, 258–265. New York: Routledge, 2000.

Burke, Ashley. "Crisis on Ice: What You Need to Know about the Hockey Canada Scandal." CBC, July 29, 2022. www.cbc.ca/news/politics/hockey-canada -sexual-assault-crisis-parliamentary-committee-1.6535248.

Burnett, Mark, creator. *The Apprentice*. Featuring Donald Trump. Aired 2004–2017 on NBC.

Campion, Jane, and Gerard Lee, writers. *Top of the Lake*. Featuring Elisabeth Moss. Aired 2013 on BBC UK TV and BBC Two.

———. *Top of the Lake: China Girl*. Featuring Elisabeth Moss. Aired 2017 on BBC UK TV and BBC Two.

Capehart, Jonathan. "'The First White President' Is a 'Bad Dude.'" *Washington Post*, September 18, 2017. www.washingtonpost.com/blogs/post-partisan /wp/2017/09/18/the-first-white-president-is-a-bad-dude.

Carrilho, André. "American Psycho." *New Statesman* (cover), March 9, 2016.

Casselot, Marie-Anne. "L'habillement est un piège pour les femmes en politique." *Le Devoir*, December 22, 2018. www.ledevoir.com/societe/le-devoir-de /544175/l-habillement-est-un-piege-pour-les-femmes-en-politique.

CBC News. "What about the Squash? Female Player Weighs In on Debate Over Men's-Only Winnipeg Squash Racquet Club." CBC News Manitoba, January 17, 2018. www.cbc.ca/news/canada/manitoba/winnipeg-squash-racquet -club-men-only-1.4491162.

Cennini, Cennino. *Treatise on Painting*. Translated by Mary P. Merrifield [Originally Tambroni 1437]. London: Edward Lumley, 1844. archive.org/details /atreatiseonpain00merrgoog/page/n11/mode/2up.

Chambers, Ross. "The Unexamined." In *Whiteness: A Critical Reader*, edited by Mike Hill, 187–203. New York: New York University Press, 1997.

Chambraud, Cécile. "Les sénateurs adoptent un 'amendement UNEF' permettant de dissoudre les associations faisant des réunions non mixtes racisées." *Le Monde*, April 2, 2021. www.lemonde.fr/societe/article/2021/04/02/les -senateurs-adoptent-un-amendement-unef-permettant-de-dissoudre-les -associations-faisant-des-reunions-non-mixtes-racisees_6075311_3224.html.

Chang, Emily. *Brotopia: Breaking Up the Boys' Club of Silicon Valley*. New York: Portfolio/Penguin, 2018.

Churchill, Ben, dir. *Drag King*. 2015; Radio Trip Pictures.

Coates, Ta-Nehisi. *We Were Eight Years in Power: An American Tragedy*. New York: One World, 2017.

Collin, Françoise. "La démocratie est-elle démocratique?" In *Anthologie québé-coise, 1977–2000*. Montréal: Remue-ménage, 2014.

———. *Parcours féministe: Entretiens avec Irène Kaufer*. Brussels: Labor, 2005.

Confessore, Nicholas, Maggie Haberman, and Eric Lipton. "Trump's 'Winter White House': A Peek at the Exclusive Members' List at Mar-a-Lago." *New York Times*, February 18, 2017. www.nytimes.com/2017/02/18/us/mar-a -lago-trump-ethics-winter-white-house.html.

Le Corbusier. *The Decorative Art of Today*. Translated by James I. Dunnett. Cambridge, MA: MIT Press, 1987.

———. *The Modulor: A Harmonious Measure to the Human Scale, Universally Applicable to Architecture and Mechanics*. Translated by Peter de Francia and Anna Bostock. [Originally two vols., 1954, 1958.] Basel: Birkhäuser, 2000.

Cornwell, Alicia. "Making the Man: 'Suiting' Masculinity in Performance Art." *Eagle Feather* 2 (2005): 1–10.

Corriveau, Jeanne. "Au nom des femmes." *Le Devoir*, December 23, 2014. www .ledevoir.com/politique/montreal/427477/toponymie-au-nom-des-femmes.

Criado Perez, Caroline. *Invisible Women: Data Bias in a World Designed for Men*. New York: Abrams Press, 2019.

Cubitt, Allan, creator. *The Fall*. Directed by Jakob Verbruggen and Allan Cubitt. Featuring Gillian Anderson. Aired 2014–2016 on BBC Two, RTÉ One, and ZDTneo.

Dargis, Manohla. "Review: *The Hunting Ground* Documentary, a Searing Look at Campus Rape." *New York Times*, February 27, 2015. www.nytimes.com /2015/02/27/movies/review-the-hunting-ground-documentary-a-searing -look-at-campus-rape.html.

———. "What the Movies Taught Me About Being a Woman." *New York Times*, November 30, 2018. www.nytimes.com/interactive/2018/11/30/movies /women-in-movies.html.

De Beauvoir, Simone. *The Second Sex*. Translated by Howard M. Parshley. New York: Vintage Books, 1989.

Delporte, Yvan, and Peyo. "The Smurfette." In *The Smurfs 3 in 1 #2: The Smurfette, The Smurfs and the Egg, and The Smurfs and the Howlibird*, 7–46. No translator. New York: Papercutz, 2018.

Delvaux, Béatrice and Joëlle Meskens. "Les Racines élémentaires de Mona Chollet: 'J'ai vu des mecs bien blancs, bien cultivés se comporter de manière horrible.'" *Le Soir*, September 1, 2023. www.lesoir.be/534593/article/2023

-09-01/les-racines-elementaires-de-mona-chollet-jai-vu-des-mecs-bien
-blancs-bien.

"Democalypse 2016." *The Daily Show*. Aired June 16, 2015, on Comedy Central.

Denord, François, Paul Lagneau-Ymonet, and Sylvain Thine. "Aux dîners du Siècle, l'élite du pouvoir se restaure." *Le Monde diplomatique*, February 2011. www.monde-diplomatique.fr/2011/02/DENORD/20132.

Derrida, Jacques. *The Truth in Painting*. Translated by Geoffrey Bennington and Ian McLeod. Chicago: University of Chicago Press, 2020.

Despentes, Virginie. *Baise-moi*. Paris: Florent Massot, 1994.

———. *King Kong théorie*. Paris: Grasset, 2006.

Dick, Kirby, dir. *The Hunting Ground*. 2015; New York: RADiUS-TWC.

———. *The Invisible War*. 2012; Los Angeles: Chain Camera Pictures, Independent Lens, Rise Films, ITVS, Fork Films, Cuomo Cole Productions.

Didi-Huberman, Georges. *L'œil de l'histoire*. Vol. 2 of *Remontages du temps subi*. Paris: Les Éditions de Minuit, 2010.

Didion, Joan. *Sentimental Journeys*. New York: HarperCollins, 1993.

Duffau, Hélène. *Trauma*. Paris: Gallimard, 2003.

Duras, Marguerite. *Practicalities*. Translated by Barbara Bray. New York: Grove Press, 1992.

DuVernay, Ava, creator. *When They See Us*. Premiered May 31, 2019, on Netflix.

Eisenstein, Sergei. *The Eisenstein Reader*. Translated by Richard Taylor and William Powell. London: Bloomsbury Publishing, 2019.

El Mokhtari, Mouna. "La ville est faite par et pour les hommes." *Le Monde*, March 8, 2018. www.lemonde.fr/societe/video/2018/03/08/la-ville-est-faite -par-et-pour-les-hommes_5267465_3224.html.

Ellen, Barbara. "Cécile Duflot: A Woman In a Dress? Mon Dieu, Whatever Next?" *Guardian*, July 22, 2012. www.theguardian.com/commentisfree/2012/jul/22 /barbara-ellen-cecile-duflots-dress.

Ellis, Bret Easton. *White*. New York: Knopf Doubleday, 2019.

Ellis, Bret Easton, Mary Harron, and Christian Bale. "American Psycho," interview by Charlie Rose, *Charlie Rose*. Aired April 13, 2000, on PBS. charlierose .com/videos/1102.

Federici, Silvia. *Beyond the Periphery of the Skin: Rethinking, Remaking, and Reclaiming the Body in Contemporary Capitalism*. Oakland, CA: PM Press, 2019.

————. *Le capitalisme patriarcal*. Translated by Étienne Dobenesque. Paris: La Fabrique, 2019.

Filipovic, Jill. "What Donald Trump Thinks It Takes to Be a Man." *New York Times*, November 2, 2017. www.nytimes.com/2017/11/02/opinion/sunday/donald-trump-masculinity.html.

Fins, Antonio. "Trump Indictment and Mar-a-Lago: How Much Is Membership, What's It Like Inside, Do You See Melania?" *Palm Beach Post*, June 12, 2023. www.palmbeachpost.com/story/news/trump/2023/06/12/trump-mar-lago-florida-membership-cost-melania-celebrity-photos/70309203007.

Flanagan, Caitlin. "The Dark Power of Fraternities." *Atlantic*, March 15, 2014. www.theatlantic.com/magazine/archive/2014/03/the-dark-power-of-fraternities/357580.

Foucault, Michel. "The Confessions of the Flesh." In *Power/Knowledge: Selected Interviews and Other Writings*, edited by Colin Gordon. Translated by Colin Gordon, Leo Marshall, John Mepham, and Kate Soper. New York: Pantheon Books, 1980. 194–228.

————. *Security, Territory, Population: Lectures at the Collège de France 1977–1978*. Translated by Graham Burchell. London: Palgrave Macmillan, 2007.

France Info. "#SciencesPorcs: La militante féministe Anna Toumazoff dénonce le 'choix délibéré' des IEP 'de laisser les violeurs dans l'impunité.'" February 10, 2021. www.francetvinfo.fr/societe/harcelement-sexuel/sciencesporcs-la-militante-feministe-anna-toumazoff-denonce-le-choix-delibere-des-iep-de-laisser-les-violeurs-dans-l-impunite_4291057.html.

Friedman, Vanessa. "A Primer on Power Dressing From *House of Cards*." *New York Times*, June 8, 2017. www.nytimes.com/2017/06/08/fashion/house-of-cards-power-dressing-melania-trump-claire-underwood.html.

Fuss, Diana. *Essentially Speaking: Feminism, Nature and Difference*. New York: Routledge, 1989.

Gadsby, Hannah. "Hannah Gadsby Full Speech: 'The Good Men' & Misogyny | Women in Entertainment." *Hollywood Reporter*, December 5, 2018. YouTube video. 8:13. youtu.be/OEPsqFLhHBc.

Gallagher, Brenden. "*American Gigolo* and the Rise of the Armani Generation." Grailed, February 27, 2018. www.grailed.com/drycleanonly/american-gigolo-rise-of-armani.

Garner, Dwight. "In Hindsight, an 'American Psycho' Looks a Lot like Us." *New York Times*, March 24, 2016. www.nytimes.com/2016/03/27/theater/in-hindsight-an-american-psycho-looks-a-lot-like-us.html.

Gay, Roxane. *Hunger: A Memoir of (My) Body.* New York: HarperCollins, 2017.

———. "Louis C.K. and Men Who Think Justice Takes as Long as They Want It To." *New York Times,* August 29, 2018. www.nytimes.com/2018/08/29 /opinion/louis-ck-comeback-justice.html.

Gayte, Aurore. "Cyberharcèlement: D'où viennent ces emojis médaille qui inondent des comptes Instagram?" Numerama, February 25, 2021. www.numerama.com /politique/691419-cyberharcelement-dou-viennent-ces-emojis-medaille-qui -inondent-des-comptes-instagram.html.

Gentleman, Amelia. "Garrick Club Votes to Accept Female Members for First Time." *Guardian,* May 7, 2024. www.theguardian.com/uk-news/article /2024/may/07/garrick-club-votes-to-accept-female-members-women.

———. "Time, Gentlemen: When Will the Last All-Male Clubs Admit Women?" *Guardian,* April 30, 2015. www.theguardian.com/news/2015/apr/30/time -gentlemen-when-will-last-all-male-clubs-admit-women.

Germain, Isabelle. "'#Salepute': Comment les cyberharceleurs musellent les femmes." *Les Nouvelles News,* June 23, 2021. www.lesnouvellesnews.fr /salepute-comment-les-cyberharceleurs-musellent-les-femmes.

Ghomeshi, Jian. "Reflections from a Hashtag: My Path to Public Toxicity." *New York Review of Books,* October 11, 2018. www.nybooks.com/articles/2018 /10/11/reflections-hashtag.

Girard, François dir. *Hochelaga, Land of Souls.* 2017; Montréal: Max Films.

Glamour. "A History of Melania Trump's Most Talked-About Fashion Moments." August 26, 2020. www.glamour.com/gallery/melania-trump-most-talked -about-fashion-moments.

Glover, David, and Mark Raphael, producers. *Trump: An American Dream.* Episode 1. "Manhattan." First aired in the UK November 2017 on Channel 4.

Guggenheim, David, creator. *Designated Survivor.* Featuring Kiefer Sutherland. Aired 2016–2019 on ABC and Netflix.

Haberman, Maggie, and Peter Baker. "Trump Taunts Christine Blasey Ford at Rally." *New York Times,* October 2, 2018. www.nytimes.com/2018/10/02/us /politics/trump-me-too.html.

Hainaut, Florence, and Myriam Leroy, dirs. *Sale pute.* 2021; Brussels: Kwassa Films.

Hamblin, James. "Trump Is a Climax of American Masculinity." *Atlantic,* August 8, 2016. www.theatlantic.com/health/archive/2016/08/trump-masculinity -problem/494582.

Hanisch, Carol. "The Personal is Political." *Notes from the Second Year: Women's Liberation: Major Writings of the Radical Feminists* (1970): 76–77.

Harron, Mary, dir. *American Psycho*. 2000; Los Angeles: Edward R. Pressman Productions and Muse Productions.

Hartmann, Heidi. "The Unhappy Marriage of Marxism and Feminism: Towards a More Progressive Union." *Capital & Class* 3, no. 2 (1979): 1–33.

Hawgood, Alex. "The Men Powerful Enough to Wear the Same Thing Every Day." *New York Times*, April 3, 2015, www.nytimes.com/interactive/2015 /04/02/fashion/mens-style/The-Men-Powerful-Enough-to-Wear-the-Same -Thing.html.

Hawken, Abe. "Mayfair's Savile Club Bends 150-Year-Old 'Men Only' Rule to Allow a Transgender Member to Stay On after a Sex Change to a Woman (But Don't Get Your Hopes Up Ladies, It Is a One Off Only)." *Daily Mail*, November 5, 2017.

Hayden, Dolores. "What Would a Non-Sexist City Be Like? Speculations on Housing, Urban Design, and Human Work." In "Women and the American City." Supplement, *Signs* 5, no. 3 (1980): S170–S187.

Hill, Jordan, dir. *Beyond Boundaries: The Harvey Weinstein Scandal*. 2018; London: Entertain Me.

Irigaray, Luce. "Ce sexe qui n'en est pas un." *Les Cahiers du GRIF* 5 (1974): 54–58.

Jaggar, Alison M. "Responding to the Evil of Terrorism." *Hypatia* 18, no. 1 (2003): 179.

Jannic-Cherbonnel, Fabien. "'Ligue du LOL': 'Les mises à pied c'est bien mais on veut des embauches de femmes et de minorités aux postes à responsabil-ité.'" *Komitid*, February 11, 2019. www.komitid.fr/2019/02/11/ligue-du-lol -les-mises-a-pied-cest-bien-mais-on-veut-des-embauches-de-femmes-et-de -minorites-aux-postes-a-responsabilite.

Jenkins, Barry, dir. *Moonlight*. 2016; New York: A24, Plan B Entertainment, and Pastel Productions.

Jones, Simon Cellan, dir. *Jessica Jones*. Season 1, episode 8. "AKA WWJD?" Written by Scott Reynolds. Premiered November 20, 2015, on Netflix.

Kaplan, Jonathan, dir. *The Accused*. 1988; Los Angeles: Paramount Pictures.

Katz, Jackson. "Violence Against Women: It's a Men's Issue." Ted, November 2012. www.ted.com/talks/jackson_katz_ violence_against_women_it_s _a_men_s_issue.

Kay, Richard. "Fishy politics: Charles's club bans women." *Daily Mail*, October 21,

Works Cited   227

2012. www.dailymail.co.uk/news/article-2221229/Prince-Charless-Flyfishers
-Club-Bans-Women.html.

Keegan, Rebecca. "Why Emily Blunt's 'Sicario' Role Was Almost Rewritten for
a Man and How the FBI Helped Her Get Tough." *Los Angeles Times*, September 24, 2015. www.latimes.com/entertainment/movies/la-et-mn-emily
-blunt-sicario-20150924-story.html.

Kegu, Jessica. "Christine Blasey Ford Says She Remembers 'Uproarious Laughter'
of Alleged Attackers." CBS News, September 17, 2018. www.cbsnews.com
/news/christine-blasey-ford-says-she-remembers-uproarious-laughter-of
-alleged-attackers-brett-kavanaugh.

Kelly, Richard, dir. *Donnie Darko*. 2001; Los Angeles: Flower Films.

Kimmel, Michael S. *The Gender of Desire: Essays on Male Sexuality*. Albany, NY:
State University of New York Press, 2005.

———. *Guyland: The Perilous World Where Boys Become Men*. New York: HarperCollins, 2008.

King, Michelle, Robert King, and Phil Alden Robinson, creators. *The Good Fight*.
Produced by Scott Free Productions, King Size Productions, and CBS Studios. Aired 2017–2022 on CBS All Access.

King, Robert, dir. *The Good Fight*. Season 3, episode 1. "The One About the Recent
Troubles." Written by Michelle King and Robert King. Featuring Christine
Baranski. Aired March 14, 2019, on CBS All Access.

Koestenbaum, Wayne. "Foreword: The Eve Effect." In *Between Men: English Literature and Male Homosocial Desire*, thirtieth anniversary ed., by Eve Kosofsky
Sedgwick, ix–xvi. New York: Columbia University Press, 2015 [1985].

Koppelman, Brian, David Levien, and Andrew Ross Sorkin, creators. *Billions*.
Aired January 17, 2016–October 29, 2023, on Showtime.

Korsh, Aaron, creator. *Suits*. Produced by Gene Klein, Gabriel Macht, Patrick J.
Adams, and JM Danguilan. Aired 2011–2019 on USA Network.

Koselleck, Reinhart. "Afterword to Charlotte Beradt's *The Third Reich of Dreams*."
In *The Practice of Conceptual History: Timing History, Spacing Concepts*,
translated by Todd Samuel Presner and others, 327–340. Stanford: Stanford
University Press, 2002.

LaBute, Neil, dir. *Billions*. Season 1, episode 5. "The Good Life." Written by Heidi
Schreck. Aired February 14, 2016, on Showtime.

———. *In the Company of Men*. 1997; Los Angeles: Atlantis Entertainment and
Company One Productions.

———. *Your Friends & Neighbors*. 1998; PolyGram Filmed Entertainment.

Lacroix-Couture, Frédéric. "Un peu plus de femmes dans la toponymie montréal-aise." *Métro*, March 4, 2020. journalmetro.com/actualites/2425327/un-peu-plus-de-femmes-dans-la-toponymie-montrealaise.

Laughland, Oliver. "Donald Trump and the Central Park Five: The Racially Charged Rise of a Demagogue." *Guardian*, February 17, 2016. www.the-guardian.com/us-news/2016/feb/17/central-park-five-donald-trump-jogger-rape-case-new-york.

Lauzen, Martha M. "Boxed in 2018–19: Women on Screen and Behind the Scenes in Television." San Diego: Center for the Study of Women in Television and Film, 2019. womenintvfilm.sdsu.edu/wp-content/uploads/2019/09/2018-19_Boxed_In_Report.pdf.

———. "It's a Man's (Celluloid) World, Even in a Pandemic Year: Portrayals of Female Characters in the Top U.S. Films of 2021." San Diego: Center for the Study of Women in Television and Film, 2022. womenintvfilm.sdsu.edu/wp-content/uploads/2022/03/2021-Its-a-Mans-Celluloid-World-Report.pdf.

Layden, Anthony. "Chairman Anthony Layden's Report to Travellers Club Members." *London Evening Standard*, April 9, 2014. www.standard.co.uk/news/londoners-diary/chairman-anthony-layden-s-report-to-travellers-club-members-9248509.html.

LDV Studio Urbain. "Saviez-vous que l'urbanité était genrée?" Demain la ville (website), March 8, 2016. www.demainlaville.com/saviez-vous-que-lurbanite-etait-genree.

"Leaked Steubenville Big Red Rape Video." Don Carpenter, January 2, 2013. You-Tube video. 12:28. youtu.be/W1oahqCzwcY.

Leamer, Laurence. *Mar-a-Lago: Inside the Gates of Power at Donald Trump's Presidential Palace*. New York: Flatiron Books, 2019.

Lecaplain, Guillaume, and Anaïs Moran. "Lycée Saint-Cyr: Une machine à broyer les femmes." *Libération*, March 22, 2018. www.liberation.fr/france/2018/03/22/lycee-saint-cyr-une-machine-a-broyer-les-femmes_1638211.

Lechner, Julia. "Donald Trump's Favorite Movies." CBS News, December 6, 2016. www.cbsnews.com/pictures/donald-trumps-favorite-movies.

Lee, Spike, dir. *Jungle Fever*. 1991; Brooklyn, NY: 40 Acres and a Mule Filmworks.

Leitch, Luke. "Last Trump for the Suit?" *Economist*, August 4, 2016. www.econo-mist.com/1843/2016/08/04/last-trump-for-the-suit.

Leonhardt, David, and Stuart A. Thomson. "Trump's Lies." *New York Times*, updated December 14, 2017. www.nytimes.com/interactive/2017/06/23/opinion/trumps-lies.html.

Leriche, Chloé, dir. *Before the Streets*. 2016; Montréal: Les films de l'autre and Telefilm Canada.

Levinas, Emmanuel. *Totality and Infinity: An Essay on Exteriority*. Translated by Alphonso Lingis. Pittsburgh: Duquesne University Press, 1969.

Levy, Ariel. "Trial by Twitter." *New Yorker*, July 29, 2013. www.newyorker.com /magazine/2013/08/05/trial-by-twitter.

Lewis, Tim. "Tom Ford: 'I Wore a Suit on Set. It's a Uniform ... I Feel Weak in Trainers.'" *Guardian*, October 23, 2016. www.theguardian.com/film/2016 /oct/23/tom-ford-suit-set-film-nocturnal-animals-director.

Liberman, Anatoly. "The Etymology of *boy, beacon* and *buoy*." *Journal of Germanic Linguistics* 12, no. 2 (2000): 201–234.

Lieber, Marylène. *Genres, violences et espaces publics: La vulnérabilité des femmes en question*. Paris: Presses de Sciences Po, 2008.

Livingston, Jennie, dir. *Paris is Burning*. 1990; New York: Academy Entertainment and Off-White Productions.

Lodhia, Sharmila. "From 'Living Corpse' to India's daughter: Exploring the Social, Political and Legal Landscape of the 2012 Delhi Gang Rape." *Women's Studies International Forum* 50 (2015): 89–101. www.scu.edu/media/ethics -center/business-ethics/Lodhia-From-Living-Corpse-to-India's-Daughter -Women's-Studies-International-Forum.pdf.

Loofbourow, Lili. "Brett Kavanaugh and the Cruelty of Male Bonding: When Being One of the Guys Comes at a Woman's Expense." *Slate*, September 25, 2018. slate.com/news-and-politics/2018/09/brett-kavanaugh-allegations -yearbook-male-bonding.html.

———. "The Female Price of Male Pleasure." *Week*, January 25, 2018. theweek. com/articles/749978/female-price-male-pleasure.

———. "The Male Glance." *VQR*, Spring 2018. www.vqronline.org/essays-articles /2018/03/male-glance.

———. "The Year of the Old Boys." *Slate*, December 21, 2018. slate.com/human -interest/2018/12/old-boys-trump-kavanaugh-moonves-epstein-childish -masculinity.html.

Los Angeles Times. "Read the Complete Transcript of President Trump's Remarks at Trump Tower on Charlottesville." August 15, 2017. www.latimes.com/pol- itics/la-na-pol-trump-charlottesville-transcript-20170815-story.html.

Lumet, Sidney, dir. *12 Angry Men*. 1957; Los Angeles: Orion-Nova.

Lupien, Anna, with Francine Descarries and Réalisatrices équitables. *L'avant et l'arrière de l'écran: L'influence du sexe des cinéastes sur la représentation des hommes et des femmes dans le cinéma québécois recent.* Réalisatrices équitables, 2013. annalupien.com/L-avant-et-l-arriere-de-l-ecran.

MacKinnon, Catharine A. *Are Women Human?: And Other International Dialogues.* Cambridge, MA: Belknap Press of Harvard University Press, 2006.

——. *Butterfly Politics: Changing the World for Women.* Cambridge, MA: Belknap Press of Harvard University Press, 2017.

Malabou, Catherine. *Changing Difference: The Feminine and the Question of Philosophy.* Translated by Carolyn Shread. Malden, MA: Polity Press, 2011.

Markman, Tiffany. "An Analysis of President Donald Trump's Use of Language." Medium, February 9, 2020. tiffanymarkman.medium.com/an-analysis-of -president-donald-trumps-use-of-language-74a76c3d062b.

Marsh, Jan. *Gender Ideology and Separate Spheres in the 19th Century.* London: Victoria and Albert Museum, n.d.

Martin, Kristen. "Donald Trump's Sentimental Journey to the Top." Literary Hub, March 22, 2016. lithub.com/donald-trumps-sentimental-journey-to-the-top.

Massé, Manon. "Féministe, puisqu'il le faut encore." *Le Devoir*, March 8, 2018. www.ledevoir.com/opinion/idees/522117/feministe-puisqu-il-le-faut-encore

Mayer, Jane. "Donald Trump's Ghostwriter Tells All." *New Yorker*, July 18, 2016. www.newyorker.com/magazine/2016/07/25/donald-trumps-ghostwriter -tells-all.

McClelland, Sara. "Intimate Justice: Sexual Satisfaction in Young Adults." Ph.D. diss., New York University, 2009.

McKinley Jr., James C. "Killings in '89 Set a Record in New York." *New York Times*, March 31, 1990. www.nytimes.com/1990/03/31/nyregion/killings-in-89-set -a-record-in-new-york.html.

Mill, John Stuart. *The Subjection of Women.* New York: D. Appleton and Company, 1870. books.google.ca/books?id=fVwSsCdK26AC&pg=PP5&source=gbs _selected_pages&cad=1#v=onepage&q&f=false.

Miller, Michael E. "All-American Swimmer Found Guilty of Sexually Assaulting Unconscious Woman on Stanford Campus." *Washington Post*, March 31, 2016. www.washingtonpost.com/news/morning-mix/wp/2016/03/31 /all-american-swimmer-found-guilty-of-sexually-assaulting-unconscious -woman-on-stanford-campus.

Milne-Smith, Amy. "A Flight to Domesticity? Making a Home in the Gentlemen's Clubs of London, 1880–1914." *Journal of British Studies* 45, no. 4 (2006): 796–808.

Milot, Marie-Ève, and Marie-Claude St-Laurent. *La place des femmes en théâtre:*

Chantier féministe. Montréal. L'ESPACE GO, April 8 to 13, 2019. espacego
.com/les-spectacles/2018-2019/la-place-des-femmes-en-theatre-chantier
-feministe.

Moix, Yann. "Yann Moix: 'J'aime les femmes plus jeune, je n'en suis responsable et
je n'en ai pas honte!'" *On n'est pas couché.* YouTube video. Originally aired
January 13, 2019, on France 2. youtu.be/Iy3-1YrCqyY.

Le Monde. "Ligue du LOL: 6 journalistes écartés après des accusations de cyber-
harcèlement." February 11, 2019. www.lemonde.fr/pixels/article/2019/02/11
/ligue-du-lol-un-journaliste-de-liberation-mis-a-pied-a-titre-conservatoire
_5422027_4408996.html.

Moore, Michael, dir. *Bowling for Columbine.* 2002; Dog Eat Dog Films.

———. *Fahrenheit 9/11.* 2004; Dog Eat Dog Films.

———. *Fahrenheit 11/9.* 2018; Midwestern Films.

———. *Roger & Me.* 1989; Dog Eat Dog Films.

Morrison, Toni. "Making America White Again." *New Yorker,* November 14, 2016.
www.newyorker.com/magazine/2016/11/21/toni-morrison-trump-election
-making-america-white-again.

Mukherjee, Sreenita. "Women, Architecture and Education: Experiences of Women
in the UK's Architectural Space." Medium, February 9, 2021. medium.com
/architectonics/women-architecture-and-education-e44f90cc5b38.

Nadau, Louis. "Affaire 'Ligue du LOL': Le crash des journalistes 'caïds de Twitter.'"
Marianne, February 11, 2019. www.marianne.net/societe/affaire-ligue-du-lol
-le-crash-des-journalistes-caids-de-twitter.

National Inquiry into Missing and Murdered Indigenous Women and Girls.
*A Legal Analysis of Genocide: Supplementary Report of the National Inquiry
into Missing and Murdered Indigenous Women and Girls.* June 3, 2019. www
.mmiwg-ffada.ca/wp-content/uploads/2019/06/Supplementary-Report
_Genocide.pdf.

———. "News Release." June 3, 2019. www.mmiwg-ffada.ca/wp-content/uploads
/2019/06/News-Release-Final-Report.pdf.

Navarro, Pascale. *Femmes et pouvoir: Les changements nécessaires. Plaidoyer pour
la parité.* Montréal: Leméac, 2015.

Neel, Andrew, dir. *Goat.* New York: Great Point Media, Killer Films, and Rabbit
Bandini Productions, 2016.

New York Times. "Donald Trump Too Tame for You? Meet Britain's Boris Johnson." June 29, 2019. www.nytimes.com/2019/06/29/opinion/sunday/boris
-johnson-britain-trump.html.

————. "Transcript: Donald Trump's Taped Comments About Women." October 8, 2016. www.nytimes.com/2016/10/08/us/donald-trump-tape-transcript.html.

New York Times Magazine. "The Way We Live Now: 7-4-99; What They Were Thinking." July 4, 1999. www.nytimes.com/1999/07/04/magazine/the-way-we-live-now-7-4-99-what-they-were-thinking.html?searchResultPosition=1.

NewsHunter29. "Donald Trump Movie Review – Orson Welles's *Citizen Kane.*" August 20, 2015. YouTube video. youtu.be/aeQOJZ-QzBk.

Nicolas, Lison. "Florence Parly et le sexisme à l'Assemblée: 'Il valait mieux porter un uniforme tailleur-pantalon.'" *Gala,* March 12, 2021. www.gala.fr/l_actu/news_de_stars/florence-parly-et-le-sexisme-a-lassemblee-il-valait-mieux-porter-un-uniforme-tailleur-pantalon_464832.

Nussbaum, Emily. "Reacting to the Louis C.K. Revelations." *New Yorker,* November 9, 2017. www.newyorker.com/culture/cultural-comment/reacting-to-the-louis-ck-revelations.

Nuzzi, Olivia. "Former Donald Trump Executive: 'He's a Supreme Sexist.'" *Daily Beast,* updated July 12, 2017. www.thedailybeast.com/former-donald-trump-executive-hes-a-supreme-sexist.

Oliver, Kelly. *Hunting Girls: Sexual Violence from* The Hunger Games *to Campus Rape.* New York: Columbia University Press, 2016.

Oppenheim, Maya. "Misogyny Is a Key Element of White Supremacy, Anti-Defamation League Report Finds." *Independent,* July 26, 2018. www.independent.co.uk/news/world/americas/misogyny-white-supremacy-links-alt-right-antidefamation-league-report-incel-a8463611.html.

Ordre des architectes du Québec. *Esquisses* 24, no. 2 (summer 2013). www.oaq.com/esquisses/archives_en_html/balades_au_fil_de_leau/tout_le_reste/portrait_chiffre.html.

Panofsky, Erwin. "Style and Medium in the Moving Pictures" (1934). In *Aesthetics: A Critical Anthology,* edited by George Dickie and R.J. Sclafani. 351–365. New York: St. Martin's Press, 1977.

Park, Alice. "Yale Opts Out of DKE Punishment." *Yale Daily News,* January 17, 2019. yaledailynews.com/blog/2019/01/17/analysis-yales-unmoved-response-to-allegations-at-dke.

Patmore, Coventry. *The Angel in the House, parts 1 and 2.* London: Macmillan & Co., 1863. catalog.hathitrust.org/Record/009247273.

Peeters, Sofie, dir. *Femme de la rue.* Aired July 26, 2012, on Canvas.

Pelletier, Francine. "La zone gris foncé." *Le Devoir*, January 20, 2016. www.ledevoir
.com/opinion/chroniques/460628/la-zone-gris-fonce

Perrier, Brice. "À Paris, plongée dans des clubs au genre très masculine." *Le Paris-*
ien, June 23, 2019. www.leparisien.fr/societe/a-paris-plongee-dans-des-clubs
-au-genre-tres-masculin-23-06-2019-8100678.php.

Perry, Grayson. "Grayson Perry: The Rise and Fall of Default Man." *New States-*
man, October 8, 2014. www.newstatesman.com/long-reads/2014/10/grayson
-perry-rise-and-fall-default-man.

Philipps, Dave. "'This Is Unacceptable': Military Reports a Surge of Sexual Assaults
in the Ranks." *New York Times*, May 2, 2019. www.nytimes.com/2019/05/02
/us/military-sexual-assault.html.

Pilkington, Ed. "'Stand Back and Stand By': How Trumpism Led to the Capitol
Siege." *Guardian*, January 6, 2021. www.theguardian.com/us-news/2021
/jan/06/donald-trump-armed-protest-capitol.

Plante, Caroline. "'Boys club': Des propos de Manon Massé décriés." *Le Droit*,
March 15, 2018. www.ledroit.com/2018/03/15/boys-club-des-propos-de
-manon-masse-decries-7d88442734551c29d893c92f87984a6b.

Pogrebin, Robin. "I Am Not the Decorator: Female Architects Speak Out." *New*
York Times, April 12, 2016. www.nytimes.com/2016/04/13/arts/design/female
-architects-speak-out-on-sexism-unequal-pay-and-more.html.

Pollitt, Katha. "Hers; The Smurfette Principle." *New York Times*, April 7, 1991. www
.nytimes.com/1991/04/07/magazine/hers-the-smurfette-principle.html.

———. "Why We Need Women in Power." *Nation*, March 3, 2016. www.thenation
.com/article/archive/why-we-need-women-in-power.

Polytechnique commemoration ceremony. Montréal, Québec. December 6, 2014.

Ponciau, Ludivine. "Alice Barbe, insultée et menacée pour avoir pris la parole en
faveur des migrants: 'Elle doit aimer le vis nègre.'" *Le Soir*, September 6, 2018.
www.lesoir.be/177058/article/2018-09-06/alice-barbe-insultee-et-menacee
-pour-avoir-pris-la-parole-en-faveur-des-migrants.

Portolano, Marie, and Guillaume Priou, dirs. *Je ne suis pas une salope, je suis une*
journaliste. 2021; Issy-les-Moulineaux: Canal+.

Pouyat, Alice. "Architectes, faites de la place aux femmes!" WE demain (website),
March 8, 2018. www.wedemain.fr/dechiffrer/architectes-faites-de-la-place
-aux-femmes.

Preston, Jennifer. "How Blogger Helped the Steubenville Rape Case Unfold
Online." *New York Times*, March 18, 2013. archive.nytimes.com/thelede

.blogs.nytimes.com/2013/03/18/how-blogger-helped-steubenville-rape-case -unfold-online.

Raibaud, Yves. *La ville faite par et pour les hommes: Dans l'espace urbain, une mixité en trompe-l'œil.* Paris: Editions Belin, 2015.

Rand, Ayn. *The Fountainhead.* New York: Penguin, 1996 [1943].

Ransom, Jay. "Trump Will Not Apologize for Calling for Death Penalty Over Central Park Five." *New York Times,* June 18, 2019. www.nytimes.com/2019 /06/18/nyregion/central-park-five-trump.html.

Rayfield, Jillian. "Wesleyan Sued over 'Rape Factory' Frat." *Salon,* October 7, 2012. www.salon.com/2012/10/07/wesleyan_sued_over_rape_factory_frat.

Reeser, Todd W. *Masculinities in Theory: An Introduction.* Hoboken, NJ: Wiley-Blackwell, 2013.

Regnier, Isabelle. "Stéphanie Dadour: 'Les étudiantes en architecture sont demandeuses de modèles de femmes reconnues par la profession'." *Le Monde,* June 8, 2020. www.lemonde.fr/culture/article/2020/06/08/stephanie-dadour -les-etudiantes-en-architecture-sont-demandeuses-de-modeles-de-femmes -reconnues-par-la-profession_6042102_3246.html.

Reiner, Rob, dir. *A Few Good Men.* 1992; Beverly Hills, CA: Castle Rock Entertainment.

Relman, Eliza, and Azmi Haroun. "The 26 Women Who Have Accused Trump of Sexual Misconduct." Business Insider, updated May 9, 2023. www.businessinsider.com/women-accused-trump-sexual-misconduct-list-2017-12.

Renck, Johan, dir. *Chernobyl.* Created and written by Craig Mazin, produced by Sanne Wohlenberg. Aired May 6–June 3, 2019, on HBO and Sky Atlantic.

Res, Barbara A. *All Alone on the 68th Floor: How One Woman Changed the Face of Construction.* New York: CreateSpace Independent Publishing Platform, 2013.

———. *Tower of Lies: What My Eighteen Years of Working With Donald Trump Reveals About Him.* Los Angeles: Graymalkin Media, 2020.

Right to Be (website). righttobe.org.

Rocah, Mimi, Barbara McQuade, Jill Wine-Banks, Joyce White Vance, and Maya Wiley. "Brett Kavanaugh Allegations: Why They Are Not Simply a 'He Said, She Said' Situation." NBC News, September 18, 2018. www.nbcnews .com/think/opinion/allegations-against-brett-kavanaugh-are-not-simply -he-said-she-ncna910771.

Rosenberg, Melissa, creator. *Jessica Jones.* Featuring Krysten Ritter. Aired 2015– 2018 on Netflix.

Works Cited

Ruskin, John. *Sesames and Lilies: Two Lectures delivered at Manchester in 1864.* New York: J. Wiley & Son, 1865. www.biblio.com/sesame-and-lilies-by-ruskin-john/work/34918.

Ryan, Erin Gloria. "Infamous 'Rapebait' Frat Disbanded for Being Entirely Too Rapey." Jezebel, April 4, 2014. jezebel.com/infamous-rapebait-frat-disbanded-for-being-entirely-t-1558252895.

Sanders, Joel. *Stud: Architectures of Masculinity.* New York: Princeton University Press, 1996.

Sansot, Pierre. *Poétique de la ville.* Lausanne: Payot, 2015.

Sarkeesian, Anita. *Tropes vs. Women in Video Games.* Feminist Frequency. YouTube. 2009–2017.

The Savage Club (website), 2024. www.savageclub.com.

Scherfig, Lone, dir. *The Riot Club.* 2014; London: Blueprint Pictures, Film4, Han-Way Films, and Pinewood Films.

Schrader, Paul, dir. *American Gigolo.* 1980; Los Angeles: Paramount Pictures.

Sciences-Po Ad-Hoc students' Collective. "Affaire Duhamel: 'Nous, étudiantes et étudiants, demandons la démission du directeur de Sciences-Po Frédéric Mion'." *Libération*, January 13, 2021. www.liberation.fr/debats/2021/01/13/affaire-duhamel-nous-etudiantes-et-etudiants-demandons-la-demission-du-directeur-de-science-po-frede_1815892.

Scorsese, Martin, dir. *The Wolf of Wall Street.* 2013; West Hollywood, CA: Red Granite Pictures, Appian Way Productions, Sikelia Productions, and EMJAG Productions.

Segal, David. "What Donald Trump's Plaza Deal Reveals About His White House Bid." *New York Times*, January 17, 2016. www.nytimes.com/2016/01/17/business/what-donald-trumps-plaza-deal-reveals-about-his-white-house-bid.html.

Shepard, Richard, dir. *Girls.* Season 6, episode 3. "American Bitch." Written by Lena Dunham. Aired February 26, 2017, on HBO.

Silverman, David, dir. "Trumptastic Voyage." *The Simpsons.* 2015; Los Angeles: Gracie Films.

Smith, Dorothy E. "A Peculiar Eclipsing: Women's Exclusion from Man's Culture." *Women's Studies International Quarterly* 1 (1978).

Solnit, Rebecca. "Men Explain *Lolita* to Me." Literary Hub, December 17, 2015. lithub.com/men-explain-lolita-to-me/.

———. *Men Explain Things to Me.* Chicago: Haymarket Books, 2014.

Spielberg, Steven, dir. *Munich*. 2005; Universal City, CA: Amblin Entertainment, Kennedy Marshall, and Alliance Atlantis.

Stack, Liam. "Light Sentence for Brock Turner in Stanford Rape Case Draws Outrage." *New York Times*, June 6, 2016. www.nytimes.com/2016/06/07/us/outrage-in-stanford-rape-case-over-dueling-statements-of-victim-and-attackers-father.html.

Stone, Oliver, dir. *Wall Street*. 1987; American Entertainment Partners and Amercent Films.

Stratigakos, Despina. *Where Are the Women Architects?* Princeton, NJ: Princeton University Press, 2016.

"Take the Pledge." It's On Us. Civic Nation, 2023. www.itsonus.org/get-involved/take-the-pledge.

Tate, Gabriel. "London Spy Recap: Episode Three – 'I knew you'd make a lot of mistakes.'" *Guardian*, November 23, 2015. www.theguardian.com/tv-and-radio/tvandradioblog/2015/nov/23/london-spy-recap-episode-three-danny-mistakes-nightmare.

Tauber, Matt, dir. *The Architect*. 2006; Denver: HDNet Films and Sly Dog Films.

Tesquet, Olivier. "Pour en finir avec la culture web." *Télérama*, November 10, 2017. www.telerama.fr/medias/pour-en-finir-avec-la-culture-web,n5338155.php.

Tessier, Liane. "Gossip Within the Male Dominated Workplace." Disappointing the Boys' Club (blog), July 18, 2015. lianetessier.wordpress.com/2015/07/18/gossip-within-the-male-dominated-workplace.

TF1 Info. "Ligue du LOL: Une association féministe saisit le procureur de Paris." May 20, 2019. www.tflinfo.fr/societe/ligue-du-lol-association-feministe-prenons-la-une-saisit-le-procureur-de-paris-2121626.html.

Thévenoud, Thomas. "Alice Coffin: Le neutre, c'est la subjectivité des dominants." *Revue Charles*, December 8, 2020. revuecharles.fr/100-politique/entretiens/femme-d-influence/alice-coffin-le-neutre-cest-la-subjectivite-des-dominants.

Thiolay, Boris. "La guerre des ladies." *L'Express*, March 2, 2006. www.lexpress.fr/monde/europe/la-guerre-des-ladies_482861.html.

Tiger, Lionel. *Men in Groups*. New York: Routledge, 2017 [New York: Random House, 1969].

Times of India. "What is Nirbhaya case?" December 18, 2019. timesofindia.indiatimes.com/india/what-is-nirbhaya-case/articleshow/72868430.cms.

Tolentino, Jia. "Brett Kavanaugh, Donald Trump, and the Things Men Do for Other Men." *New Yorker*, September 26, 2018. www.newyorker.com/news

Works Cited

/our-columnists/brett-kavanaugh-donald-trump-and-the-things-men-do
-for-other-men.

Trump, Donald. "Bring Back the Death Penalty, Bring Back Our Police." Advertisement, *New York Times*, May 1, 1989.

———. "Executive Branch Personnel Public Financial Disclosure Report, (OGE
Form 278e)." United States Office of Government Ethics. May 16, 2016.
web.archive.org/web/20190902113525/https://assets.documentcloud.org
/documents/2838696/Trump-2016-Financial-Disclosure.pdf.

———. Interview by Nancy Collins. *Primetime Live*. Aired March 10, 1994, on
ABC. www.youtube.com/watch?v=WktcHktNbN8.

———. Interview by Phil Donahue. *The Phil Donahue Show*. Aired December 15,
1987, in syndication. www.youtube.com/watch?v=RSb4CmeZd08.

———. Interview by Rona Barrett. *Washington Post*, October 6, 1980. www.washing-
tonpost.com/wp-stat/graphics/politics/trump-archive/docs/rona-barrett
-1980-interview-of-donald-trump.pdf.

———. *Trump: The Art of the Deal*. With Tony Schwartz. New York: Random
House, 1987.

Twitchell, James B, with photographs by Ken Ross. *Where Men Hide*. New York:
Columbia University Press, 2006.

Ukoha, Ezinne. "How *American Psycho* Serves As the White Man's Code for
Behavioral Dysfunction." Medium, February 10, 2018. nilegirl.medium.com
/how-american-psycho-serves-as-the-white-man-s-code-for-behavioral
-dysfunction-acf0eb58abe0.

United States Marine Corps. "We're Looking for a Few Good Men." Television
advertisement, 1985. youtu.be/YC82SwuDrcE.

United States of America. "Jeanne Clery Disclosure of Campus Security Policy
and Campus Crime Statistics Act." Pub. L. No. 101–542, 20 U.S.C. § 1092,
34 CFR 668.46 (1990).

Uzel, Jean-Philippe. "Le montage: De la vision à l'action." *Cinéma: Revue d'études
cinématographiques* 9, no. 1 (1998): 63–78.

Valenti, Jessica. "Frat Brothers Rape 300 percent More. One in 5 Women
Is Sexually Assaulted on Campus. Should We Ban Frats?" *Guardian*,
September 24, 2014. www.theguardian.com/commentisfree/2014/sep/24
/rape-sexual-assault-ban-frats.

Vallée, Jean-Marc dir. *Dallas Buyers Club*. 2013; Truth Entertainment and Voltage
Pictures.

Vaubien, Florise, and AFP. "Montpellier: Une enquête ouverte pour harcèlement moral et sexuel à l'École d'architecture." *RTL France*, December 16, 2020. www.rtl.fr/actu/justice-faits-divers/montpellier-une-enquete-ouverte-pour-harcelement-moral-et-sexuel-a-l-ecole-d-architecture-7800941410.

Verbruggen, Jakob, dir. *London Spy*. Season 1, episode 3. "Blue." Written by Tom Rob Smith. Aired November 23, 2015, on BBC Two.

Verduzier, Pauline. "Quels sont ces clubs de 'gentlemen' qui n'acceptent pas les femmes?" *Le Figaro Madame*, July 20, 2015. madame.lefigaro.fr/societe/quels-sont-ces-clubs-tres-prives-reserves-aux-hommes-170715-97505.

Verica, Tom, dir. *Scandal*. Season 5, episode 9. "Baby, It's Cold Outside." Written by Mark Wilding. Aired November 19, 2015, on ABC.

Verkaik, Robert. "To Drain the Swamp of Men-Only Clubs There Must Be a Public Register of Members." *Guardian*, January 27, 2018. www.theguardian.com/commentisfree/2018/jan/27/to-drain-the-swamp-ofmenonlyclubsthere mustbeapublicregister.

Vidor, King, dir. *The Fountainhead*. 1949; Burbank, CA: Warner Bros.

Villeneuve, Denis, dir. *Sicario*. 2015; Los Angeles: Black Label Media and Thunder Road.

Vogels, Emily A. "Teens and Cyberbullying 2022." Pew Research Center, December 15, 2022. www.pewresearch.org/internet/2022/12/15/teensand cyberbullying2022.

Walters, Suzanna Danuta. "Why Can't We Hate Men?" *Washington Post*, June 8, 2018. www.washingtonpost.com/opinions/whycantwehatemen/2018/06/08/fla3a8e0645111e8a69cb944de66d9e7_story.html.

Washington Journal. "Barbara Res on *Tower of Lies*." Aired on *CSpan*, December 26, 2020. www.cspan.org/video/?5075373/barbararestowerlies#!.

Way, Katie. "I Went on a Date with Aziz Ansari. It Turned into the Worst Night of My Life." Babe, January 14, 2018. babe.net/2018/01/13/azizansari28355.

Weiner, Matthew, creator. *Mad Men*. Aired July 19, 2007–May 17, 2015, on AMC.

Welles, Orson, dir. *Citizen Kane*. 1941; New York: RKO Radio Pictures Mercury Productions.

West, Simon, dir. *The General's Daughter*. 1999; Los Angeles: Paramount Pictures.

Westfall, Sammy, and Asha Prihar, "Ford Quotes Spray Painted around Campus." *Yale Daily News*, October 24, 2018. yaledailynews.com/blog/2018/10/24/fordquotesspraypaintedaroundcampus.

Wigley, Mark. "Untitled: The Housing of Gender." In *Sexuality & Space*, edited by Beatriz Colomina. New York: Princeton Papers on Architecture, 1992.

Williams, Gilda. "What Are You Looking At? The Female Gaze." Tate Etc. 2 (Autumn 2004). www.tate.org.uk/tateetc/issue2autumn2004/whatareyou looking.

Williams, Zoe. "'Raw Hatred': Why the 'Incel' Movement Targets and Terrorises Women." Guardian, April 25, 2018. www.theguardian.com/world/2018/apr /25/rawhatredwhyincelmovementtargetsterroriseswomen.

Willimon, Beau, creator. House of Cards. Featuring Kevin Spacey. Aired 2013–2018 on Netflix.

Willis, Charlotte. "Men Shamed on Tumblr Site for Taking Up Too Much Space on the Train." Courier Mail, September 20, 2013. www.couriermail.com.au /entertainment/celebrity/menshamedontumblrsitefortakinguptoomuch spaceonthetrain/newsstory/8217f0c17486af271fda4d019f-b8fe85.

wilson, cintra. "A Brief History of the Power Suit." Medium, October 11, 2018. gen .medium.com/abriefhistoryofthepowersuit544ed4dee095.

Wilson, Mabel O., and Julian Rose. "Changing the Subject: Race and Public Space." Artforum, Summer 2017. www.artforum.com/features/changingthe subjectraceandpublicspace234352.

Woolf, Virginia. A Room of One's Own. London: Penguin, 2019 [1929].

———. Three Guineas. Penguin Books, 1977 [1938].

Woolsey, Amy. "Total Carnage: The Timely Anger of The Riot Club." Film School Rejects (website). November 1, 2018. filmschoolrejects.com/timelyanger theriotclub.

Wright, Megh. "Hannah Gadsby Calls Out Hollywood's 'Good Men' for Their Hot Takes on Misogyny." Vulture, December 5, 2018. www.vulture.com/2018/12 /hannahgadsbyhollywoodreporterbadmensexismmisogyny.html.

Xu, Victor. "The Full Letter Read by Brock Turner's Father at His Sentencing Hearing." Stanford Daily, June 8, 2016. stanforddaily.com/2016/06/08/the fullletterreadbybrockturnersfatherathissentencinghearing.

Yancy, George. Look, a White!: Philosophical Essays on Whiteness. Philadelphia: Temple University Press, 2012.

Yee, Vivian. "Statutory Rape, Twitter and a Connecticut Town's Divide." New York Times, April 4, 2013. www.nytimes.com/2013/04/05/nyregion/generational divideintorringtonconnoversexassaultcase.html.

Young, Iris Marion. "Gender as Seriality: Thinking about Women as a Social Collective." Signs 19, no. 3 (Spring 1994): 713–738.

Index

Index

Novelist and essayist **Martine Delvaux** is a central figure in Québec literary feminism. She is the author of five novels, including *Thelma, Louise & moi*, which was shortlisted for the Prix des libraires, and nine books of non-fiction, the most recent of which is *Pompières et pyromanes*. *Le boys club* won the Grand Prix du livre de Montréal. Five of Delvaux's works have been translated into English, including *Blanc dehors*, translated as *White Out* by Katia Grubisic.

Photo by Emilie Pelletier

Katia Grubisic is a writer, editor, and translator whose work has appeared in various Canadian and international publications. Her collection *What if red ran out* was shortlisted for the A.M. Klein Prize for Poetry and won the 2009 Gerald Lampert Memorial Award for best first book. Her translations of David Clerson's *Brothers* and Alina Dumitrescu's *A Cemetery for Bees* were both shortlisted for the Governor General's Literary Award for translation, and her translation of Clerson's *To See Out the Night* won the Cole Foundation Prize for Translation.